Virtual
Schools

Virtual
Schools

PLANNING FOR SUCCESS

Edited by Zane L. Berge and Tom Clark

Foreword by Julie Young

Teachers College, Columbia University
New York and London

Published by Teachers College Press, 1234 Amsterdam Avenue, New York, NY 10027

Library of Congress Cataloging-in-Publication Data

Virtual schools : planning for success / edited by Zane L. Berge and Tom Clark; foreword by Julie Young.
    p. cm.
    Includes bibliographical references and index.
    ISBN 0-8077-4572-3 (cloth : alk. paper)—ISBN 0-8077-4571-5 (pbk. : alk. paper)
    1. Distance education—United States—Computer-assisted instruction—Case studies. 2. Distance education—United States—Planning—Case studies.
    3. Virtual reality in education—United States—Case studies. I. Berge, Zane L.
    II. Clark, Thomas A., 1952–

    LC5803.C65V58 2005
    371.3'58—dc22
                                                                    2004059826

ISBN 0-8077-4571-5 (paper)
ISBN 0-8077-4572-3 (cloth)

Printed on acid-free paper
Manufactured in the United States of America

12 11 10 09 08 07 06 05   8 7 6 5 4 3 2 1

Contents

PART III: Summing Up

Foreword

THIS BOOK comes to us at a time when public education is being challenged as never before. Demands for measurable results are now every educator's reality, and this has already spurred change. In order to meet this ongoing challenge, how do we ensure that all children have access to the highest quality of education regardless of where they live, their race, or their socioeconomic status? We must find a creative way to bring outstanding education to every student—and we have done so with online learning.

If I sound optimistic about online learning, it is because I contend that more virtual options will facilitate change in traditional public and private schools. Why? Because online learning steadily steers the focus away from process and place and toward results. Online learning also provides flexible options for the diverse educational needs of students and their families in ways not previously possible.

The success of online learning will continue to drive change in traditional models. In fact, I can envision schools within schools where some students come and go at odd hours and teachers work from both their homes and school buildings or other sites, depending on their students' schedules and needs. It's more than a virtual possibility—it is a virtual reality.

I have also watched online learning meet difficult challenges with overwhelming success in providing educational choice, promoting the use of technology in learning, dealing with large increases or decreases in student enrollment, and producing students who have the knowledge and skills to succeed in postsecondary education or the workforce.

In short, online learning has become a proven and viable tool to meet the demands that student-centered, results-oriented learning presents. However, many districts are dealing with technology plans that are more focused on putting out fires than on incorporating online learning into their course offerings.

If you are interested in the details of launching virtual learning options for your school, district, region, or state, you likely have more questions than answers. Where do you begin? What kind of personnel will you need? What is already out there, in terms of providers and resources? What is involved in development? How do you hire and train teachers? What kinds of policies do you need to address and have in place? What are the costs involved? What are the pitfalls to avoid? Where can you go for answers as more questions arise? This volume was designed to answer questions like these.

When my own online school, Florida Virtual School, began in 1996, there were no road maps, no rules, and few experiences to look to for guidance; we simply took the most logical approach to making it up as we went along. This book would have helped, for it is an amazing collection of wisdom and actual strategies from many of the pioneers in K–12 online education. What makes this collection of knowledge so powerful is the fact that all of the chapters are written by real practitioners and experts in the field. They share proven techniques for developing and managing an effective online instructional service. And not only is the book useful as a guide for those who are in the planning phases of building a virtual school, it is also a great collection of fresh ideas for many of us who have been at it for a while, providing new perspectives and different points of view.

I have had the pleasure of working with many of the contributors. They are visionary educators who are dedicated to making a difference. Once you've read this book, you will walk away armed with new ideas and energized by the possibilities for kids. After all, isn't that why we all became educators?

—Julie Young
President and CEO, Florida Virtual School

Introduction

BECAUSE K–12 online learning experiments in the late 1990s were mainly focused on high school curricula, the term *virtual high school* came into common use. But now that middle and elementary school students are also participating in online courses the term *virtual school* more accurately describes the phenomenon as a whole, with *virtual schooling* denoting all K–12 online courses. Virtual schooling is part of a larger phenomenon, K–12 e-learning. The term *e-learning* properly applies to all types of education and training utilizing electronic technology, and we use the term *K–12 e-learning* here to mean the use of technology to support teaching and learning in elementary and secondary education.

In a study sponsored by WestEd's Distance Learning Resource Network, Clark (2001) sought to estimate the number of K–12 learners participating in virtual schooling by contacting known virtual school course providers, and concluded that about 40,000 to 50,000 students were taking online courses in the school year 2000–01. It is likely that several times as many are taking them now. An accurate estimate of the scope of school and student involvement will require a large national survey of the schools themselves. The results of a national survey on K–12 distance learning by the U.S. Department of Education will soon be released, providing a more accurate estimate of how many U.S. schools have students enrolled in online courses and how many students overall are enrolled in credit-granting courses via electronic distance learning.

DISTANCE EDUCATION, E-LEARNING, AND VIRTUAL SCHOOLS

The virtual school can be seen as the newest form of *distance education*, defined as formal education in which a majority of instruction occurs while teacher and learner are separate. Two kinds of distance education methods are pertinent to a discussion of virtual schooling: those using electronic media for teaching and learning, and those using nonelectronic media, such as correspondence or independent study. E-learning is usually considered to include only electronic distance education methods.

But e-learning is more than just electronic distance learning. The term *e-learning* is commonly used to describe not only online courses and other forms of electronic distance learning but also technology integration throughout the virtual learning environment, technology-based professional development, and other uses of technology to support teaching and learning.

Many common uses of technology in learning are not really distance education because they are part of an on-site teacher's lessons, but they are e-learning. For example, an interactive computer-based reading program used by second graders, an e-mail sharing activity between seventh graders and the sixth graders who will attend their school the following year, and Channel One newscasts watched by high school students in a social studies class are all e-learning.

The single concept of e-learning may come to replace the perception of distance learning and technology use in education as two separate modes of online learning. Virtual schools operate within an overall K–12 e-learning environment, located wherever the school community lives and learns. Technology vendors are beginning to describe their products as K–12 e-learning solutions. The U.S. Open e-Learning Consortium, led by 15 state departments of education, has sought to "accelerate the deployment of statewide, interoperable e-learning and decision support platforms" (Colorado Center for Teaching, Learning and Technology, 2002). States are exploring ways to package educational content, teaching resources, and test items as exchangeable learning objects that can be automatically aligned with state-level standards and assessments. Many states are using the Internet to meet the changing professional development and certification needs of teachers (Clark, 2000a).

PURPOSE AND SCOPE OF THE BOOK

While many resources are being invested in virtual schools, and in K–12 e-learning generally, there is no guarantee of success in meeting intended goals and sustaining such efforts. The uniqueness of individual virtual schools, as evidenced in this book, means that well-informed independent decision making is needed to succeed in planning and operating a successful virtual school.

A primary purpose of this book is to provide strategic advice to managers and planners of virtual schools that will help them plan for success. These individuals may work in K–12 schools, in state education or other governmental agencies, or in nonprofit or for-profit enterprises. While the focus is on practical knowledge and planning, the book should also be useful to those interested in studying or understanding the phenomenon of virtual schools and e-learning, such as students and faculty in graduate education programs, policymakers, and educational researchers.

As the editors, we have many years of experience in distance learning and e-learning. With our readers, we share an interest in better understanding the evolving phenomenon of virtual schools, and in managing virtual school enterprises. To that twofold end, we have included two types of contributed chapters: (1) analyses of key issues or components of virtual schools and (2) case studies of particular virtual schools. Both groups of chapters reflect the unique viewpoints of virtual school administrators and experts in the field.

Nine issues or components have been identified as among those important in virtual school success: access and equity, technology, funding, administration and policy, marketing and public relations, curriculum, instruction and teacher development, academic services, and program assessment (Clark, 2001). Chapters 2 through 6 examine the first five issues (the remaining four are addressed more informally in the case studies), with each chapter exploring the context of one of the key aspects of virtual schooling and describing how a variety of virtual schools are handling that aspect. The authors of these chapters sought to provide broad coverage of the issue or component, including its place within the virtual school/e-learning context, practical examples of its role in virtual schools and e-learning, and its strategic implications in planning for success.

The case study chapters explore in depth how particular virtual schools have planned for success. The case study authors sought to provide a strategic overview of the virtual school program and its context, a systematic review of how the organization addresses issues relevant to success, and a focus on how the organization has planned for success, with particular emphasis on those components it addresses in an exceptional manner. For example, Chapter 8 emphasizes curriculum and instruction issues, Chapter 9 highlights teacher development, and Chapter 12 discusses the school's approach to program assessment in some depth.

ORGANIZATION OF THE BOOK

Part I lays out the context for virtual schools with an overview of their development and operation and five chapters on key issues. In Chapter 1, we provide an overview of the growing phenomenon of virtual schools in American elementary and secondary (K–12) education, exploring their benefits and limitations. We describe approaches to planning for success and steps in beginning the planning process.

Chapters 2 through 6 are the "issues" chapters and are intended to provide practical advice from administrators and experts. In Chapter 2, Hernandez addresses the issue of ensuring access and equity in virtual schools. In Chapter 3, Freedman describes the role of technology in virtual schools and discusses key factors in making good technology decisions. Funding is a key part of the success formula for virtual schools; in Chapter 4, Cavalluzzo delves into funding models and the politics inherent in funding issues. Policy and administrative practice are essential to virtual school development and operation; in Chapter 5, Blomeyer and Dawson explore important policy and practice issues. In Chapter 6, Stefanski describes how marketing and public relations impact stakeholder support and build audiences for virtual school offerings.

Part II profiles seven virtual school or K–12 e-learning efforts. The virtual schools selected for these case studies represent different kinds of organizational control. In Chapter 7, Friend and Johnston profile the Florida Virtual School, a widely recognized state-level virtual school. Virtual schools operated by a collaborative consortium are well represented in Chapter 8 by the Virtual High School, as described by Pape, Adams, and Ribeiro. In Chapter 9, Baker, Bouras, Hartwig, and McNair profile a virtual charter school, the Colorado Virtual Academy, which relies upon a private for-profit provider, K12, Inc., for its curriculum. In Chapter 10, Jordan describes a virtual school operated by a local education agency, the Cumberland County Schools Web Academy. In Chapter 11, Smalley provides a case study of the University of Missouri–Columbia High School. The case studies conclude with two profiles of K–12 e-learning efforts supported by a state university or state government: In Chapter 12, Vrasidas and Chamberlain explore university roles in virtual schools and describe a partnership between a university and a statewide school consortium to offer online curriculum to schools via the LUDA Virtual High School, and in Chapter 13, Simonson describes a statewide effort to integrate technology into K–12 instruction via the Digital Dakota Network.

Part III, containing the final chapter, synthesizes the information presented in the book. We summarize how virtual schools are addressing key issues in planning for success, as well as the important lessons learned by different types of virtual schools; set forth a detailed basic road map for success for schools considering virtual learning; and discuss the implications for the future of virtual learning.

In the next chapter, we begin to look at the context for virtual schools and planning for success, by examining perspectives on virtual schools.

PART I

Context

Perspectives on Virtual Schools

Tom Clark & Zane L. Berge

VIRTUAL SCHOOLS are a rapidly growing phenomenon in American elementary and secondary (K–12) education. They are the latest and potentially the most controversial manifestation of the e-learning revolution in schools. As Clark and Else (2003) have noted, "For the foreseeable future, the World Wide Web . . . is likely to serve as an umbrella technology uniting distance education media for distributed learning. . . . Virtual schooling is the next wave" (pp. 35–36).

The term *virtual school* is generally applied to any educational organization that offers K–12 courses through Internet- or Web-based methods (Clark, 2001). The World Wide Web Consortium (2003), which creates Web standards, defines the Web as the "universe of network-accessible information." Virtual school courses involve online, or virtual, learning that can occur not only via the Internet, but also via schools' local and wide area networks.

A virtual school is a form of distance education in which teacher and learner are separate and instruction is mediated. It is also a type of e-learning, being one of the many ways in which educational technology is integrated into teaching and learning. In other forms of e-learning, the teacher may be on-site with the student, and the technologies used may be online or off-line. For example, computer-based learning facilitated by a local teacher and technology integration in K–12 classrooms are examples of e-learning, but not of distance learning or virtual schooling. The use of such e-learning approaches is growing rapidly in schools and deserves to be studied. Many e-learning initiatives are being led by universities or state government.

NEW CHALLENGES FOR SCHOOLS

In the first decade of the twenty-first century, schools face sterner challenges than ever before. These include new federal mandates, inadequate funding, and unimaginative use of technology.

New Demands for School Improvement and Educational Equity

Under the January 2002 reauthorization of the Elementary and Secondary Education Act, called No Child Left Behind (NCLB), all K–12 schools must make Adequate Yearly Progress (AYP) in meeting school improvement goals, with 100% of students demonstrating academic proficiency on state tests by 2013–14, including low-income, minority, and disabled students and students with limited English proficiency. Each state education agency is required to develop a statewide plan, which must be approved by the U.S. Department of Education, that defines its AYP. Schools not making AYP within 2 years are required to devote 20% of their federal Title I funding to providing Educational Choice options for students in failing schools (after 3 years they are also required to provide Supplemental Education Services). Under Educational Choice, parents have the option of moving students enrolled in failing schools into other schools, including charter schools. In some states, these include virtual charter schools, although only a limited number of parents can provide the kinds of home supervision needed, and the capacity of virtual charter schools to accept students is also limited.

High schools need to improve graduation and dropout rates to meet their states' NCLB plan. NCLB also sets the goal of a "highly qualified" teacher in every classroom by 2005. However, there are many problems implementing NCLB in the real world. Schools with low-scoring students will need large improvements annually to meet AYP, and a single low-scoring subgroup means a school's AYP is not met. As a result, a large percentage of public schools, including schools designated as exemplary, are not making AYP. School districts often have far more students in schools not meeting AYP than viable Educational Choice slots in non-AYP schools.

Funding Constraints and Limited Resources

Federal Title I funding is less than the amount authorized and insufficient for the mandated school improvement tasks under NCLB. Depressed state and local economies have inadequate discretionary seed funding for new programs, including virtual school programs. The new federal program,

Enhancing Education Through Technology, provides limited state pass-through funding for technology use in schools. Schools vary widely in the amount of state and local funding available to meet school improvement needs.

Limited Impact of Technology

Schools have made extensive investments in technology infrastructure, but the impact of technology on improving teaching and learning is still in question. Becker (2000) concludes in a national study that "computers are clearly becoming a valuable and well-functioning instructional tool" (p. 29). But Becker also finds that "computers have not transformed the teaching practices of a majority of teachers, particularly teachers of secondary academic subjects" (p. 29), lending credibility to the arguments of critics such as Larry Cuban. In *The Principal as Technology Leader*, Creighton (2003) summarizes the responses of hundreds of school administrators and staff to the question "Why do technology programs fail?" He identifies four causes of failure:

- Failure to tie technology to institutional mission and priorities
- Inappropriate leadership—too little or too much
- Failure to get the right people on board
- Moving too fast (p. 21)

BENEFITS OF VIRTUAL SCHOOLS

Virtual schools can play a role in ensuring equitable access to high-quality learning opportunities for K–12 learners. They can help schools improve student outcomes and skills and provide new educational choices for parents and students.

Expanding Educational Access

The ability to provide an expanded curriculum is probably the most frequently cited benefit of virtual schools. Like previous forms of electronic distance education, virtual schools can make courses accessible to students who could not otherwise take them. For example, some schools offer low-enrollment advanced elective courses via online learning. Schools may offer online dual enrollment courses in collaboration with community colleges. Virtual courses can potentially be offered anywhere, anytime via Internet-capable computers. Students may be able to select their pace of interaction with content, instructor, and fellow learners, within a given structure, and may fulfill course or diploma requirements more quickly.

Policymakers and virtual school advocates have touted the potential benefits of online learning for minority, low-income, rural, inner-city, and small-school students as well as for remedial and alternative learners and other targeted populations. Some virtual schools, such as the Florida Virtual School and the University of California College Preparatory Initiative, have made low-income and minority student recruitment a priority and have had substantial success in these efforts.

High-Quality Learning Opportunities

A virtual school may be perceived as most beneficial when it offers courses that enrich the curriculum through their high quality and challenging nature and help students meet measurable state and national standards of learning. The idea here is to go beyond expanding access to "equivalent" educational experiences through distance learning, to create a learning environment that raises the bar for the quality of education for all learners. In virtual learning, instructional methods, content, and interaction can be individualized to best meet the needs of the learner. Virtual schools have the potential to assist every learner in meeting individual educational goals, while tracking progress electronically. Some of the leading virtual schools have developed extensive processes for ensuring high-quality courses. The National Education Association's *Guide to Online High School Courses* (2002) proposes quality measures and standards for such courses and provides helpful planning information for stakeholders involved in online learning.

Improving Student Outcomes and Skills

Schools are under great pressure to improve student outcomes, especially with the advent of No Child Left Behind. Some local schools are using virtual schools and e-learning as part of their Supplemental Education Services strategies for assisting students in schools that have not made the required Annual Yearly Progress on NCLB goals. Many virtual school providers offer courses and delivery methods tailored to remedial or alternative student populations.

While meeting NCLB requirements is the current crisis facing schools, administrators continue to look for ways to improve the long-term educational and career outcomes of students. Federal funding is helping increase low-income and minority student access to online Advanced Placement (AP) courses and exam review. Students completing online AP courses and passing AP exams can boost their grade point averages and receive early college credit. Student outcomes can also serve as measures of quality. For example, as more students take online AP courses, the quality of their online learning would be reflected in the percentages passing AP exams compared with peers in regular AP courses.

Participation in virtual learning can also help students build the kinds of skills needed for rewarding careers in the twenty-first century, such as digital age literacy, inventive thinking, effective communication, and high productivity (Metiri Group, 2003). Digital age literacy includes basic literacy in reading and math. Since large amounts of time are spent reading Web pages and responding to postings and course materials, the reading skills of virtual learners may be strengthened. Researchers in a 3-year study found that low-income K–12 students who spent more time on the Web performed better on standardized tests of reading achievement than nonparticipating peers (Michigan State University, 2003). Virtual schoolers may learn more effective teaming and collaboration skills online. They may develop stronger self-discipline and time management skills, as most do not have an on-site teacher to ensure that they stay on pace. Their technology and Internet proficiencies may also be improved, including skills in troubleshooting computer problems.

Educational Choice

A key benefit of virtual learning for some students and their parents is the expansion of educational choice. In spring 1999, an estimated 850,000 students, or about 1.7% of students nationwide, were being homeschooled (Bielick, Chandler, Broughman, 2001), and the number appears to be growing. For those students who attend a virtual school rather than a regular school, or who combine online courses with home study, virtual schooling may be seen as a safer, more supportive alternative to regular schooling. In large-scale surveys of homeschoolers enrolled in virtual schools and their parents, both cited dissatisfaction with public schools as a key reason for participation in virtual schooling (Optimal Performance, 2001; Barker & Wendel, 2001). Some private virtual schools offer a curriculum integrating family or faith-based values, or approaches to education that parent and child prefer.

Online charter schools are one of several options for educational choice supported by the U.S. Department of Education under No Child Left Behind—an array that then Undersecretary of Education Eugene Hickok described as "this promising new mix that, I believe, will help deliver the excellent education that all children deserve" (K12, Inc., 2001). Most media attention and public awareness focuses on the virtual charter school phenomenon. It appears safe to conclude, however, that at present most virtual school participants are enrolled in regular schools and using online courses to supplement regular instruction.

LIMITATIONS OF VIRTUAL SCHOOLS

It is important to consider not only the potential benefits of virtual schools, but also their limitations. These include high start-up costs, continuing inequities of access, differentials in student readiness, higher dropout rates, difficulties in obtaining accreditation, and low levels of public and stakeholder support.

Program Costs

As Morris (2002) notes, start-up costs for virtual school programs can be quite intimidating. Technology infrastructure, content, and staff salaries will need to be dealt with before per-student state funding becomes available based on enrollments. Many schools have used grant funding for start-up. A continuation budget may need to draw in part upon general district funds, which requires the buy-in of key internal stakeholders. Obtaining such funding is becoming more challenging as district budgets tighten.

Student Access Issues

The "digital divide" between rich and poor schools in networked computer access for students has greatly lessened in recent years. Kleiner and Lewis (2003) have reported that in fall 2002, 99% of U.S. public schools and 92% of instructional rooms in U.S. public schools had Internet access, although large city schools lagged somewhat, with 88% of instructional rooms connected. The ratio of students to Internet-connected instructional computers was 4.8 to 1 overall, and 5.5 to 1 for schools with the highest poverty concentrations. About 73% of high schools made Internet access available outside regular school hours, including high-poverty schools.

However, the divide continues in home computer use (see Figure 1.1). DeBell and Chapman's (2003) analysis of 2001 Census Bureau survey data found wide ethnic, family income, and parental education differentials in the use of computers at home by children aged 5–17. About 41% of Black and Hispanic children used computers at home, compared to 77% of White and 76% of Asian children. Only 31% of children from families with annual incomes of less than $20,000 used computers at home, compared to 89% of those whose families had annual incomes over $75,000. About 26% of children whose parents did not complete high school used computers

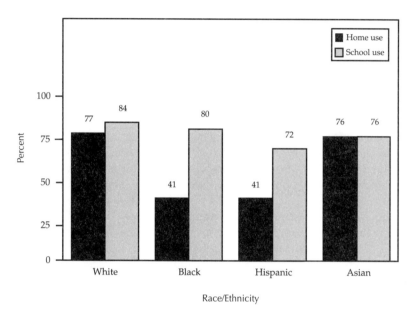

Figure 1.1. Percentage of children and adolescents using computers at home and at school by race/ethnicity, 2001. *Sources*: U.S. Census Bureau, *Current Population Survey*, September 2001; DeBell & Chapman, 2003.

at home, compared with 90% of those living with at least one parent who had attended graduate school.

Many virtual charter school program providers, such as K12, Inc., and Connections Academy, provide free home computer setups for their students. About 18% of public high schools loaned laptops to their students in 2002, but high-poverty and predominantly minority schools offered less access, and the total percentage of public schools offering laptop access actually decreased from 2001 to 2002 (Kleiner & Lewis, 2003). The alternative for public schools is to rely upon expanded hours of computer lab access for students in virtual courses, which may not totally bridge the divide. Given that the percentage of students enrolled in public schools who participate in supplemental virtual courses is still fairly low, schools might consider targeting laptop or computer loan programs to those virtual students with inadequate home access to the Internet. Without free or low-cost Internet access, a computer is of little use for virtual schooling. It is optimal for students to dial into the school network, if students reside in the local calling area. However, these kinds of costs may be difficult to cover.

Access to virtual learning does not guarantee success. Strategies for helping low-achieving students "stay on track" for graduation through online remedial education or for increasing college eligibility of low-income and minority students through online AP courses may be destined for failure unless attention is paid to helping these students be successful in virtual learning.

Student Readiness Issues

Virtual schooling may not be a good fit for some students, due to learning style, academic and technology skills, motivational levels, or other factors. Students with low reading and comprehension skills are unlikely to thrive in online courses. As Berge (2001) noted, "For some students, 'any-time learning' becomes 'no-time learning' because they have not developed the skills to structure and manage their own time" (p. 10). Students who are less proficient in technology use or who have limited access to technology at home or school may also do less well in virtual courses.

While online learning can give students new opportunities for collaborative learning, many students report feeling isolated or missing regular classroom interaction when they take a virtual course. Students may be resistant to changes in teacher and learner roles that give them additional responsibility for their own learning. Instructors may be unaware that a student is in trouble in the absence of contextual clues, and students may not realize they need to proactively seek help in the online learning environment (Kennedy, 2002).

Many virtual schools administer self-screening surveys on readiness issues to potential students. Virtual school programs may develop criteria for the students they permit to take virtual courses, such as grade point average or reading scores. Where policy allows, it makes sense to devise screening methods that help identify students who are intrinsically motivated to succeed in their courses. For example, some programs require students to ask an administrator to sign off on the application, or to complete a short essay on why they want to enroll. Some virtual schools offer short courses that let students practice online learning and study skills before enrolling in courses for a grade. Under No Child Left Behind, all students must exhibit basic technology use skills in the eighth grade by 2006; meeting this goal will help ensure that high school students have one of the baseline skills needed to take a virtual course. The sense of isolation may be addressed to some extent through local tutoring and, if multiple local students are participating in virtual learning, through informal peer mentoring. Providing more intensive on-site support may help address student readiness issues generally.

Retention Issues

Students taking an online course may never get on track, which can contribute to high dropout rates and poor grades. Some virtual schools have documented high dropout rates in their early stages, although retention appears to improve over time (Bigbie & McCarroll, 2000; Clark, Lewis, Oyer, & Schreiber, 2002). High school students may be more likely than college students to drop out of online courses (Roblyer, 1999). Research on other forms of electronic distance learning suggests that online high school students who are not high achievers may drop out at higher rates (Kirby & Roblyer, 1999).

Virtual school programs offer different pacing options for students. While some continue to offer courses that students can start and complete at any time, many align courses with the regular academic year. Some virtual schools issue automated prompts to instructional and support staff when a student falls behind in completion of assignments and active participation. A well-thought-out plan for screening potential students, monitoring and supporting enrolled students, and encouraging appropriate pacing in coursework may lessen retention and failure problems.

Accreditation Issues

State approval or regional accreditation for a virtual school's program, especially at the high school level, can play a role in its acceptability to students, parents, schools, and colleges. Where courses are taken through the local public school, this is generally less of a problem. Typically, the school approves the course and grants the grade and credit locally. A local teacher acts as the virtual school instructor or tutor and is the instructor of record. However, if the virtual school is providing courses directly to the student, colleges and employers may not accept its high school diploma. Virtual schools operated by local education agencies such as public schools can attain approval and accreditation more easily than private schools or nonschool entities. Universities have long experience with obtaining regional accreditation for academic programs, but in some states they have found it difficult to obtain state approval for their virtual high school diploma programs. Private schools often turn to alternative certification agencies not recognized by postsecondary institutions (Clark, 2001).

Low Levels of Public Support and Stakeholder Buy-In

Two recent Phi Delta Kappa polls have found only 30% of the general public in favor of students' participating in virtual charter schools or online courses without attending a regular school (Rose & Gallup, 2000, 2002). Those seeking to operate virtual school programs that supplement regular school instruction often encounter confusion from people who assume all virtual schools are virtual charter schools that serve only homeschoolers. Concerns that online learning will reduce funding for public schools or replace teachers or regular schools have been expressed by teacher unions and public school advocates. An effective communication plan can proactively address the concerns of these key stakeholders.

PLANNING FOR SUCCESS

Planning for success begins with the initial exploration of offering a virtual school program. What are some things that an educational administrator needs to consider? At a basic level, the same considerations apply to a virtual school program operated by a local, regional, or state education agency.

Approaches to Virtual School Planning

Several publications have focused on virtual school planning. Zucker, Kozma, Yarnell, and Marder (2002) describe the Virtual High School, a national collaborative of schools, providing rich detail from a multiyear evaluation. For those planning to create a local virtual school program "from scratch," Morris (2002) has developed a fine descriptive overview from the program administrator's viewpoint of the experience of one local virtual school program. Morris's book includes a chronology of the operational details in creating the Wichita eSchool. Many of these details are also of use to virtual schools that rely more upon external providers in developing their programs than did Wichita.

A simple, systematic approach to working with external providers and making strategic decisions about the virtual school program is offered by Newman, Stein, and Trask (2003). Newman and his colleagues discuss planning approaches for virtual school programs, briefly profile several schools, and profile vendors that provide services to virtual school programs. They provide a framework for making "build or partner" decisions on curriculum, instruction, and program management components, and indicate in some detail the capabilities of each profiled external provider in these areas. Some may be put off by the report's focus on partnering with vendors, and it should be noted that it was funded in part by six e-learning providers. However, it does provide valuable information and a systematic approach.

"Follow Your Own Path" Approach

These publications do not focus on a local process for determining whether a virtual school program is a viable option for addressing school improvement needs. The main issue for the local school may be whether it can maintain ownership of the process if it decides to work with external vendors too early on. Because vendors often have experience in many components of operating a virtual school, there may be a tendency to rely excessively on their expertise in planning the virtual school program.

We recommend a "follow your own path" approach. Consider external partnerships only after a local process has established the need for and feasibility of a virtual school program. Use external partnerships to meet specific local needs, rather than allowing them to drive the process. Keep the focus on how a virtual learning option can assist with school improvement.

CONCLUSION

Virtual schools are a rapidly growing phenomenon in K–12 education. Even as their budgets are becoming more limited, schools face new challenges in areas such as school improvement and equity. The impact of technology on improving teaching and learning is still in question, including the impact of virtual schools.

The potential benefits of virtual schools include increasing educational access, providing high-quality learning opportunities, improving student outcomes and skills, and expanding options for educational choice. Limitations and challenges include program costs, differing levels of student access, lack of student readiness or fit for virtual learning, student dropout, and improving acceptability and support among stakeholders and the public.

Those planning to offer a virtual school program have many resources and options to consider. We recommend a "follow your own path" approach for local schools that keeps the focus on how a virtual learning option helps meet school needs.

Equity and Access:
The Promise of Virtual Schools

Francisco J. Hernandez

T HIS CHAPTER will review the policy issues of equity and access in the context of the virtual school movement. In particular, I review California's lack of equitable access to a college preparatory curriculum as an illustration of the impact of skewed equity and access as well as a result of specific conditions within the state. An understanding of the California situation is important because there are areas of California that reflect the racial and ethnic makeup predicted for the entire United States by the year 2030. I also examine the experience of the University of California College Preparatory (UCCP) Initiative, with special attention to the lessons learned from that project. The chapter concludes with a set of recommendations for ensuring that equity and access will be at the center of virtual school planning and implementation.

EQUITY AND ACCESS ISSUES

The issues of equity and access involve attempting to bridge a "set of divides, cutting in different directions like the tributaries of a river . . . those inequities involve not so much access to computers, but the way computers are used to educate children."

—*Education Week*

Clark (2000b) argues that equity and access are the critical issues facing those planning for virtual schools. These issues have been discussed and debated since the first schools were established in the United States and educational technology took the form of a writing tablet. The latest revolution in technology has presented a great promise of increased educational attainment for all students. However, the combination of the rapid growth of the U.S. minority communities and the rapid rise of e-learning as an educational opportunity has created a crucial issue that demands the attention of all virtual school planners—the disproportionate access to technology along racial, ethnic, and gender lines and the opportunities that equity of access can offer to a diverse population.

Access to Technology

Recent years have seen the rapid deployment of computers in all schools including those that serve poor and minority students. Along with the spread of computers has come increased access to the Internet and to computer-based instructional materials. For example, between 1998 and 2000, Internet access for African American households rose from 11.2% to 23.5% (U.S. Department of Commerce, 2000). Use of computers will continue to rise rapidly as hardware, software, and access costs continue to drop. However, the "set of divides" continue to trouble e-learning architects: As more computers are put into schools, minority and poor students have less access than their majority counterparts. The U.S. Department of Commerce (2000) report contends that as more computer-based educational materials become available, minority and poor students have access only to the oldest, not the latest and greatest; consequently, these students do not use technology as much as they should to increase their level of educational attainment.

About 35% of U.S. children are members of minority groups and that figure will increase to more than 50% by 2040 (U.S. Census, 2004). If equal access to these new e-learning opportunities is not provided, virtual education will increase educational gaps rather than provide the means to close them. Because virtual education has so much promise as a key provider of educational opportunity, it has drawn both the fascination and ire of educational technology critics. However, because virtual education has the potential to challenge fundamental education tenets, it deserves special attention as a means to overcome barriers for minority and poor students.

The Web-based Education Commission (2000) issued a call to action among state and federal educational agencies to increase opportunities for all students to access e-learning resources. That call to action was answered in the form of federal and state legislation that provided funds for computers, Internet connections, and the creation of online learning materials. The federal legislation also created the opportunity for e-learning private-public partnerships. Several state educational agencies allocated funds for addressing the gaps in access to e-learning. Virtual school architects need to ensure that e-learning access and equity trends mirror the tremendous gains in Internet access and utilization in recent years.

Access to a College Preparatory Curriculum

> For too long in this country, we made assumptions about students' abilities based on the color of their skin, or their parents' lack of education, or the country they came from, or whether they came to school in a wheelchair. We even made assumptions about ability based on gender. As a result of this tyranny of low expectations, many students were never encouraged to take challenging or Advanced Placement courses.
> —Richard Riley, former U.S. Secretary of Education

One of the most glaring examples of disparate access to educational resources is the differential access to a college preparatory curriculum. One key indicator of that disparity is the dearth of Advanced Placement (AP) courses in high schools with a large percentage of minority or low-income students. At the best high schools, the availability of AP courses improves the students' chances of getting into colleges and universities; for example, high school students can earn college credits and increase their grade point averages for college admissions (the most selective universities assign extra grade points for AP and honors courses) by successfully completing AP courses and scoring well on the associated tests. And as colleges and universities have become more selective, that edge has become increasingly important. But a student's access to AP curriculum varies from none to more than 20 courses depending on the high school he or she attends. Put bluntly, as with other college preparatory offerings, access to AP courses is not equitable across ethnic, socioeconomic, or racial groups. Given that when universities make admissions decisions, a student who takes many AP (or honors) courses has a distinct advantage over one who doesn't, that inequity is a significant problem for minority students, who tend to be in the high schools with few if any AP courses.

We know, for example, that White students are four times more likely to take AP tests than Black students and twice as likely as Hispanic students. To address the need for increased access to AP courses, the federal government created several programs to increase access to college preparatory courses (No Child Left Behind Act, 2002). One program, the Advanced Placement Incentive Program (APIP), is designed to increase the level of participation in AP courses by poor and minority students. This federal initiative is two-pronged, providing for test fee waivers for poor students and also for additional AP courses. The fee waiver program is designed to increase the number of students who take the AP tests after they have successfully completed the AP courses. The additional courses would result from the following activities:

1. Additional teacher professional development in subject matter areas
2. Pre-AP-level course development, especially in mathematics and sciences
3. Coordination and articulation between grade levels to prepare students for academic achievement in Advanced Placement courses
4. Increasing the availability of, and participation in, online AP courses

The last set of activities caught the attention of educational agencies working in the e-learning arena. The APIP follows initiatives in several states that led to the development of online high school curriculum. Clark (2000b) has chronicled the history of these virtual school leaders and has documented the extent of their engagement with access and equity issues. Florida, for example, invested in a statewide online high school. Many of the students in this online school are from rural areas and do not have access to college preparatory courses. "One of their major motivations for doing this was equity in access," said William R. Thomas, the director of educational technology for the Atlanta-based Southern Regional Education Board (Sandham, 2001). Thomas singles out Florida for its commitment to online learning and notes, "the vast majority of states are in process of addressing digital-divide issues, and this is one way they're doing it." The Florida Virtual High School addressed access by allowing students from rural and low-performing schools to register before students from other public, private, or home schools. When the state of Florida announced an end to affirmative action for minority students, its online high school was one of the initiatives to increase minority enrollment in Florida colleges. The governor of Florida proposed to expand access to a college preparatory curriculum by increasing funding for the state's virtual high school. Later he also proposed an increase in funding for computers and Internet connections for poor and low-performing schools. This dual approach of increasing the availability of virtual learning curriculum as well as providing additional computers with Internet connections could be found across the country as each state grappled with access and equity issues.

Kentucky took a similar approach. In January 2000 the Kentucky Virtual High School was launched to provide "equal opportunity for rigorous coursework" to all students in Kentucky. Initially, the Kentucky Virtual High School marketed its services to poor schools, urban schools with minority populations, and schools with high dropout rates. In the summer of 2000, Kentucky was awarded a $1.1 million federal grant to provide AP courses for high-poverty and minority students. Kentucky also developed an online community of decision makers to address the gap in minority student achievement (Clark, 2000b).

States have banded together to address issues of equity of access to a college preparatory curriculum. A grant to the Western Interstate Commission for Higher Education (WICHE) expanded access to AP and honors courses for students in the western states. Through funding from the federal Advanced Placement Incentive Program (APIP), WICHE's Western Consortium for Accelerated Learning Opportunities (WCALD) provided funding for Arizona, Colorado, Hawaii, Idaho, Montana, New Mexico, Oregon, South Dakota, and Utah. The consortium was created so that these states could provide Advanced Placement programs for low-income and rural students.

THE CALIFORNIA EXPERIENCE

The state of California is one of the most ethnically and racially diverse in the country and its school population reflects that diversity. The profile of California schools has changed rapidly over the last 20 years: In 1981–82, Whites represented 56% of the student population; by 2003, Whites represented only 34.8% of the population, with Hispanic students comprising 44.2% of California's elementary and high school students (California Department of Education, 2003).

Unfortunately, the different ethnic and racial groups have different rates at which they complete the course prerequisites for college admissions. For example, White students comprise 44% of public high school graduates but 50% of those who complete a college preparatory curriculum; in contrast, Hispanics comprise 32.8% of public high school graduates but only 21% of those who complete a college preparatory curriculum (California Department of Education, 2003).

A study by the California State University Institute for Education Reform (1999) reported some disturbing statistics:

- About 20% of all high school students in California's public schools were enrolled in schools that had 4 or fewer AP classes, and about 40% were enrolled in schools with 12 or more AP classes.
- More than 90% of California's high schools offered AP courses, but many students across all ethnicities and socioeconomic strata had limited AP opportunities.

- In schools across all levels of AP program size, Hispanics and African Americans generally participated in AP classes at rates substantially below their share of total school enrollment.

This unequal access was the impetus for a 1999 lawsuit that was instrumental in shaping the virtual school approach within California (Rasheda Daniel, 1999). The American Civil Liberties Union (ACLU) noted in its lawsuit that at Inglewood High School students had access to 3 AP courses while the students at Beverly Hills High had access to 45 AP courses. The ACLU concluded that the lack of access to AP courses was a violation of the Equal Protection Clause and the Education Clause of the California Constitution.

Another factor contributing to unequal access was a significant decrease in the level of enrollment of ethnic/racial minorities on University of California campuses. A state referendum, Proposition 209, prohibited consideration of either race or ethnicity in university admissions. Because of an immediate drop in enrollments of ethnic/racial minorities at university campuses, the California legislature provided additional funding for early outreach efforts throughout the state. These efforts were designed to increase the number of minority students who qualified for admission to California colleges and universities.

The drop in university enrollments among minority students, coupled by a concern over the lack of access to college preparatory courses led to a legislative initiative to increase college preparatory course offerings with special emphasis on AP courses. The California legislature funded several efforts to increase both the number of courses offered and the accessibility of those courses to minority students. One of those efforts was the University of California College Preparatory (UCCP) Initiative (http://www.uccp.org). The focus of the UCCP Initiative was to use Internet technologies under development as a part of the state's Digital California Project (an initiative to provide high-speed Internet connectivity to every school) to provide AP and honors courses to students in California high schools that did not have access to those courses.

Establishment of the University of California College Preparatory Initiative

To encourage our young people to pursue science and technology, we will offer distinguished scholar awards of $2,500 to any high school student who also scores a 5 on the Advanced Placement math exam and one AP science exam. If AP classes are not yet available, then we will

allow the student to qualify for a scholarship by obtaining an equivalent score on the Golden State Exam.

But that won't last long, because I'm calling on the Legislature to
provide the funds to make at least one AP class available to every student in California by this fall. . . .

By the following year, however, I don't want to hear any more ex-
cuses. I propose spending $20.5 million to ensure that at least four core
AP classes will be available to every high school student. No child in
California capable of taking AP classes will be held back because we
couldn't get the job done.

Gray Davis, State of the State, 2000

In 1997, well before Governor Davis made that promise, the UCCP Initiative had been funded after a year and a half of planning. California has
had several efforts to create high schools that used online learning as a
means to reach students outside of the regular high school setting. For
example, Choice 2000 was one of the original charter schools to provide
its curriculum fully online to California students. Other schools in the
Clovis, Poway, and San Diego school districts had also launched online
courses for their students.

The University of California (UC) sponsored initiatives to develop
additional charter schools as part of its efforts to increase the number of
minority students who qualified for admission. Two different feasibility
studies were funded: One study resulted in the Pruess Charter School situ-
ated on the UC–San Diego campus. The second examined the potential of
a virtual school that would serve the entire state—the Santa Cruz campus
took the lead in this feasibility study for a virtual charter school (Hernandez
et al., 1998). That study had components:

- An examination of the distance learning opportunities available to
  California high school students that met the course requirements
  necessary for admission to the University of California
- A survey of high schools to determine the need for distance learning
  courses and the technological readiness of participating high schools
- An assessment of the best distance learning delivery methods
- A strategic plan for funding the creation of the courses and their
  use in high school or alternative settings
- An appraisal of the alternative organizational models for operating such a statewide project

The feasibility study culminated in a virtual school conference held
in June 1998 on the Santa Cruz campus. That conference brought together
educators from California high schools, colleges, and universities to dis-

cuss the creation of a virtual high school sponsored by UC and made available to the entire state. The conference featured demonstrations of other successful virtual school efforts including the nationwide Concord Consortium and the University of Nebraska's CLASS project.

Two concurrent developments were to affect the initial character of the UCCP Initiative. First, the UC regents were considering a proposal to change the course requirements for University admissions while maintaining the extra weight and credit given for AP and honors courses at admission. Second, the American Civil Liberties Union was preparing a suit against the state of California because of the unequal access to AP courses in minority and high-poverty high schools. Both of these events only increased the already strong pressure to increase the offerings of AP and honors courses in California high schools.

AP Online

> Access and equity are at the heart of the UCCP Initiative.
> —Interim evaluation report

Because the leadership of the initiative had plans for developing online offerings in AP subject areas, the UCCP Initiative was positioned to become one of the several efforts supported to increase AP and honors course offerings. The UCCP Initiative secured initial funding of $400,000 from the UC president's office in fall 1998 with the stipulation that the program offer its first AP courses in January 1999. By spring 1999, the UCCP Initiative had come to the attention of the state educational leadership. As a result, it was awarded additional funds to provide AP and honors courses to students from targeted high schools. In order to ensure that this investment was focused on access and equity (especially for poor and minority learners), UCCP developed an eligibility policy. To participate, high schools had to meet at least one of the following criteria:

1. School identified for potential state corrective action
2. School with an academic performance index of 1 through 5
3. School with less than 20% of its graduates matriculating to a 4-year college or university
4. School with more than 50% of its students receiving free or reduced-price lunch
5. School in the University of California School-University Program

The dual issues of access and equity were firmly engrained in the selection of schools and students to receive the initial UCCP services. The first two criteria focused on low-performing schools; the third criterion addressed the needs of students in schools not sending many graduates to higher education; the fourth criterion addressed the needs of low-income students; and the fifth criterion focused on schools allied with the university in school change efforts. The UC School-University Program was focused on teacher training and academic support activities in schools with low college-bound rates. The great majority of these schools had high proportions of poor and minority students.

To ensure that poor and minority students would have access to UCCP services, UCCP staff developed strategic partnerships with several statewide efforts. For example, legislation directed the UCCP Initiative to establish a partnership with the Advancement Via Individual Determination (AVID) program. AVID is a 20-year-old program designed to increase the number and percentage of underserved students attending higher education. The program began in San Diego with one school and 32 students. It now serves 1,000 schools and over 70,000 students in California. Providing both academic and motivational activities to support the students' aspirations for higher learning, AVID has grown to serve students both nationally and internationally. AVID students enroll in college preparatory courses, including AP courses, and in an elective course on preparing for college.

Other partnerships were established with the Mathematics, Engineering, Science Achievement (MESA) program, Puente Project, and the Early Academic Outreach Program. Each of these programs provides academic, motivational, and informational activities to minority and low-income students. These services include the following:

1. Academic support in the form of tutorials or how-to-study workshops
2. Motivational activities in the form of college field trips or guest speakers
3. Informational activities in the form of college application workshops or advising on financial aid for parents
4. College counseling in the form of course selection and admissions test preparation
5. Advocacy in the form of recommendations to high school counselors and to college and university admissions counselors

UCCP is able to provide complementary academic services by enrolling these students in credit-bearing courses, by providing online mentoring and tutoring, and by providing online access to AP examination review and ACT and SAT test preparation modules. This partnership—along with its special relationship with UC and other outreach efforts—enabled the UCCP Initiative to create communication channels between students, teachers, and counselors who were strong advocates for college-bound students.

The UCCP Initiative was also able to recruit a diverse staff experienced in academic programming designed to increase access and equity in educational settings. These staff members brought both experience and passion to the initiative. That experience and passion, combined with the additional perspective provided by their diverse ethnic and racial backgrounds, ensure that each program element considers access and equity as key drivers for making program decisions. For example, the program provides bilingual staff to meet the needs of Spanish-speaking students and their parents.

When students were asked why they enrolled in UCCP courses, they responded that they wanted to take a challenging course, that their school did not offer the AP course then needed, or that they needed the course to enhance their eligibility for college. This finding confirms that the UCCP Initiative has targeted the schools and students with the most need. Our analysis shows that more than half of the schools eligible for UCCP services have taken advantage of the UCCP services to offer online courses for their students. At present, use of UCCP services is greater in rural, small high schools than in the urban schools.

The racial/ethnic mix of participants in UCCP programs is shown in Figure 2.1. This diversity among student participants reflects the program's strong efforts at reaching minority and low-income populations. However, additional inroads still need to be made: A recent study by an outside evaluator found that the project needs to develop stronger communication links with minority students in urban high schools. The findings indicate that minority students in urban schools are not taking advantage of UCCP

Hispanic/Latino	30%
White/Caucasian	38
Black/African American	6
Asian/Pacific Islander	16
American Indian/Alaska Native	1
Other/Two or More Races	3
No Response	7

Figure 2.1. Race/ethnicity distribution of UCCP participants.

services at a level matching their need for AP and honors courses. As a result, the UCCP Initiative will need to redouble efforts in urban schools in order to increase the number of minority and low-income students who take advantage of online services.

LESSONS LEARNED

The University of California College Preparatory Initiative was created with the specific intent to serve minority and low-income students who, because of the high school they attend, did not have access to a solid college preparatory curriculum. Like other states, California has many efforts and programs to address this educational gap: Some efforts are focused on school improvement, others on providing additional training for teachers, and still others on providing additional services directly to students and their parents. The UCCP Initiative is distinctive in that the program is designed to use computing technology and the Internet to accomplish these goals.

Challenges

In launching a program to meet the education needs of minority and low-income students, UCCP faced many formidable and daunting challenges. Even so, the UCCP Initiative experience revealed some noteworthy information of relevance to others involved in the virtual school movement.

Paucity of research. There is a paucity of research, case studies, and documentation on efforts to address the dual challenges of closing an education gap and bridging the digital divide. At the same time, there is a great volume of research on efforts to bridge the education gap for minority and low-income students, and on the efficacy of technology use in education. While much has been written about the digital divide, little has been written about how to build bridges across that divide. And there is little research (and, particularly unhelpfully, few case studies) on efforts to address the education gap with virtual schooling. To maximize its successes, the virtual school movement needs to engage in ongoing analysis of program efforts in order to improve such efforts whether or not they included cyber teaching or e-learning. I recommend a coordinated and comprehensive effort to sponsor research chronicling these efforts, comparing their approaches, and documenting their successes.

Barriers for minority and low-income students. Barriers for minority and low-income students exist within the virtual schools as much as within other schools. I recommend that the types of communication channels with minority and low-income students be increased beyond those now available within their schools. I also recommend communication with and support from other advocates for access and equity. These include the following:

- Federal programs, such as Gear Up, Talent Search, and Upward Bound
- State programs, especially those that provide outreach services to minority communities from institutions of higher education
- In-school advocates, including minority administrators, counselors, and teachers
- Interested parent groups

Need for additional support. Minority and low-income students can be successful in virtual schooling if they are challenged and if they receive sufficient support. These students were responsive to efforts by UCCP staff to recruit them to enroll for online services. Although they faced many barriers as indicated above, these students persisted and overcame the barriers by asking for—and sometimes demanding—assistance from both UCCP and school staff. With additional and adequate support, minority and low-income students could succeed in the completion of online courses. Additional academic support services were designed to meet the needs of these students. The program provided additional online tutoring and assigned cyber mentors to provide additional assistance for these students. I recommend that online schools provide demanding and rigorous courses and academic support services, and tailor their services to meet the special needs of minority and low-income students.

Training school personnel. School personnel are not always prepared to meet the technology needs of students taking courses online. For those students without access to computers at home, virtual (and regular) schools need to provide adequate access to school computers. They should also provide someone who can address student's questions in a timely manner. Online teachers, as well as the course management system they use, must be flexible enough to adjust for limited access to computers. For example, course management systems must allow for downloading and printing assignments for work off-line. School staff must be prepared to provide students with information about how to access computers in the community in which they reside. The virtual school needs to provide both student and teacher orientations that emphasize best practices in the use of technology use for online teaching and learning.

Intermittent availability of online assistance. The course materials were available anytime and anyplace. However, mentors, online teachers, and technical assistance were not. In order to provide the necessary support for online learners, virtual schools need to create additional support mechanisms. I recommend the following mechanisms:

- Online tutorials in the subject matter and in general skill areas of mathematics and writing
- Online tutorials on technical issues
- Peer-mentoring structures
- Subject matter–based student study groups
- Regular, scheduled opportunities for students to check in with online tutors, mentors, and teachers

Staff-student communication. On-site school personnel and online teachers, tutors, mentors, and support staff did not always communicate adequately to address the needs of online learners. Especially with regard to minority and low-income students, all school staff involved with online learners need to establish formal and regular communication channels both within and external to the course management system. Online tutors, mentors, student-support staff, and cyber teachers need access to a student's progress report. I recommend the development of timely communication among the students' course delivery team to address issues that include the delivery of the textbook, the completion of course assignments, computer access, and finally, the successful completion of the course.

Diversity by Design

> All secondary school students deserve access to a wide variety of high-quality courses. Yet many schools—especially smaller, rural and resource-poor urban schools—can offer little more than a basic curriculum. For their students, these limited offerings can translate into a limited future.
> —Julie Z. Aronson and Mike J. Timms, *Net Choices, Net Gains*

Virtual schools must lead the educational community in the attempt to address the significant gaps in educational opportunity afforded to students in the United States. The additional powers of instructional technologies must be used to bridge these educational gaps rather than build more divides—digital or otherwise. To that end, virtual schools should have policies and practices specifically designed to address those gaps.

Virtual schools should set as a goal that their student bodies reflect the ethnic/racial makeup of their related area of service. Further, each virtual school should have cost structures that provide equal access to educational technologies for low-income students and to schools comprised of significant numbers of minority and low-income students.

Virtual schools should establish strong partnerships with federal, state, and local programs designed to increase educational opportunities for poor and minority students. These partnerships should include linkages for student recruitment, for information to parents, and for the additional support services provided by these programs. Similar partnerships should be established with programs designed to increase the access to hardware, software, and connectivity for minority and low-income communities.

Virtual schools should establish as a goal the recruitment of ethnically/ racially diverse personnel. Such personnel will help establish a strong connection to minority communities, which in turn will yield positive results in the recruitment of students and in the design of support services necessary to serve those students.

Virtual schools should establish national dialogues about access and equity issues. They must help each other identify, confront, and overcome each of the many obstacles present in e-learning for minority and low-income students.

Virtual schools should band together to establish interstate programs to expand educational opportunity beyond their individual state boundaries. Through collaboration, successful virtual schools can offer educational opportunities to students regardless of state boundaries while simultaneously enhancing the opportunities for students within their state. State boundaries should not present yet another obstacle to increasing educational opportunity.

Virtual schools should develop national legislation to assist in the creation of interstate policies that support the sharing of educational resources for the benefit of minority and low-income students.

Virtual schools should establish a national dialogue with institutions of higher education leading to partnerships for the benefit of minority and low-income students. These partnerships should identify educational technologies developed for higher education that can be adapted and extended for the benefit of high school students.

CONCLUSION

The issues of equity and access have a long history within the educational history of the United States. Of the many programs and educational reforms that have been developed in an attempt to ameliorate the effects of a lack of equity and access for minority and low-income students, the virtual school movement promises to be a significant force in the building of bridges over the educational divides that affect minority and low-income students.

It is clear that e-learning and virtual high schools have much to offer all students. That promise also comes with additional responsibilities for those of us involved with virtual high schools. If we are to contribute to the solution for the education gap and the digital divide, we must dedicate our efforts, coordinate our activities, share our resources, and place access and equity issues at the front of all our planning and design efforts.

Virtual Schools:
Technology and Transformation

Gordon Freedman

HISTORICALLY, TECHNOLOGY has been used to enhance or supplement education, from preelectronic times to the digital age. When technology is incorporated into education from the foundation up, unifying learning and administration into one process or system, a new type of education culture is created: virtual education.

This chapter describes how technologies act as the foundation of virtual schools, contributing to a systemic change, or transformation, in school structure and function not found in earlier forms of distance education, educational technology, or alternative education.

VIRTUAL SCHOOL PROCESSES

Virtual schools introduce a new set of dynamics into educational practice. Virtual schools are giving rise to a new kind of education culture from their unique capacity to organize practice, policy, and performance coherently through the use of Internet technologies. In a short period, virtual schools have made an entrance, established themselves, and are now leading the way to establishing new and effective models for changing the creation, delivery, administration, and measurement of education in the United States.

Creation

The creation of virtual school courses and course materials often happens in a well-thought-out process that is transparent and open to inspection at all stages. This process begins with teams of teachers, instructional designers, subject matter experts, and course developers working together. This process alone is transformational: It collapses many separate activities spread across traditional education into one horizontal process. Traditionally, course creation is vertically organized, much of it inaccessible and closed from view. While this process uses technology, what is far more significant is the end-to-end nature of the single process for creating and distributing education.

Delivery

Educational delivery utilizing the Internet or intranets is point to any point—home, office, and classroom—and can include a network where there is either central control or decentralized control. It is not bound to the school site though it can be centered in the school; it can be expressed at a single school site or across a number of sites. This hallmark of virtual education—anywhere, anytime learning—brings with it many more attributes than just convenience, in particular, adaptability. This new education environment is computer-centric, not classroom-centric. In this environment, delivery is not simply one teacher facing a group of students, but the interaction between online learners and the instructor, and learners with each other.

Administration

State-funded virtual schools bring new solutions to the complex social realities of school management. Virtual schools arrive at a time when education, as a whole, is severely challenged on many fronts. There are shortages of qualified (or even certified) teachers, new demands for improved student achievement, and budget shortfalls of staggering proportions. Virtual schools are well suited for substituting for or augmenting physical schools. They hold tremendous promise for managing scheduling difficulties, filling in curricular gaps, and offering new professional development options.

Performance Monitoring

Virtual schools are data-driven. Every student's keystroke or page view creates user data. This data can be subjected to real-time analysis to determine across a cohort of users whether the curriculum is producing the right results and, if not, what issues need to be addressed. In the age of testing, No Child Left Behind, high teacher qualifications, and high student performance, virtual schools are designed to produce and monitor multiple forms of data. While traditional educational settings have to retrofit and establish layers of reporting structures, virtual schools can be designed with data collection and monitoring as a central feature of their structure.

Combined, the electronic creation, delivery, administration, and measurement of education create the basis for a new education culture, one that concentrates, by design, directly on the educational mission and the management of performance rather than on formalistic structures and traditional hierarchical organization. The culture of the administration, teaching, and learning that comes to life in virtual schools is akin to other social activities of today's generation that use the Internet to its full potential.

INTERNET TECHNOLOGIES AND VIRTUAL SCHOOLS

Virtual schools are bound to and defined by the structure and presence of the Internet, the culture of its use, and the software applications that run on it. The incorporation of the Internet into the life of schools is not so much a reliance on technology itself, but on the philosophy of the Internet. The Internet allows for the equitable distribution of content and interaction to many individuals and, at the same time, allows those individuals to define how they use the Internet. The Internet, Web pages, e-mail, e-commerce, instant messaging, stock trading, dating services, searching, and obtaining official information and news are all part of a separate and growing cultural transformation. For the most part, schools have been left out of the cultural embrace of the full power of the Internet; they tend to use e-mail, Web searching, and portals, but do not transpose the experience of school to something new. Virtual schools offer a cultural experience as part of the educational experience. Students often get to know more about teachers and peers through candid online discussions or the sharing of assignments than they would in a regular class.

Virtual schools rely on the Internet for delivery of instruction, interaction, administration, and other services. The software that powers virtual schools is server-based, requiring little more of the student, or teacher, than a connected computer with a Web browser. However, the software for hosting virtual schools is complex and ranks among the largest expenses of virtual schools. Virtual schools maintain a central course and resource development repository, a central distribution system, and a set of methods for local school and single student engagement.

Five primary Web-based software applications make up the foundation for virtual schools, enabling the new electronic administration and the new teaching and learning culture to flourish: a school portal, a student information system, a course management system (CMS), course content, and an assessment system. Each of these will be discussed later in this chapter, with special emphasis on the CMS and the course content as the unique elements of a virtual school. A sixth component of the virtual school would be the purely administrative functions of human resources, finance, and state reporting. While there are software packages for these functions and some of the more sophisticated portal products have them, virtual schools tend to use a mix of products and no one package is commonly used or commonly defined.

Many schools have portals and have Web-based or digital student information systems. Many also use Web-based courses. The addition of and reliance on the course management system differentiates the virtual school from other à la carte educational technologies.

The School Portal

There are a variety of portals, ranging from simple Web pages and common electronic calendars for a school to sophisticated software for managing the school's entire electronic infrastructure. The first use of the portal in a school environment has been to post activity in every classroom, including assignments, access to grades, and reference material. Such use of portals for schools is growing. The virtual school uses the portal as the front door and the organization of the online school. From the portal, the students, teachers, and administrators go to their individual online activities or monitor the activities of others. The portal, as the name implies, is the opening into the virtual school.

The Student Information System

All schools by law have official student record systems whether they are server-based database systems or Web-based "enterprise" systems that are accessed and used via the Internet. The Web-based systems, which are getting more popular at physical sites, are gaining in sophistication and will be expected to hold performance data that can share statistics with state and federal offices. For the virtual school, the student information system is critical. It is the connection to the student that the virtual school may never meet personally. In the virtual schools the portal, course management system, and student information system must all be able to "talk" to each other and exchange data. At the center of these interoperations, the record of the student is the primary product of the virtual school. Student information system products are sold by commercial vendors or developed by individual virtual schools.

THE COURSE MANAGEMENT SYSTEM

If the student school information system is the back office filled with student records, the course management system is the classroom and teacher's office filled with content and communication. Course management systems brought the reality of virtual schools to the Internet. These systems, which will be described later in detail, bring together in one technology platform the course content, class and assignment scheduling, class communication, grade posting, and office hours. The virtual school really got its start when the CMS software could support the functions of school in one virtual package that had the feel, the content, the interactions, and the information exchange typical of a school classroom course.

The Course Content

Schools are about course content. Whether it is in the textbook, the lesson plan, research assignments, or calculations, content is what drives schools. Virtual schools use a CMS to house course content. In the case of some virtual schools (Florida is a good example), textbooks are not even used. Instead, the content in the course embodies what would otherwise be in a textbook. Other virtual schools, such as the University of California College Preparatory Initiative, do not require a textbook for their Advanced Placement and honors courses; they supply books for students who are more comfortable with a textbook.

The Assessment System

Since virtual schools are online, normal testing can be built into the course management system or acquired as a separate software package that will communicate with the CMS and the student information system. As these systems—either in the CMS or integrated with it—become more capable, real-time data for communicating test results and performance statistics will become a more common feature. For all schools, accountability data is all-important. For the virtual schools, it becomes a routine report because these schools are primarily data-driven. While some tests may be proctored at a physical site, other forms of verification are being used online.

Rapid Evolution

The companies that develop the course management system software, at the heart of virtual school operations, and the developers of related Internet education technologies acknowledge that the ways their products are used is evolutionary and not static. In contrast, much of the classroom educational technology is fixed and set for its particular software release and use. The CMS software, on the other hand, is constantly evolving, and while there are fixed releases, the feedback from user groups is constant. In short, the culture of users is affecting how the software is built so that the software, in time, accommodates the users' needs. This dynamic process is part of the development of the virtual education culture.

The rolling development of CMS and other Web-based education applications is part of the pattern of the rapid evolution of the Internet. As time passes, the underlying technologies develop more quickly and become more stable, facilitating the rapid addition of new functions in all software. Today, in course management system, student information system, and portal products, modular elements can be added and subtracted. In these products functionality has been altered incrementally, sometimes abruptly in a new product release, until now there is a stable complex of technical solutions and a stable base of technology that approximates, or exceeds, the interactions and functions achieved in a physical school setting and surpasses what could be done with simpler educational technologies.

A key feature of "enterprise" or Web-based systems on the Internet is their ability to distribute evenly and to get feedback instantaneously, resulting in constant, ongoing improvements to the central service, whether it is a course management system, student information system, assessment system, or some other Web-based product. This cycle of improvement is the hallmark of the Internet. This means that virtual schools and other virtual education settings can be designed to be learning organizations.

The Higher Education Model

Colleges and universities have a 5–7-year head start on their K–12 school counterparts in terms of their adoption of CMS technology for instructional support on campus or distance education off-campus. Today, on most college campuses, the course infrastructure is managed by CMS software as a part of the overall campus infrastructure. On the modern campus there is a merger between the course and portal infrastructure housing the syllabus, course calendar, key content provided by the professor, office hours, discussion boards, access to grades, and site for turning in assignments; the administrative infrastructure houses human resources, finance, and the student information system. In many cases, the single campus technology structure that is used to support the teaching, learning, and administration also supports the online college and university distance education operated by campus continuing education or extension operations. Course management systems, almost a universal on college and university campuses, often rely upon the same software used in virtual schools.

Newly arriving college freshmen encounter a total electronic culture as they leave the bricks-and-mortar confines of high school. There are approximately 4,000 colleges and universities in the United States. The two largest CMS providers in the college market, Blackboard and WebCT, each claim approximately 2,000 customers, which are predominantly physical campuses, not online distance programs. The third largest CMS company, eCollege, is the leader in servicing distance education programs, concentrating on the for-profit universities and the public college online distance education programs. Technology that helps students enroll, take courses, coordinate calendars, communicate to groups, classes, and individuals, interact in online office hours, and get announcements—all inherent functions in CMS—is a big part of postsecondary life characterized by committed budgets, chief information officers, and students who are in touch but still mobile.

The virtual schools are following the model of the university or college online distance education program or that of the fully online university, such as the University of Phoenix online or Capella University. On the other hand, a growing number of mainstream, bricks-and-mortar high schools are following campus-based colleges and universities in putting up the course and portal technologies to augment the schools' physical campus by allowing access to school from any location after school hours or for those who are not able to attend.

It is also interesting to note that the pattern for virtual education in the college and university setting grew up from the historical use of distance and correspondence education. Those units—typically university continuing education, university colleges, or extensions—were necessitated and in some cases mandated to provide education to farm students and other remote learners who could not travel to class every day. With the passage of time, the continuing education arms of colleges and universities adopted each new technology, from audiotapes to videotapes, to the use of e-mail.

In fact, it was on college campuses that the two major course management systems were spawned. Blackboard was developed at Cornell and American University, and WebCT originated at the University of British Columbia. Blackboard and WebCT were the first systems to automate professors' class Web pages; and Prometheus (now part of Blackboard), a product developed by George Washington University, pioneered the system-wide use of course management system technology.

THE CENTRAL TECHNOLOGY DECISION

Virtual schools are built upon and grow out of a technology foundation unprecedented in school environments, but commonplace in colleges and universities. The principal technology, the course management system, is an enterprise, systemwide, server-based software application sometimes referred to as a learning management system (LMS). The LMS, more preva-lent in corporate training environments, is designed for single users who are not interacting with a class, group, or cohort of students taking the same course. The significant quality of CMS and LMS technology in compari-son with other individual technologies or database products is that it is comprehensive and encompassing, whereas other education technologies are specific and isolated in their functions and purpose.

Most virtual schools use CMS software as the primary delivery sys-tem. There are a growing number of vendor options available, or virtual schools have the option to build their own CMS. CMS platforms may be outsourced to the vendor, using the application service provider (ASP) model, or run inside the virtual school, using a software license or hosted license model. Vendors used by some well-known virtual schools help il-lustrate the two models. eClassroom, which was chosen by the Illinois and Kentucky virtual high schools, is an outsourced model, hosted from its data center in Denver. Although a student may be in Illinois or Kentucky, the server and the 24/7 services are in Colorado. This ASP model means the state does not invest in technology and operators, but pays a per-student fee to eClassroom, a division of eCollege. UCCP and Michigan Virtual High School (MVHS), in contrast, use Blackboard, which has a school-based software licensing model. Their parent organizations license the software, and use their own hardware and employees to operate the system inside their institutions.

While UCCP and MVHS could physically exchange courses easily because they are both on Blackboard and they could run those courses on their Blackboard server, they could not necessarily network their course offerings together because they are running separate servers. eClassroom, on the other hand, because it runs one data center with one CMS appli-cation at the location, could link two or more virtual schools on their platform should those schools request the ability for interoperability. eClassroom also has a content solution that allows courses created with different CMS's to be accessed through the eClassroom platform.

Course management system software is dominated by three vendors: Blackboard, WebCT, and eClassroom (eCollege). This class of software application generates, to some extent, its own culture because the CMS houses the functions that model certain school functions. Unfortunately each system does it a little bit differently and locks out easy access to courses developed outside the specific platform; thus Blackboard courses do not operate inside WebCT and vice versa. At one time, as standards were being promulgated in the higher education environment, it was hoped that this problem could be mitigated. However, it is not in the interest of the CMS companies to do so, nor do the different applications make this easy to accomplish. As the school market develops further, a new standard, the School Interoperability Framework (SIF), is likely to attack the problem of mobility of courses once again.

Together, the functions of a CMS embody a coherent system, constituting what could be described as an "educational operating system," experienced by its users as more than the sum of its parts. The course management system is the home of the education environment, creating an educational ecology within its software. While CMS systems are not perfect, the multiplicity and coherence of core functions that are in a single software application are significant. There are also downsides to the CMS that are significant, leading to the thought that this generation of products, developed for higher education and adapted for school use, is really the first generation of good products.

The next generation of products will model learning needs more than modeling the school. Because of the origin of the CMS as a way to automate professors' Web pages in the university, and because of the limitations of the technology and bandwidth at the time, the CMS became primarily a text-based system that could be augmented with pictures and video and audio clips. These systems, in many ways, are not all that different from textbooks. Many practitioners, designers, and learning theorists hope that this model could give way to CMS models that are more versatile and engaging.

Because the CMS systems were largely designed for higher education, the companies are willing to make modifications that better suit the K–12 markets, yet they are still course-centric in design. Additionally, the main companies are still unwilling to make one product for school use and another for higher education. Ultimately, course management systems are better suited for the delivery of courses than for the operation of classrooms, the needs of school administration and reporting, or the distribution of interactive media like CD-ROM's. The distinction lies in the word *management*: The CMS, above all, is a management system. In the future, it is hoped that the CMS will provide a richer set of interactions with resources and incorporate more features that are unique to schools and more able to be adjusted as learning environments.

CMS Decisions

Each virtual school must make choices based on differences in the course management system vendor's approach to its product. The first choice is the core decision on whether the customer (school, district, county, state agency) will manage the CMS locally or contract for it to be hosted remotely. Understanding the true level of service that will flow from a vendor relationship is critical to a new virtual school that will be charting new ground with little guidance. Some virtual schools are constituted with a large IT staff, allowing for large internal technology operations. Others, for many reasons, are not inclined to run the virtual school software application internally. In the past, the choice of vendor was fairly simple: Select either a provider with a software license model like Blackboard or one like eCollege that uses a hosted services model. In recent years, however, other smaller companies have become popular in final choices as well, such as Desire 2 Learn and Course Compass. WebCT, the other large presence in higher education, only passively markets into the K–12 marketplace.

The CMS decision is a difficult one for virtual school operators. The systems are costly and thus the stakes are high. There is always the possibility that the choice of a single vendor in a large state could later conflict with the free exchange of courses, content, and services developed by other smaller virtual schools in the state. This may make it more difficult to exchange and use in common courses designed for all the students in the state.

Are Course Management Systems the Whole Answer?

Choosing a course management system is a big part of setting up a virtual school. It is, in fact, the largest single nonpersonnel budget item for virtual schools. The competition between the primary vendors is intense and the rise of alternate CMS providers is constant. The intensity of the competition may even obscure some of schools' more basic needs that are not being addressed by the CMS software. Unlike their university counterparts, schools are more about resources used for teaching. Best practices of teaching are, in large part, the mastery of the right resources for the particular curricular or student need. Schools need repositories for resources and non-course-related content. However, these are not part of current course management systems.

The cost and quality of courses vary widely. A simple text and picture–based course could cost less than $30,000 to develop internally. A graphically rich and pedagogically researched course could cost several hundred thousand dollars to develop internally. The same richly populated course could cost more than $500,000—as some of the University of California College Prep courses have, from custom developers inside and outside the University of California—or as little as $30,000—as some courses from Florida Virtual School have. Moderately priced courses from vendors could run around $100 per student per semester or as much as $500 per student.

Two factors are implicit in all current virtual school CMS discussions. The first is that virtual schools revolve around courses that have limited interactive content; they have a cohort of students who will interact online and teachers who are trained both in teaching with technology and in teaching their subject online. This model may be sufficient now, but because of No Child Left Behind, needs are evolving to require sophisticated data-reporting and data-analysis tools that have the ability to easily link into repositories with modules of content that are aligned by state and federal standards. The second factor is that, for now, virtual schools and their traditional counterparts do not run joint activities where the same technology is utilized both for distance virtual education and *at the same time* in a physical, school-campus installation. They are separate worlds. Virtual schools are external. Education technology in the classroom is internal. It is hoped that these two worlds will move closer to each other with maximum support being offered to students and teachers, regardless of which world learners occupy or whether they mix these worlds.

TRANSFORMATION: FROM VIRTUAL SCHOOLS TO VIRTUAL INFRASTRUCTURE

Virtual schools, as external and distributed entities, can provide new models to physical schools, as internal and local entities. The question is how centrally developed expertise can be married to the authority of the local school environment in an ongoing process of education. This would return schooling to where it was a century ago when the expertise of the local teacher was part and parcel of the authority of the locally controlled school. At that time, local students became local workers. Today, more than likely, students educated with the Internet as part of their education will be workers who use technology and the Internet in their work lives, just as the missions of virtual schools suggest. As they move around the country or the world, virtual education can help today's students maintain a sense of continuity in a modern mobile society.

Costs, Funding, and the Provision of Online Education

Linda Cavalluzzo

POLICYMAKERS WHO are interested in exploring online education for their public K–12 school systems must confront a variety of issues surrounding costs and funding. The goal of this chapter is to help policymakers reach informed decisions about providing Web-based educational services through public K–12 school systems. It pays particular attention to how different models for the provision of services are likely to affect costs and equitable access to these services.

CURRENT EDUCATION FINANCE ISSUES THAT IMPACT VIRTUAL SCHOOLS

Three aspects of education finance for traditional public schools have important implications for virtual public schools:

- Limited budgets
- Inequitable distribution of educational resources
- Students not attending public schools

Limited Budgets

According to the National Conference of State Legislatures, states are dealing with the most challenging fiscal conditions in decades. The trend toward shifting funding responsibilities from local to state governments and the legal obligation of states to ensure "adequacy" (i.e., providing sufficient funding to allow all schools to meet established performance measures) have added further pressures to ever-shrinking state budgets (Smith & Pettersen, 2002).

Making budget challenges more difficult, the demands on limited school resources are rising. New federal provisions under the No Child Left Behind Act for accountability, school choice, supplemental services, and teacher quality come with inadequate funding to pay for them and carry a threat of loss of funding under current federal programs for education.

What are the implications for virtual school programs? Education leaders who see a possible role for online education in their school systems should begin by assessing student needs and identifying clear objectives for the program. Once these objectives are defined, education leaders will want to consider factors that affect the costs and effectiveness of such programs. In addition, they will need to identify funding sources and methods that can be used to launch and maintain their programs. These challenges have been addressed in a number of different ways by different school districts and states.

Inequitable Distribution of Educational Resources

K–12 public education in the United States is almost always furnished by a locally controlled education system that sets budgets, goals, and objectives within the context of state and federal regulations. According to National Education Association (2003) research, on average, 46% of funding for public schools comes from local revenue sources that rely almost exclusively on property taxes, which, in turn, are closely tied to local wealth. States contribute an average of 49% of K–12 public school budgets, but that amount varies widely across states. At the extremes, Nevada contributes 28% to K–12 education, while Michigan contributes 78%. Hawaii—which operates a single statewide school district—furnishes 89% of total funding. The federal government provides funding through categorical aid programs, such as Title I for schools with high proportions of economically disadvantaged students, the free and reduced-price lunch program, and aid for children with learning disabilities. Those programs tend to target poor children, but account for barely 8% of total spending for operating public schools. As a result of differences in funding sources and levels, school funding varies widely across states and across districts within a single state, and favors students from wealthier areas.

Advocates for poor and minority students have seized on state-level funding reform as a way to ensure adequate funding and reduce the gap in educational outcomes among public school students. Nevertheless, local wealth and value of property are still significant elements of school finance and a key contributor to inequality in intrastate spending across school districts (Augenblick, Myers, & Anderson, 1997; Evans, Murray, & Schwab, 1999; Minorini & Sugarman, 1999).

Spending inequality also occurs among schools in a single district. In most districts, funding is allocated to cover the cost of resources, rather than on a per-student basis. Consider the implications for instruction: Frequently, the number of funded teaching positions per school is determined by student enrollments and targeted class sizes. The district imputes the wage bill based on the number of approved teaching positions and the cost of each of those positions. Across-school funding disparities arise because schools with the most difficult working conditions tend to have the least experienced and, consequently, the lowest paid teachers (Sugarman, 2002).

What are the implications for virtual school programs? Web-based classes have the ability to reduce resource disparities within and across districts because they can easily traverse geographic and political boundaries to bring the same qualified teacher and curriculum—indeed the very same courses—to students from different districts and schools. But simply setting up a virtual school will not guarantee equity.

If the virtual school is designed as an out-of-school program, enrollments will be limited to those students who have access to a computer and the Internet. Almost 92% of students with family incomes of $75,000 or more use computers with Internet access at home, compared with only 46% of students with family incomes under $20,000 (DeBell & Chapman, 2003). In the case of virtual charter schools, which typically furnish a full-time, home-based alternative to traditional schools and include computer and Internet access, disparate opportunities to participate can result from the inability of low-income families to provide daytime supervision or to coach their children through lesson plans. Moreover, "equitable access" to virtual school programs may not address responsibilities to ensure "adequacy." Students from poorly performing schools may be at greater risk of failure in their online courses if class scheduling is too unstructured, if qualified instructional support is thin, or if inexpensive courseware is used that does not accommodate multiple learning styles or customize lessons to help remediate deficiencies.

It may be preferable for school systems that place a priority on equity to schedule their courses during the regular school day and use school computer labs (or other school facilities) to provide access to those courses. In addition, those schools could keep their facilities open before or after school to allow students time to complete Internet-based assignments or to provide additional scheduling flexibility. Students who want to take a course online could access it through the lab when it fits their schedule. With online education, it isn't necessary for students who use the computer lab to be enrolled in the same online course, or for students in the same online course to be in the lab at the same time.

Students Not Attending Public Schools

Approximately 10% of K–12 students across the United States attend private schools (7%) or are being homeschooled (3%). Parents of these students have opted out of publicly funded education for a wide range of reasons, but predominately to provide religious training to their children as part of their formal education (Alt & Peter, 2002). Many of these students could benefit from access to high-quality online programs; in many states and localities, they do.

What are the implications for virtual school programs? Eligibility policies vary across states and have important implications for enrollments and costs. Some states (e.g., Arkansas, Minnesota, and Pennsylvania) permit formerly homeschooled or privately schooled students to enroll in publicly funded online schools, while other states (e.g., Michigan and Illinois) expressly prohibit funding for such students.

When eligibility rules permit, publicly funded virtual charter schools, which provide a full-time online alternative to traditional schools, are enormously popular among formerly homeschooled students, who thus reenter the public school system, benefit from curriculum and instructional materials that meet state standards for learning, and continue to learn from home. In Arkansas, for example, 72% (282 of 392 students) of students in Grades 1–12 who enrolled in the publicly funded school program for the virtual charter school, Arkansas Virtual School, came from homeschools (63%) or private schools (9%). Only 24% of students came from traditional public schools (Barnett Reed, 2004). Florida's eligibility rules go a step farther. The state has two pilot programs for virtual charter schools, which have attracted large numbers of formerly homeschooled students, and operates its own virtual school. Courses offered by the state-run Florida Virtual School are free to any Florida student, regardless of whether the student is schooled publicly, privately, or at home. Such a policy is consistent with Florida's school voucher program, which allows students to take public dollars to private schools of their choice.

In states with virtual charter schools, funding policies are typically designed around a brick-and-mortar model of education, and funding formulas specifically for virtual charter schools have not yet been adopted. Observers in Arkansas and elsewhere have questioned the resulting per-student costs. These questions take on added importance because many of the newly formed state virtual charter schools are not-for-profit organizations tied to a for-profit parent company. Assigning a funding formula to virtual charter schools is further complicated by the potential for widely varying program designs and widely varying costs.

THE COST OF FURNISHING ONLINE EDUCATION

This section focuses on costs associated with the development of online programs. Of course, eligibility policies can also have important implications for the costs of enrollments in online learning through public schools.

Types of Costs

Two kinds of costs are relevant to policymakers who are considering making online education available through their school systems: fixed and variable. *Fixed costs* refer to those one-time expenses that the provider must incur in order to offer any courses online. These costs are fixed in the sense that they do not change with the number of enrollments over large ranges. *Variable costs* increase as the number of units of output (course seats) increases. Whether a function that must be provided through the online school is fixed or variable can depend on how the online school goes about providing it. In general, online schools will be better off purchasing services and avoiding substantial fixed costs if enrollments are expected to be low, which may be the case in small schools or districts or if the goal of the program is to serve a relatively small or special-needs population. If a large number of students are expected to take advantage of available courses (either because the school system is large, or because the system anticipates selling access to products it creates), fixed costs can be spread over these enrollments, reducing the fixed cost per course seat to a negligible amount.

Below, the elements that need to be furnished in order to deliver courses online are described. Some of the options and costs associated with these functions are noted to give the reader a feel for their size and character. For a more thorough treatment of different options and their costs, the report to the Colorado Online Education Programs Study Committee is a good resource (Adsit, 2003).

Course Development and Maintenance Costs

Many district and state online schools develop their own courses. The range of expenditures dedicated to this activity is striking. At the low end, the district-run Cumberland County Schools Web Academy in North Carolina uses standard templates and teachers who are experienced at course development, and spends $1,500 per course. A more common figure is $4,500 per course developed in district-based programs, using one or two state-licensed and experienced teachers without previous online course development experience. That expenditure excludes the cost of training teachers to develop those courses and other related expenses (Cavalluzzo, Fauntleroy, & Eline, 2003; Morris, 2002).

At the high end, the state-financed Florida Virtual School (FLVS) used teams of three or more teachers to develop each course around a motif or story that engages students in an interesting set of problems. Students solve these problems as they work their way through the course. FLVS estimates that it spent from $50,000 to $100,000 per course to develop a set of highly interactive courses. These courses include inquiry-based assignments that account for different learning styles, the use of the Web, and other supporting materials (Young, 2003).

In addition to the costs of course development, funds should be allocated for course maintenance for three reasons: (1) Web addresses change, (2) textbooks change, and (3) technology changes. No good teacher reuses the same materials from year to year without reviewing notes and lesson plans and thinking about ways to improve or update them for the new round of students. The same is true for online education. For courses that have already been developed, the Wichita eSchool pays teachers $1,000 each time a course is reused to check the validity and update Web addresses, and spends $2,000 if a new textbook has been introduced (Morris, 2002). Even these costs overlook the investment that one should plan to make from time to time to completely revisit a course in light of the availability of new technologies, new learning objectives, or new ideas that will keep a course fresh, up-to-date, and interesting.

The fixed costs of course development and maintenance can be converted to variable costs by leasing rather than developing or buying content. There are a number of ways to do this, including purchasing course seats from providers that operate classes meeting the needs of local students or purchasing licenses for use of content. Apex Learning is a commercial provider that offers Advanced Placement, foreign language, and other courses. The company makes large investments in course development—at the high end, $500,000 for its AP calculus course (R. Hanley, personal communication, October 16, 2001), and charges $950 per course seat for Apex-staffed AP courses or $500 per seat if the local school provides the instructor (Apex Learning Website, 2003).

Course Platform and Delivery System Expenses

Another important fixed expense is associated with course management and delivery systems. These include a "platform" that is used to structure the content and provide access to various services for the online teacher and student, such as threaded discussion, chat room, grades, assignments, and e-mail. The platform is, in effect, the e-classroom. Commercial vendors license use of these Internet-based platforms. An annual licensing fee of $5,000 per year for an unlimited number of users is typical, but adding a server and associated support can increase the total cost by $15,000 to $20,000 (Adsit, 2003).

Some programs build their own platform, operate their own server, or provide their own technical support. Unless the program is a large one, platform quality or system reliability is likely to suffer at the hands of low spending for these inputs. A bare-bones platform may reduce the quality of the learning experience, while poor system reliability will frustrate students and teachers and threaten completion rates.

Program Management and Administration Costs

A final source of fixed costs is staff salaries for the basic administrative functions:

- Hiring and obtaining training for course developers and instructors
- Handling student registrations
- Marketing
- Maintaining student records
- Reporting grades to each student's traditional school
- Collecting data to help guide program, teacher, and course improvement
- Evaluating new curricula, services, and technologies
- Negotiating contracts with vendors

These costs may vary little whether 100 or 500 students are enrolled in online classes (Adsit, 2003).

Costs of Instruction

The largest source of variable costs is salaries for instruction. Many virtual schools that are operated by districts or states place no more than 20 students per teacher in an online high school class. That is because the online classroom, as currently designed, requires a great deal of communication, assignments, and feedback to ensure that students remain engaged in their coursework and stay on track for timely and successful completion. Evidence suggests that maintaining a rapport and regular communication with students is the key to successful course completions. Without these connections, students are prone to losing interest or postponing their work. In addition, online teachers may communicate regularly with parents.

Because online classes are often smaller than traditional classes, staffing them with qualified (state-certified and experienced) full-time teachers can cost more on a per-student basis than staffing a traditional classroom. As a result, some online schools use part-time teachers because these teachers generate lower payroll expenses inasmuch as fringe benefits do not have to be paid. This solution, however, is not as simple as it may seem. First, part-time teachers may raise teacher union issues in some districts. More to the point, the savings from using a part-time staff is less than one might expect, because online teachers typically receive a full complement of hardware and software (personal computer, fax, scanner, high-speed Internet connection) to allow them to work effectively from a home office. By my calculations, if five part-time teachers are used in place of one full-time teacher, the savings may be on the order of only 3%, if all classes are fully enrolled. Higher savings would result from staffing with part-time personnel if those teachers taught more than one class each (thus reducing hardware and software costs), or if part-time teachers were paid according to the number of students enrolled (since full-time teachers receive full pay even if their classes are only partially filled).

It is not surprising, then, that sliding pay scales for part-time online teachers are popular. This pay structure, which begins with a base amount and a minimum enrollment and then adds incrementally as enrollments increase, recognizes the direct link between class size and the level of work for the teacher, in the form of grading and individual communication. As a result, it is seen as a fair way to determine pay. In addition, some programs allow their online teachers to cap their classes below the maximum set by the online school, and a sliding pay scale allows them to implement that policy in a fair way. Sliding pay scales also recognize that revenue from tuition varies with the number of students enrolled in a course: If online teachers were paid under the assumption that classes were full when they were not, tuition-based programs would have difficulty covering their operating costs.

Implications for Virtual School Programs

It is clear that course developers have a great deal of flexibility in deciding how to design their online courses and how much to invest in course development. These decisions will affect course quality. Low-end expenditures are more likely to use technology to deliver content in traditional (textbook/worksheet) formats, and they may be better suited to programs that are designed to support test preparation. More expensive courseware can incorporate higher quality graphics to articulate concepts more clearly and in different ways. Motifs, like those developed by the Florida Virtual School, create problem-based, student-centered learning experiences and address multiple learning styles. While course designs like this are expensive to develop, many programs have found grants to help fund course development costs, or have obtained government appropriations to cover them (Lane, 2000). Nevertheless, such expenses are hard to justify if the number of students who will use them is expected to be small.

The high fixed costs required to produce and maintain online programs has led to a variety of models for furnishing those services, including the creation of large statewide programs, collaborations among smaller district- or school-based programs, and leasing services from large providers to reduce the need for investment funds. The next section considers the advantages and challenges to the viability of these models, as well as equity issues that were introduced earlier in this chapter.

MODELS FOR THE PROVISION AND FUNDING
OF ONLINE EDUCATION

District-as-Producer Model

Small districts that produce their own courseware typically hold down investment expenditures by limiting the rate at which they produce new courses and the amount they spend on development of individual courses. By seeking out experienced teachers who are excited about the new technology, and paying a fixed fee for course development, districts have been able to create software that they judge to be moderately high in quality. As a result, it could prove to be more cost-effective to furnish homebound or other eligible students with online instruction than to provide those students with home visits by a qualified public school teacher. Many districts charge tuition if the online course is taken as a course overload or is taken by a student from outside the district.

Consortiums and Partnerships

Small providers, such as individual schools or districts, may establish a consortium for sharing online resources. Such systems are motivated by common needs, scarcity of resources, and the desire to avoid duplication of effort. A successful consortium has the potential to make more efficient use of resources and to accelerate development of a rich menu of courses that meet common needs of participants. Consortiums will have the best chances of success if they adhere to common design standards that require an equal per-course commitment of resources and result in courses that are comparable in quality. Consortiums will be difficult to establish and maintain if potential members cannot agree on the level of investment that should be made in building their portfolio of courses. Disagreements are more likely if districts have different goals for their online program or different budget constraints. For example, larger or wealthier districts are likely to want to invest more per course than their smaller or less wealthy counterparts. Similarly, programs that seek to serve only a few students may wish to invest less per course than programs that wish to serve larger numbers of students. Even when investment of resources is equal, loosely structured consortiums that allow participants to trade courseware or course seats and that set only minimum standards for design are not likely to succeed.

The Virtual High School, now VHS, Inc. (http://www.govhs.org), is an example of a successful consortium. It was funded under a 5-year U.S. Department of Education Technology Innovation Challenge Grant awarded to Hudson (Massachusetts) Public Schools in October 1996. In partnership with the not-for-profit Concord Consortium, the district set up a consortium in which participating schools contribute a new Web-based course developed by a qualified teacher who has received graduate-level professional development in course design and online instruction through the consortium. Once the course is developed, evaluated, and approved, the teacher offers the course through the consortium. Enrollments are capped at 25 seats per course, and the contributing school receives 25 course seats that can be used, in turn, in any Web-based courses offered by the consortium. Since the expiration of the original grant, the consortium retained its basic model, but added participation fees for members.

State-Level Models

Given the potential for significant cost savings from economies of scale, and the need for an organizing agent or administrator to help realize those economies, state-level models are a natural alternative to district-level programs for furnishing education online. In addition to cost savings, another important advantage of state-level programs is the elimination of inequities in quality of content and instruction for these online courses across districts if access can be ensured.

Because traditional instruction is primarily covered by local education districts, states need to set prices for the online courses they offer. In the short term, below-cost pricing can play an important role in the development of an effective and robust online education system. However, providing online courses at little or no cost to districts may result in their being seen as being of low value, leading districts to continue to offer traditional courses even in those instances when, from the point of view of the overall education system, it is wasteful to do so.

Cavalluzzo and Higgins (2001) discuss different ways to allocate costs between states and districts for state-sponsored programs and different ways to reach policymakers' goals for their online education program. If state policymakers want to grow their program as quickly as possible, they could provide courses at no cost to districts or their students, or even pay districts to try some of their online classes. By providing online courses below cost, states could encourage districts to test the quality and effectiveness of online courses for themselves.

Below-cost pricing will encourage experimentation and could lead to innovative ways to use online education to improve student outcomes. For example, schools would be more likely to experiment with the use of online course materials in the context of traditional classes if those course materials were free. If the state collected and analyzed data on student outcomes from those courses, and then compared them with outcomes for students in traditional classes, they could determine if their investment resulted in improved student outcomes. They could also determine if the strategy was more effective for particular types of students, or if it improved effectiveness of different types of teachers.

Once the uses and effectiveness of online courses are well understood, state programs could charge districts prices that cover their costs per course seat. This price would encourage districts to use online education when it makes economic sense to do so, for example, when a traditional course would not have enough students enrolled to justify a traditional teaching slot.

State as broker. Some states (e.g., West Virginia) have set up virtual schools with little investment by acting as a resource broker and executive agent for online courses. In this model, the state identifies, evaluates, and qualifies course providers. In addition, it sets policy, familiarizes districts with the program, negotiates statewide prices for services, and collects and analyzes data to support program improvement. Local districts purchase course seats required by their students at these negotiated prices.

The primary objective of the West Virginia Virtual School (WVVS) is to bring all students in this rural state high-quality opportunities for education. The school offers traditional satellite and Internet-based courses. While districts are responsible for course costs, the state has set up a grant program to help cover the costs of online courses. Under the grant program (http://access.k12.wv.us/vschool), the state pays 75% of the cost of tuition and materials. The district pays the remaining 25%. Funding for the program comes from the shifting of state-appropriated technology funds for distance learning from satellite to online education.

From the standpoint of costs and effectiveness, the state-as-broker model appears to be a promising approach. By acting as a large-scale buyer and not limiting themselves to a single vendor, the state can take advantage of competition among providers to get the best courses at the best possible prices for their students. The use of grants to help pay tuition encourages use of online courses, and provides the state department of education access to data that can be used to monitor effectiveness and identify best practices. Challenges associated with this approach include the difficulty of finding content that aligns with state curriculum standards, and evaluating and approving courses quickly so that they can be made available to students.

State as producer. A number of states produce their own content and other services, or use both in-house and commercially developed products to furnish online courses.

Michigan Virtual High School (MVHS) was launched with a $17-million appropriation from the state legislature in July 2000. Under the legislation, the Michigan Virtual University (a private, not-for-profit Michigan corporation) would operate MVHS for a 3-year period. After 18 months, the corporation sought an alternative funding model to sustain its operations. MVHS now operates from revenue derived from à la carte tuition charges in addition to a subscription membership system. Member schools are charged a base fee, ranging from $1,000 to $5,000, depending on school size as measured by enrollment, plus 50 cents per student. The flat annual fee provides member schools with 60 course seats in MVHS courses, plus unlimited access to test review tools for 12 different AP subjects, college entry exams (ACT, SAT, and PSAT), and the high-stakes 11th-grade state exam in reading, writing, and math. In addition, each subscriber school receives onsite training and implementation services, as well as a scholarship to train one teacher in online education methods. MVHS reports that the shift to a flat-fee subscription model was accompanied by a boom in course enrollments (K. Middleton, personal communication, January 23, 2003).

The best known state-run virtual school is undoubtedly the Florida Virtual School, with 75 in-house-developed courses in its portfolio. Florida students enroll online, without needing to go through a public school. FLVS charges no tuition to in-state students, but sells access to its courses, as well as other products and expertise, to out-of-state customers. A review of the FLVS Web site (http://flvs.net) shows the school's keen interest in sales (for example, courses can be ordered in traditional semester formats or in block schedule formats) and in organization growth (apply for a franchise).

In this business model, profits from out-of-state sales can be used to reduce costs of education for state taxpayers. In addition, legislators see online education, accessed "anyplace" (i.e., outside of school), as a way to reduce the need for new schoolhouses to accommodate their growing school-aged population.

Virtual Charter Schools

Virtual charter schools, also referred to as cyber charter schools, are full-time, publicly funded alternatives to traditional brick-and-mortar schools. Such schools may be granted a state or district charter to operate, and they are well suited to students who cannot attend, have not thrived in, or do not wish to attend traditional public schools. This model for delivery of elementary and secondary education has created a great deal of controversy and presents a range of policy and funding issues that need to be considered.

In all but four states—California, Colorado, Ohio, and Pennsylvania—virtual charter schools operate under the same state laws as other charter schools (Anderson, 2002). For funding purposes, that means that virtual charter schools receive the same per-student amount as traditional brick-and-mortar charter schools, although the cost structure of virtual charter schools is much different. Revisions to funding formulas are needed for these new forms of education delivery. Ideally, these formulas will recognize the range of designs provided through different programs and will accommodate their various cost structures. In addition, education leaders should consider restructuring funding to accommodate students who attend traditional public schools but would like to enroll in an occasional online course. With the exception of students in California, such students are left out of the mix.

Some charter schools—particularly those serving students in the primary grades—rely on parents for instruction and provide as few as one teacher for every 50 students (Barnett Reed, 2004). Although parents are thrilled to receive free materials and guidance to help their children learn, these delivery models have raised concerns about the distinctions between fully funded virtual charter schools and old-fashioned correspondence courses, and whether these distinctions add enough value to justify their added cost.

CONCLUSIONS

Virtual schools have the capacity to reach across geographic and political divides to help reduce inequities in the quality of instruction and breadth of choices faced by students in disparate districts and schools. Virtual schools also have the capacity to support student instruction outside the traditional schoolhouse. Education leaders who want to create an online program to better meet the needs of their students must begin by defining the goals of the program and then selecting a model for financing and delivering online education that aligns with those goals. They must also pay special attention to the far-reaching effects that state policies for online education can have on the shape of public education.

Districts or schools may develop their own courses, but economies of scale in the development and management of online programs suggest that larger programs will be more cost-effective and have the potential to provide a broader range of higher quality courses. Consortiums, formed to take advantage of scale economies, are more likely to be successful if participants have common needs and a willingness to make equivalent investments to build and sustain the program.

State-run virtual schools may build their own courses, or they may act as a broker, selecting courses for quality and alignment with state standards from commercially available sources. States should be able to use their large size and vendor competition to obtain high-quality products at lower prices than districts would be able to negotiate on their own. Broker models have the added benefit of flexibility: They can change suppliers when cost or quality considerations dictate, and use multiple suppliers to provide different courses or to support other aspects of the program.

States, such as Florida, that are interested in rapid program growth and in promoting school choice make online courses directly available to students and do not charge tuition to students who live in the state, regardless of whether those students are enrolled in public schools, private schools, or homeschools. In the long term, Florida leaders expect to use profits from sales of services outside the state to help fund the program, and they expect to use its "any place" design to reduce the need to build new schoolhouses for its growing school-age population. Programs like this are especially popular among parents of homeschoolers, but they may not meet the needs of underserved minority students.

Where charter school legislation is in place, virtual charter schools may be granted permission to operate by a state or district (or other approved chartering body). But several aspects of charter-school legislation, formulated with traditional bricks-and-mortar schools in mind, have caused controversy where such programs have been initiated. One concern is that, in most states, funding formulas do not take into account differences in the cost structure of virtual charter schools. Some of those schools have few teachers, and rely on parents to support their child's instruction, causing critics to ask how these fully funded charter schools—often run by not-for-profit organizations tied to for-profit parent companies—differ from correspondence courses, and to question the spending of public dollars for what amounts to private education. Making such issues more pressing, district-chartered cyber schools can attract students—and their public education dollars—from across the state, impacting local districts. It is important for planners to consider the funding implications of different types of virtual school programs they might implement. But in a broader sense, policymakers should consider the impact of virtual schools on the funding of public education.

Virtual Schools: Policy and Practice Considerations

Robert L. Blomeyer & Matt Dawson

IMPORTANT ISSUES concerning online learning have been examined in great depth in recent years, and comprehensive guidelines for online learning policy have been suggested as a result of this research. In this chapter we present a synthesis of the key policy and practice considerations for virtual school planners, as well as a review of the major organizations participating in the research.

ORGANIZATIONS EXPLORING POLICY AND PRACTICE

Several organizations have sought to provide policy and practice guidance for policymakers and decision makers charged with the investigation and deployment of online learning in K–12 schools. Three of these organizations will be discussed here.

NCREL: Examining the Issues Involved in e-Learning

North Central Regional Education Laboratory (NCREL) at Learning Point Associates (LPA) has conducted significant research on policy and practice issues and developed technical assistance for education agencies based upon this research. In a special issue of *NCREL Policy Issues,* NCREL (2002) summarized the crucial e-learning education policy issues, provided a review of the existing research and professional literature describing "what works," and offered a series of recommendations, including the following:

- Technology leaders in the e-learning movement and established state education policy leaders need to establish a real basis for national or state-level communication and dialogue on critical policy issues relating to K–12 online learning.
- Good traditional teachers can become effective facilitators of online learning when provided quality professional development opportunities and supervised online clinical experience.
- Hybrid courses (combining face-to-face and online instruction) with smaller enrollments and clear linkages to approved curriculum practice seem to offer higher completion rates and arguably better quality learning outcomes than online courses alone.
- Optimal resource configurations and instructional design practices that promote effective e-learning outcomes in K–12 learning environments need to be better recognized, more widely understood, and more uniformly agreed upon by e-learning producers, consumers, and education policy leaders.
- Existing educational research and program evaluations that examine and analyze the outcomes and impact of online learning in K–12 learning environments presently are very limited and need to be expanded.

Since that time, other organizations have begun to address some of these important issues and questions. But many of the issues summarized above remain partially or wholly unaddressed.

NACOL: Exploring Policy Issues and Obstacles Facing Virtual Education

Much of the recent work on online learning policy has resulted from initiatives undertaken by the recently organized North American Council for Online Learning (NACOL). In April 2003 NACOL announced its formation and the appointment of its initial board of directors (NACOL, 2003). In October 2002, under the sponsorship of the U.S. Department of Education in partnership with various corporate sponsors, NACOL had brought together a group of key stakeholders to identify specific challenges, policy issues, and regulatory obstacles facing virtual education. That working group produced a policy document, *Virtual Schools Forum Report* (Center for Digital Education, 2003).

The principal findings and conclusions from this report provide detailed guidance for developing federal and state educational policies that would ideally remove many of the obstacles presently limiting expanded use of online high school courses as a widely available instructional "choice" in many of our nation's secondary schools. The four major themes considered by the working group participants were accountability, equity, funding, and quality:

- *Accountability* includes a broad range of concepts from measuring effective student outcomes using accountability systems to define data standards, indicators, and metrics for online learning. Better measures and evidence of effectiveness are needed.
- *Equity* is often described as making everything equal, when it should really mean that every child has access to what he or she needs and what is "appropriate."
- *Funding* traditional K–12 education is different from the variety of models used to fund virtual learning. There is a disconnect when traditional funding models are applied to virtual school practices.
- Key *quality* issues include program quality assurance, teacher certification issues, accreditation, standards, and curriculum quality. How is course quality measured? How does one "ensure" and "assure" quality in online education?

The detailed findings and recommendations in this report suggest the development of comprehensive government policies that school districts can use to guide the implementation and expanded use of online courses. Much work remains to be done in state education agencies to adjust existing policies and procedures and (when appropriate) to implement new policies to remove the significant state and local e-learning policy barriers identified in this report.

SREB: Moving K–20 Online Learning Policy into Practice

The Southern Regional Education Board (SREB) Web site (http://www.sreb.org) has become a regional and national repository for a variety of timely publications and reports on K–20 online learning. While summarizing its extensive research on e-learning policy and practice is beyond the scope of this chapter, we would refer the interested reader to the SREB publications in the "Further Reading" section at the end of the chapter, and to the Web site itself.

CRUCIAL ONLINE LEARNING ISSUES AND QUESTIONS

Easy access on the Web to free online learning policy and practice resources from authoritative sources is very helpful, but planners may be overwhelmed by the sheer volume of information and lack the technical knowledge to interpret it. This may limit their ability to put online learning policy and practice into well-informed plans of action. In this section, we seek to lighten the burden of the growing information overload by identifying key policy and practice questions; the "Further Reading" section directs readers to recommended Internet-based resources addressing these questions in more detail.

Five crucial questions about instructional and curricular policy and practice should be addressed. These issues directly affect states' and communities' deliberations, planning, and resource allocation decisions.

1. What are the policy and practice issues that *must* be addressed before offering online courses in K–12 districts?

Many of the crucial policy and practice issues have been adequately addressed above. In response to the apparent need for a simple, clear, and unambiguous rubric or checklist to guide assessments of local schools' readiness to begin using online courses, the staff of NCREL's Center for Technology created the Online Learning Management Checklist, based on the NEA's *Guide to Online High School Courses* (National Education Association, 2002); the checklist is provided in Figure 5.1 for the reader's use.

2. What qualities or characteristics are common to "high-quality" online courses?

As software options for e-learning continue to evolve, K–12 schools must consider an increasing variety of options for obtaining e-learning courses. Typically, there are 2 choices: (1) license or purchase use of commercially developed, course-equivalent online courses from software vendors; or (2) initiate software development projects using master teachers as subject matter experts who participate in designing, developing, and implementing locally created online courses. If K–12 schools follow prevailing trends in postsecondary institutions, many online courses will be developed by teachers in local school districts.

The materials used in online courses can be obtained from commercial or not-for-profit publishers or developed locally by teachers. Even when online courses are professionally developed, online teachers often customize or support them with their own materials. But the disadvantages should be carefully considered:

- Creating online materials is very time consuming and usually requires specialized design skills and use of authoring tools.

1. Procedures exist for determining when to employ online courses. _____

2. Online instruction is aligned with an overall vision for student achievement. _____

3. Procedures exist for ensuring that online courses are aligned with state/local standards and assessments. _____

4. Procedures exist for deciding when to develop or purchase online courses. _____

5. Policies exist that specify who can enroll in online courses. _____

6. Procedures exist for online course fees payment and registration. _____

7. Course descriptions are available to students and parents/guardians. _____

8. Students have access to the appropriate hardware and software needed. _____

9. Students have reliable access to the Internet as needed. _____

10. Counseling is available to advise students about enrollment in online classes. _____

11. Teachers are adequately trained and prepared to teach online. _____

12. Procedures exist for monitoring and evaluating the performance of online teaching. _____

13. Procedures exist for teachers/staff to mentor online students and/or act as school liaisons with off-site providers. _____

14. Procedures exist to deal with cheating and to authenticate student identity. _____

15. Students and parents/guardians sign an agreement about the rights and responsibilities associated with an online course. _____

16. Policies and procedures are in place to deal with student complaints and inappropriate student behavior associated with an online course. _____

17. A secure grading system is provided with opportunities for students, parents/guardians, and administrators to review grades as appropriate. _____

18. Confidential management of student records is assured. _____

19. Students are provided feedback about their progress in an online course. _____

20. Students and teachers provide feedback on course content, support systems, and infrastructure, which is used to make improvements. _____

21. Data is available on system usage and reliability. _____

22. The online platform used for course delivery has the necessary reliability and capacity to support all learning/teaching activities. _____

23. Adequate technical support is available for students, teachers, staff. _____

24. Adequate training is provided to staff to administer online courses. _____

25. Procedures exist for reviewing and updating policies relating to online courses. _____

Figure 5.1. Online learning management checklist. *Source*: Adapted from *Online Learning Management Checklist* [Web document], by North Central Regional Educational Laboratory Center for Technology. Copyright © 2004 by North Central Regional Educational Laboratory, a wholly owned subsidiary of Learning Point Associates. All rights reserved. Adapted with permission.

- Ownership (copyright) of materials usually resides with the institution, not individuals.
- Online materials need to be matched to curriculum standards and state/federal requirements (e.g., privacy of student records).

Blomeyer (2002) summarized many of the factors influencing schools' and districts' decisions either to develop online courses locally or to obtain them from commercial and not-for-profit online course developers. Important among those factors are the significant amounts of teacher time needed to undertake online course development projects and the predictably poor quality of most initial online course development efforts undertaken by teacher-practitioners without training. Blomeyer suggests comparing the costs of creating courses with the costs of purchasing them, including the following:

- Replacement costs for teacher-developers' time (releasing them from other duties)
- High per-pupil costs for small-volume licensing of commercially developed online courses
- Cost-sharing arrangements sometimes associated with large-volume licensing or cooperative participation (i.e., contributing the time of an online teacher/administrator or locally developed online courses in exchange for shared access to a larger library of online courses)

Regardless of whether professionally developed online courses are screened and selected for local use, or course development efforts are undertaken by teachers or development teams in a school or school district, clear, understandable, and authoritative online course standards are needed to support good decisions. The National Education Association's *Guide to Online High School Courses* (2002) is generally recognized as one of the best resources presently available for thorough selection and screening of online high school courses.

The Southern Regional Educational Board also offers an online course assessment instrument on the SREB Web site. The course assessment instruments available on both the SREB and NEA Web sites may be used without modification, or items from either or both course evaluation instruments can be recombined to create derivative online course selection and screening tools that better reflect local priorities and standards.

Educators are frequently more receptive to the use of checklists and assessment rubrics if there has been an opportunity for input to the customization process. Letting reviewers add their own ideas to the construction of selection and screening instruments is probably one of the best ways to ensure that they will be used. When existing assessment tools are repurposed to give them a local flavor, remember to acknowledge your sources.

3. What knowledge, skills, and dispositions are needed for experienced teachers to become effective online teachers?

Online courses have become very popular in higher education, and with the emergence of virtual schools they are becoming common at the K–12 level (see Clark, 2001; Vail, 2001; Zucker et al., 2002). While most universities and colleges have established training programs to prepare their faculty to teach online, school systems are just beginning to address this need. As noted by McKenzie (2001), preparing teachers to teach online should involve more than the short workshops typical of most in-service training.

Hannum (2001) describes an extensive statewide initiative in Colorado. The Concord Consortium, Illinois Online Network's Making Virtual Courses a Reality (MVCR) program (Varvel, Lindeman, & Stovall, 2003), and an increasing number of online university-based programs and for-profit companies offer online teacher preparation programs and online professional development courses. A significant number of online learning system vendors also offer online teacher training programs, but these offerings tend to be platform-specific professional development.

A question that is becoming increasingly important wherever there are virtual schools and online courses is, How can we effectively prepare certified and experienced classroom teachers to become effective online teachers? To respond to this emerging national need, NCREL recently developed and pilot-tested a fully online professional development course for teachers called the NCREL/LPA Online Teaching Facilitation Course.

4. What special knowledge, skills, and dispositions are needed for educational leaders to also become effective leaders and managers for online learning projects?

The Technology Standards for School Administrators Collaborative created professional standards for school administrators that were subsequently adopted by the International Society for Technology in Education (ISTE) (2001) as the National Educational Technology Standards for Administrators (NETS*A). The NETS*A standards provide a foundational core to fundamentally orient all technology leadership, including leadership for online learning.

A common assumption about online teaching is that it takes considerably more time and effort than traditional classroom instruction, for the following reasons:

- Providing student feedback can be an open-ended task.
- Online courses are a 24/7 learning environment.
- Keeping up with technology requires a lot of time and effort.
- Teachers need to learn strategies to manage workload.
- Teachers may expect more compensation for online teaching than is typically provided.

Burnout in online teaching is likely to be a bigger concern because of the extra workload. Needless to say, the workload issue is likely to be a contentious one for teacher unions and school administration (Kearsley & Blomeyer, 2004).

Both students and teachers need a lot of support in online courses. Online learning support may include technical support (assistance with hardware and software systems), administrative support (enrollment and course management), instructional design support, counseling, and possibly support for students classified as having special needs (see Section 508 of the Americans with Disabilities Act, available online: http://www .section508.gov/).

Teachers are not expected to provide these different types of support, and they generally turn to administrators for assistance after making first contact with students who require specialized support services. A well-organized distance learning program will have properly trained staff to handle each of these types of support. Both online teachers and virtual school administrators should be able to address the following questions:

- When are online classes appropriate or inappropriate for a given subject, group of students, or school?
- When does it make sense to combine online and classroom learning?
- When should online technology be combined with other media (e.g., video or audio conferencing)?
- When is it better to use technology in the classroom but not remotely?

In response to the regionally and nationally identified need for professional development designed to prepare school administrators to assume leadership roles in K–12 online learning initiatives, the North Central Regional Educational Laboratory is developing the NCREL/LPA Management of Online Learning Course. The goal of this course is to provide school leaders with the basic knowledge, skills, and dispositions needed to provide leadership for online learning in K–12 schools and school districts. The audience for this course consists of principals, assistant principals, district and state educational staff, and school board members having little or no exposure to online learning. The performance-based objectives for the course align with the National Education Technology Standards for Administrators, as shown in Figure 5.2. Additional resources are listed in the "Further Reading" section at the end of this chapter.

5. **What available evidence (research-based or otherwise) supports claims that K–12 online learning systems support gains in achievement equivalent to academic performance standards for traditional instruction?**

With the recent push for "scientifically-based research," the assessment of student outcomes associated with online learning has increased importance. Unfortunately, research documenting and examining e-learning in K–12 settings has only recently begun to be published. Catherine Cavanaugh (2001) conducted a meta-analysis examining the effects sizes of selected quantitative educational research that examined student academic achievement as a result of using distance education in K–12 settings published between 1993 and 1997. Cavanaugh's findings indicated that distance-learning projects that used online learning to supplement and support more traditional classroom instruction, smaller sized groups, and shorter duration learning experiences show a consistently larger effect than projects using two-way videoconferencing, primary instruction via distance, long duration, and larger sized groups. Student achievement data from fully online, virtual high school courses was not available for consideration as a part of Cavanaugh's meta-analysis.

Research supports the integration of curriculum and instructional technologies. A recent meta-analysis by Valdez et al. (2000) found that computer assisted instruction (CAI) fared better if it was delivered in a content area with a well-defined subject. In addition, classrooms in which computers were used to support instruction usually showed gains in student achievement as measured by standardized achievement tests.

NCREL's new meta-analysis by Waxman, Lin, and Michko (2003) provides some of the first clear, comprehensive evidence supporting claims that effective teaching and learning with technology can lead to improvements in student academic performance. Their study examines the impact

MODULE 1: ORIENTATION

NET Standard	Performance Objectives	Activities
I. Technology Operations and Concepts	1. Be able to use typical online course discussion forums. 2. Be able to use e-mail from within a typical online course system. 3. Be able to create and use file attachments from within a typical online course system. 4. Be able to use synchronous communications systems typical of those provided by online course management systems. 5. Discuss how online learning compares to classroom learning.	✓ Post background message in forum. ✓ Participate in chat session. ✓ Complete module evaluation.

MODULE 2: TECHNOLOGY & TOOLS

NET Standard	Performance Objectives	Activities
I. Technology Operations and Concepts	1. Distinguish between synchronous and asynchronous delivery. 2. Conduct Web searches. 3. Be able to place links in messages. 4. State goals for online teaching.	✓ Identify and evaluate two Web sites relevant to teaching area/topic. ✓ Participate in chat session. ✓ Complete module evaluation.

MODULE 3: FACILITATION

NES Standard	Performance Objectives	Activities
III. Teaching, Learning, and the Curriculum	1. Discuss the importance of interactivity and feedback in an online class. 2. Discuss techniques for providing interactivity and feedback. 3. Discuss strategies for discussion forums. 4. Demonstrate strategies for discussion forums. 5. Discuss strategies for chat sessions (virtual classroom). 6. Demonstrate strategies for chat sessions (virtual classroom). 7. Explain the nature of student collaboration and learning communities.	✓ Prepare teaching moment and evaluate others. ✓ Post responses to teaching scenarios in forum and critique others. ✓ Moderate chat session. ✓ Complete module evaluation.

MODULE 4: ASSESSMENT & EVALUATION

NES Standard	Performance Objectives	Activities
IV. Assessment and Evaluation	1. Identify characteristics of successful online learners. 2. Describe accessibility issues in online learning. 3. Discuss evaluation and assessment methods for online learning.	✓ Create a lesson plan for an online class and evaluate others. ✓ Post responses to teaching scenarios in forum and critique others. ✓ Participate in chat session. ✓ Complete module evaluation.

MODULE 5: MANAGING ONLINE LEARNING

NES Standard	Performance Objectives	Activities
II. Planning and Designing Learning Environments and Experiences V. Productivity and Professional Practice	1. Identify typical problems with online learning and strategies for addressing them. 2. Describe strategies for handling the workload associated with online teaching. 3. Explain how online learning can be integrated with classroom activities.	✓ Assess management issues in lesson. ✓ Post responses to scenarios in forum and critique others. ✓ Participate in chat session. ✓ Complete module evaluation.

MODULE 6: SOCIAL, LEGAL, & ETHICAL ISSUES

NES Standard	Performance Objectives	Activities
VI. Social, Ethical, Legal, and Human Issues	1. Identify access and accessibility issues. 2. Explain privacy, piracy, and copyright issues. 3. Discuss cultural/diversity issues.	✓ Analyze lesson plans in terms of social, legal, and ethical issues. ✓ Post responses to scenarios in forum and critique others. ✓ Participate in chat session. ✓ Complete module evaluation.

Figure 5.2. Core competencies for management of online learning course. Competencies are based on the National Educational Technology Standards (NETS). *Source:* Adapted from *Management of Online Learning Course* [Web document], by North Central Regional Educational Laboratory. Copyright © 2004 by North Central Regional Educational Laboratory, a wholly owned subsidiary of Learning Point Associates. All rights reserved. Adapted with permission.

of classroom-level technology use on student academic performance and offers some of the strongest evidence available documenting a causal link between technology and academic performance. The mean of the weighted effect sizes averaging across all outcomes was .410 ($p < .001$), indicating that teaching and learning with technology has a small positive, significant effect on student outcomes when compared to traditional instruction. Constructivist applications of technologies are believed to support developing higher order thinking skills (Valdez et al., 2000). The new findings by Waxman, Lin, and Michko (2003) finally provide us with more substantial evidence supporting these assumptions.

Until significant new research becomes available that specifically examines the effectiveness and impact of K–12 online learning, there will be little scientific evidence to support claims that K–12 online learning works at least as well as traditional face-to-face classroom instruction.

SIX PRACTICAL QUESTIONS

Hearings and a draft and comment process are underway that will lead to the creation of a new version of the National Education Technology Plan for the U.S. Department of Education. The National Educational Technology Plan, first released in 2000, is being revised as part of a long-range national strategy to inform and guide the effective use of instructional technologies to improve student academic achievement, either directly or through integration with other approaches to systemic reform.

The National Technology Planning Web site (http://www.nationaled techplan.org) provides six practical questions about online learning policy and practice. These questions offer a convenient framework to summarize much of the information on online learning policy and practice.

1. What state and federal regulations are inhibiting the growth of online learning?

According to the extensive mapping of state and national online learning policies offered in the *Virtual Schools Forum Report* (Center for Digital Education, 2003), the primary state and federal regulations inhibiting the growth of online learning in the K–12 schools concern the apparent disconnect between funding and practice. In short, students seeking to enroll in online learning choices frequently encounter a variety of funding obstacles, including tuition or attendance requirements that are inconsistent across different online learning programs and across regulatory boundaries.

2. What would a checklist of "e-learning-friendly" state and federal policies include?

Building once again on the good work done on the *Virtual Schools Forum Report*, it appears that a reasonable checklist of "e-learning-friendly" federal policies might include policies supporting accountability, equity, funding, and quality. However, it is probable that federal policies supporting these broad policy goals at the federal level will still need to be translated or applied differently in nearly every state. Predictable regional variations in educational policy and practice probably make uniform implementation of federal online learning policies very difficult, if not impossible. Because local control of education is still a highly valued principle in many parts of the country, broad and easily adaptable federal policies would seemingly provide the greatest flexibility supporting online learning at the state and local levels.

3. What should a school interested in online learning be most concerned about?

Practically speaking, schools interested in online learning are well served by concentrating their efforts on researching the issues and building local expertise appropriate for responding to three of our five "crucial questions":

- What policies and technology infrastructure requirements *must* be addressed to offer online courses?
- What specific knowledge, skills, and dispositions are required for "highly effective" online teachers?
- What special knowledge, skills, and dispositions do effective online learning leaders and managers need?

4. How should one define quality and effectiveness in online learning?

This question from the National Educational Technology Plan was partly addressed in our discussion of the remaining two "crucial questions": What are the characteristics of "high-quality" online courses? and What is the evidence that online learning improves student achievement? Every state and district aspiring to make online learning one of the choices offered in its schools should strongly encourage the local customization or reinvention of course guidelines based on the work of acknowledged leaders in the field. By involving local school personnel in the process of customizing design and/or selection and screening standards, local buy-in is encouraged, and school personnel are given a real voice and role in the development and deployment of online learning at the local level.

5. What should be the role of online learning in our nation's public education system?

Online learning should become a uniformly available curricular choice throughout our national educational system. Uniform availability should include due consideration of technology infrastructure requirements and digital equity to assure that every child has equal opportunities to choose online learning, where such choices are locally appropriate and aligned to content standards and accepted curricular practices.

6. What are the best metrics for tracking the trends associated with e-learning?

In the research describing the "benchmarks and milestones" associated with tracking the quality and efficiency of online learning in higher education, the two metrics most frequently cited are scores on valid and reliable discipline-based achievement tests and retention and completion rates for the same courses. Any reasonable form of program evaluation or outcomes research looking at the impact of online learning on academic performance should take both these indicators into account.

To meet existing and emerging data reporting requirements of the No Child Left Behind Act, schools offering online courses would also be well advised to ask themselves the following questions:

- Can your school report data on student enrollments in K–12 online courses disaggregated by
    i. Race/ethnicity? (Caucasian, African American, Hispanic, Asian, American Indian)
    ii. Poverty? (qualifying for free or reduced-cost student lunch under federal guidelines)
    iii. Disability? (having a diagnosed disability qualifying for an Individual Education Plan [IEP] and related support under the Americans with Disabilities Act)
    iv. Limited English proficiency? (diagnosed as having LEP under current USDOE guidelines for the Bilingual Education Act of 1968 or after 2002 under the new Title III of NCLB)
    v. Migrant status? (served by the Migrant Education Program)

- If these data are available, how do they compare with the percentages accounted for by each subgroup within your school and district's overall student body?
- If the data are available, how does each subgroup in online courses compare with its counterpart in face-to-face classes on:

  i. Course completion? (registered at cutoff date and completing the course)
  ii. Academic attainment? (grades of students completing the courses)

CONCLUSION

No Child Left Behind sets forth a bold and systemic framework for reform to close the achievement gap: supporting stronger accountability for results, increased flexibility and local control, expanded options for parents, and an emphasis on teaching methods proven to work. At the heart of this effort is a commitment to support teachers, parents, and decision makers in refocusing and realigning their efforts to ensure that every child receives the best possible education.

A number of organizations have sought to provide policy and practice guidance and resources for decision makers and educational policy leaders charged with the investigation and deployment of online learning in K–12 schools. Substantial progress has been made in the last few years in laying the groundwork for the development of online learning policy.

Five crucial questions concerning instructional and curricular policy and practice should be addressed: What are the policy issues that *must* be addressed to offer online courses? What are "high-quality" online courses? What knowledge and skills do online teachers need? How about online learning leaders and managers? What evidence is there that online learning improves student achievement?

In addition, the new National Educational Technology Plan Web site poses six practical questions about policy: What regulations are inhibiting the growth of online learning? What would a checklist of "e-learning-friendly" policies include? What should schools interested in online learning be concerned about? How should one define quality and effectiveness in online learning? What should be the role of online learning in public education? What are the best metrics for tracking trends associated with e-learning?

We have sought to summarize current evidence and viewpoints related to these questions. We hope this review is useful to those seeking to put policy into practice by framing plans of action for online learning that help to close the achievement gap, foster school improvement, and promote education reform.

FURTHER READING

Useful summaries of online learning policy include the following online resources.

Essential principles of quality: Guidelines for Web-based courses for middle grades and high school students (SREB). Available: http://www.sreb.org/programs/edtech/pubs/PDF/Essential_Principles.pdf
NCREL e-learning knowledge base. Available: http://www.ncrel.org/tech/elearn
North American Council for Online Learning Web site: http://www.nacol.org
Principles of good practice: The foundation for quality of the Electronic Campus of the Southern Regional Education Board (SREB). Available: http://www.electroniccampus.org/student/srecinfo/publications/principles.asp
Virtual education—New opportunities, new challenges (Wisconsin Department of Public Instruction). Available: http://www.dpi.state.wi.us/dpi/dfm/pb/pdf/advis1_1.pdf

Additional information about the knowledge, skills, and dispositions needed for successful online learning leadership is available in the following recommended, fully online resources.

Behind the cameras: 10 non-instructional issues to consider when coordinating a distance education program with other institutions (Saul Carliner). Available: http://saulcarliner.home.att.net/oll/managingitv.htm
Guide to developing online student services (WCET). Available: http://www.wcet.info/resources/publications/guide/guide.htm
Managing teaching time in "flexible learning" (Learningscope–Australia). http://www.learnscope.anta.gov.au/media/Media_847.doc
Virtual realities: A school leader's guide to online education (NSBA/TLN). Available: http://www.ns2k.com/nsba/pubs/

Marketing Virtual School Enterprises: Making the Message Matter

Ronald Stefanski

V IDEO PRODUCTION capabilities, multimedia technology, and the Internet have all converged in recent years, bringing with them unparalleled opportunities for innovation in a host of industries, none more exciting or far reaching than education. When one contemplates a world with truly global reach for wireless transmission, video streaming, and enhanced collaborative capabilities, with connections to varied communities and information resources, it does not take much imagination to consider the myriad ways in which education can reach more people and set the stage to benefit societies well beyond our borders.

At the same time, one needn't look beyond local, district, or state borders to see the advantages of increasing access to education and information far and wide. So why, then, hasn't adoption of educational technology simply exploded in the K–12 sector?

A host of explanations are available, among them, the lack of widespread access to technology in the classroom, the lack of professional development training of staff and administration, the lack of technical and end-user support (Thomas, 2002). The list goes on. But at a time when it has become clear that technology can spark innovation and enhance student learning, it is easy to understand why a host of e-learning and virtual learning initiatives have been launched. As many of these virtual K–12 efforts increase, other questions will follow. How do educational organizations use technology to improve student performance? or leverage existing resources in the classroom and instructional setting? or enhance professional development for teachers? or address the demographic issues that will impact the educational community in the years to come?

Many people, with far more educational and technology experience than I, can answer some of these questions. However, the purpose of this chapter is to outline some of the ways that marketing can be used by policymakers, educators, and administrators to develop cogent business and instructional strategy. Equally important, marketing is also a critical element in communicating in targeted ways to specific audiences, and a means by which programs can be carried out to greatest advantage. Marketing allows virtual schools to plan their efforts and make their message matter. A value proposition without a receptive audience offers little value. Marketing efforts are conducted by different persons inside or outside (or both) the educational institution. Given this, not all the strategies that follow may be judged to be appropriate for the specific persons doing the marketing or for the circumstances in which the organization finds itself.

MARKETING MYTHS

Is marketing an important activity for your organization? Based on the degree to which you or your organization subscribes to some of the marketing myths listed below, marketing could be the key activity around which your organization's planning revolves.

It is important to dispel some of the more pressing myths about marketing at the outset. Marketing is not something used to "spin," "manipulate," or "exaggerate" events and developments. Rather, marketing is a key element in successful strategic planning, driven by strong, honest, and clear communication. Nowhere is this more important than with virtual education initiatives where the stakes are high, the resources limited, and the margin for error extraordinary.

In my work in education over the past 20 years as a marketing and sales executive for a variety of educational and e-learning providers, and currently as Director of Business and Partner development for the Michigan Virtual University and its K–12 initiative, the Michigan Virtual High School, I have identified a few common misconceptions that can be limiting, if not detrimental, to an organization. Consider your current enterprise, and ask whether any of the following are true:

- Marketing is often regarded as a discrete activity, separate and distinct from pricing, sales, distribution, and public relations.

- It is introduced into the equation only when something isn't happening (e.g., message isn't being conveyed effectively, or customers aren't taking advantage of the products or services available).
- It is considered less necessary because of the Web. Somehow the Internet has created the myth that if a product or service is available online, customers and constituents will "show up" for it.
- It is viewed as a commercial activity, the exclusive domain of for-profit ventures.

If any of these myths are driving your organization, a marketing plan can focus your efforts and increase your reach to a broader audience.

MARKETING PLANS

A marketing plan should be a living document, one that is adapted by organizational stakeholders across departments over time and reflects the way in which resources will be utilized toward greatest advantage. There is nothing more short-lived in its effectiveness than a strategic marketing plan that is developed and then buried in a file somewhere, so the organization can "get back to the work at hand" (Valentin, 2001). As market conditions change, plans require refinement, as a healthy part of the business development process. The method here can be simple, not complex or extraordinary. In short, it's important to plan the work, and then work the plan. Getting internal stakeholders solidly behind the effort can invariably be the more challenging prospect.

In many organizations, change is only prompted by necessity—the need to reverse serious revenue shortfalls or to alter direction because of external market conditions. But this is part of a natural process of business growth and evolution.

Numerous virtual K–12 entities have been funded over the past few years during the last days of the technology boom of the 1990s, with healthy state budget surpluses and rosy economic conditions. As these organizations grow into maturity, many are facing drastically different financial circumstances. Only those with strong capital sources and viable business models can be expected to survive over the long term. For example, the Michigan Virtual High School (MVHS) is completing a transition from a subsidized K–12 project, funded by the state legislature, to an enterprise that is client-supported. Focusing financial, technological, and human resources will be critical to emerging as a strong enterprise with sufficient capital resources to grow. Nowhere is sound and strategic marketing more vital to long-term success.

The following five elements form the basis of an effective marketing plan:

1. SWOT analysis (strengths, weaknesses, opportunities, threats)
2. Identification of target audience (primary and secondary)
3. Defining core competencies of the organization
4. Competitive analysis
5. Positioning

SWOT Analysis

The SWOT methodology (analyzing a matrix of strengths, weaknesses, opportunities, and threats) has been employed in many strategic contexts with unit leaders and senior management teams to identify key strategic issues the organization is facing (Collett, 1999). What are the strengths of the organization? Equally important, where are the weaknesses? This, of course, is the more difficult to assess. Oftentimes, when organizations conduct a SWOT analysis as a collaborative exercise (as part of a strategic retreat or off-site event), it is important to have an objective facilitator who can move the group past the defensive posture that may dominate internal discussion. A leader at the helm of a failed effort can often prove ineffectual acknowledging shortfalls in the plan. Organizations that thrive are usually those sanguine about their shortcomings, not ones without them.

It is also important to prompt discussion about future opportunities, not just evaluating those previously considered, based on ever-changing market information. This is usually the place where "out-of-the-box" thinking is encouraged; in some instances, it has even become a cliché for organizations. The trick here is to keep the focus on the customer—what do they need in order to operate more effectively? How can your program, products, or services assist them in this process?

Threats to success are a critical, and sometimes overlooked, part of this discussion. In K–12 e-learning, technology is changing at a rapid speed. School systems are launching bond issues to support significant technology infrastructure improvements. What threats might virtual schooling pose to existing offerings? Technology solutions that don't deliver can be both an internal and external threat to the business. They can drain resources, draw upon staff, and exhaust significant revenue without ever improving anything for your customer. Any initiative that doesn't increase efficiencies or drive revenue can ultimately be a considerable threat to the organization's success.

Identification of Target Audience

In planning the work, it is important to begin by identifying the primary (and secondary) target audience. Was your organization designed to support students? teachers? administrators? Very often, organizations begin going down the path of identifying the target audience, only to discover at some later point that it is different than originally anticipated. This certainly applies to the Michigan Virtual High School, an enterprise that began offering free Advanced Placement courses to all Michigan high school students, in order to impact Michigan high school districts that didn't offer an Advanced Placement curriculum. It was easy to assume that the "customer" was the student. However, MVHS is not chartered to offer a degree, certificate, or diploma, and so the primary audience is actually the educator/administrator. Why is this distinction important?

Because armed with this insight, MVHS could tailor marketing materials and communication accordingly. For example, if parents and students were the primary audience, the message would be considerably different. Figure 6.1 lists potential target audiences within the K–12 marketplace and the marketing focus for each. A review of this list shows that determining

AUDIENCE	MESSAGE FOCUS
Regional service agencies	Standards, staff development
School board	Local benchmarks, student outcomes
Superintendents	Student access, staff development
Tech directors	Technical and application support
Curriculum staff	Curriculum, product offerings
Principals	Student access, retention outcomes
Counselors	Student placement, course selection
Teachers	Classroom resources, PD programs, courses
Parents	Opportunity and program evaluation
Students	Resource options/flexibility

Figure 6.1. Tailoring the marketing message to specific K–12 audiences.

a virtual school's target audience will affect its offerings and the communication supporting them.

Defining Core Competencies of the Organization

Few organizations have the luxury of being all things to everyone. By refining the definition of their customers, organizations can focus on what they do best and outsource the rest. For start-up organizations with limited resources, this is critical.

At the Michigan Virtual University, this past year was an appropriate time to evaluate various initiatives supported throughout the organization. One of the first questions asked was, "What does the organization do best across all these varied businesses?"

It became clear that the organization's strength did not lie in being a technology company. And although course development was initially a part of the operation, it became clear that this was not an organizational competency that could be sustained over the long term—many other providers had either more capital or human resources to compete more effectively. Rather, serving as a neutral broker among vendors and aggregating resources to build e-learning initiatives identified the real value proposition, and created the best approach for delivering client-centered solutions.

An analysis of core competencies has led to a reorganization around key functions—sales, marketing, and operations—and a focus toward becoming a more efficient nonprofit service and delivery enterprise that can bring numerous offerings together in one turnkey solution for clients. Similarly, assessing core competencies can free up resources to pursue more singularly the real strengths of the organization.

Competitive Analysis

In the emerging K–12 e-learning arena, it has become the norm to suggest that many offerings are new and, as a consequence, without any meaningful competition. But there is a real danger here. Why?

It's very simple. If there isn't any meaningful competition, chances are there isn't much of a market either. Competition is a sign of health and viability. Competition also drives organizations to be stronger. Operating without competitors is an almost certain way to become lax, to begin to believe that one's offering is so invaluable that the customer must have it in order to be successful.

A competitive analysis ensures that your organization is keeping abreast of the most recent technological, operational, and product developments. Oftentimes, especially in new and emerging market arenas, one company surfaces with a "first-to-market" strategy. Another finds it is far more lucrative to imitate rather than preempt. In an emerging market, the customer may not have a clear or defined notion about what they want. It is only with time, and the ability to evaluate alternative offerings side by side, that needs become more distinct and differentiated.

In the K–12 educational field, competition is driving many new initiatives. As school districts compete for both students and funding, it is important to understand the changes in student enrollment patterns, as well as changes in funding formulas (Hendrie, 2003). As schools of choice continue to emerge and mature, and homeschooling populations continue to grow, these alternatives will continue to impact the way in which instruction is delivered.

Homeschool enrollments have been increasing in recent years for a number of reasons (e.g., issues having to do with student safety, quality of instruction, flexibility of scheduling). As students leave a district, or parents begin homeschooling, it is important for educators to better understand the reasons. This is not with the intention of viewing students as "customers," but rather to understand how instructional programs are delivering on students' individual learning needs (Boss, 2002).

Positioning

The marketplace is broad and varied. The landscape is rife with numerous competitors. It is impossible to contemplate a world in which one product serves all. Customization, globalization, and innovation have driven the consumer world to a point where one size will never fit all. Positioning a product or service simply means identifying the specific places where your offering best serves your target audience.

An example of positioning at the Michigan Virtual High School is illuminating. After developing an Advanced Placement offering, a suite of "traditional" courses to supplement schools' curriculum offerings, and courses for credit recovery, it was assumed by many internal instructional staff that "traditional" courses, with the most robust multimedia content and local instructional development, would prove to be the most popular with client schools. Experience proved otherwise.

Advanced Placement and credit recovery programs proved to be the most popular with school districts. Why? For school districts new to online learning, replacing traditional instruction with an online alternative for students wasn't in and of itself compelling. However, Advanced Placement and credit recovery programs actually served a particular need and solved a specific problem, because many of these students were under-served by their district (not by design, but by circumstance). Adminis-trators were enthusiastic about the prospects of an effective instructional alternative. This insight has assisted in better understanding and defin-ing customers' needs.

Many e-learning virtual schools support broader policy goals and larger curriculum reform or instructional transformation initiatives. Some of these efforts assume that the online course should be positioned right alongside a traditional course of instruction, as if they are equivalent. Bear in mind, it is the customer's perception that matters here. However, the research to support these claims is still inconclusive. Face-to-face instruc-tion is still clearly preferred (if not considered superior) to online forms of instruction in many settings. MVHS's suite of course offerings has been positioned as an alternative resource for schools otherwise unable to de-liver specific instruction. This has worked effectively with school districts because the offering supplements, rather than supplants, existing instruc-tional programming.

By positioning courses to align with the needs of underserved students (the gifted and talented, and those requiring credit recovery), the value proposition becomes more compelling. Additionally, by positioning these courses as a supplemental service, issues of comparison with traditional instruction can be avoided, and local administrators can together learn what works best for their students.

Summary

In today's environment where the stakes are high and the resources lim-ited, a very compelling case can be made for developing a marketing plan that serves as a living document for the organization. In addition to pro-viding critical information about the specific target audience, a strategic marketing plan recognizes the inherent limitations to available resources, and keeps the organization aligned with customers' needs.

MARKETING METRICS: THE SATISFACTION SCORECARD

How will an organization know that it has been successful? In addition to program and customer evaluations and surveys, what are the key metrics that support the organization's goals? How are "touch points" defined that signal progress toward meeting broad program objectives?

Satisfaction can be measured in a variety of ways and for a variety of program elements:

1. Course content and delivery
2. Registration and enrollment services
3. User experience (within courses and with the overall program)
4. Teacher recruitment, training, and retention
5. Student achievement (assessment, measurement, and outcome)

For many virtual school operations, funding is a critical issue. As state and local policymakers define the ways in which online learning will become part of the overall curriculum for students, numerous funding alternatives are beginning to emerge. One solution will not fit all circumstances, and it is important for virtual school administrators to identify funding sources that align with their goals and outcomes.

However, revenue and the number of students served become metrics that can track progress to date with specific initiatives, as long as they do not obscure the underlying quality and delivery issues that must be at the center of the equation.

Many virtual school initiatives have spent considerable funds developing their own courses. At the Michigan Virtual High School, the operation began creating instructional design standards (and a standards evaluation/assessment tool) and developing a model for course development that married a team of master-certified Michigan teachers with an online Web development firm and an instructional designer. However, the cost of development is high, and huge capital requirements have caused many to reevaluate this approach. By establishing quality metrics, however, MVHS is able to institute quality assessment of various online alternatives and can ensure that product, service, and curriculum offerings are aligned with Michigan state standards and benchmarks.

In the early days of the Internet, Web site traffic was initially a huge metric for many online ventures, but it has quickly become apparent that, just as in the commercial world, these metrics have little meaningful value.

Key metrics also revolve around the student—the number of those enrolling in courses or online activities, the number who actually complete these courses, and the quality of their experience. Many virtual K–12 initiatives are starting to assess metrics in this critical area. It is important to note that many comparisons remain highly subjective in nature, and further research and assessment is required before policymakers have a clear picture of how online teaching and learning stacks up against a host of other instructional strategies.

In sum, it is critical for an organization to establish clear metrics that serve as guideposts in charting progress against goals and provide key information that assists in identifying ways in which to improve and enhance its offering.

MARKETING-MIX ELEMENTS

Many educational institutions are reluctant to engage in marketing activities, often for fear that they will taint their programs by using commercial tactics to effect broad policy goals. Also, many organizations engage in a limited number of marketing activities, simply because of the available resources or existing skill set of those on staff. But it is important to look at a broad range of marketing-mix elements (outlined in brief below) to determine the combination that will work best for the organization.

BRANDING AND IMAGING STRATEGY

- Branding initiatives that support the enterprise's overall strategic plan
- Imaging strategy developed by identifying imaging statements that define what the organization does and organizational goals and values
- Broad messaging to create or increase awareness in a large, diffuse audience
- Mass market vehicles (radio, TV, newspapers, magazines)
- Web design focused on optimal customer navigation, customer recognition (e.g., by teachers, students, and administrators), and "community" resources, such as news, offerings, and information

MARKETING COMMUNICATION AND DIRECT MARKETING TARGETED TO DECISION MAKERS AND END-USERS

- Newsletter
- E-newsletter
- E-mail
- Postcards
- Marketing collateral support and presentation materials
- Marketing premiums (pens, post-it notes, giveaways)

DIRECT SELLING AND MARKETING EVENTS

- Direct sales calls and contact with prospects and key decision makers
- Key conferences and workshops that provide high profile customer contact and opportunities for interaction

- Sponsorship activities that support the organization's goals
- Panel group discussions, focus and user groups, and special events
- Local community events and sponsorship of community activities, such as parent-teacher nights, teacher recognition events, and school board orientation meetings

PUBLIC RELATIONS AND CAUSE-RELATED MARKETING

- Press releases and media conferences
- Sponsorship of key cause-related initiatives aligned with your program (e.g., literacy programs or campaigns)
- Sponsorship of online newsletter or student newspaper
- Sponsorship of public access radio program

Branding and Imaging Strategy

Strengths overplayed can quickly become weaknesses. This is apparent when organizations have lots of outgoing messages, yet it is difficult for the staff or even their strongest customer advocates to quickly articulate just what the organization does (the key value proposition). Often, when marketing, sales, and public relations exist in different units or departments, the results can be less than cohesive. A branding strategy that integrates the outgoing message and promotes marketing across the organization can exponentially increase the effectiveness of your marketing message.

Often, worries surface in an organization that individual programs will get overlooked, and the overall marketing effect will suffer. Successful organizations are able to build core brands, with common organizational values, that are supported by diverse and seemingly unconnected products and services. Again, an easy way to determine whether the marketing reach is getting too broad is to ask, Who is the target audience? How does the organization deliver value to them? How does it best reach them with existing resources?

At the Michigan Virtual High School, after identifying a core target audience—local high schools and districts—a strategy was developed for promoting a wide array of product offerings with limited financial and staff resources through a member subscription model. Some of the identifiers regarding the core mission and objectives assisted in refining this approach.

By identifying the organization's broader goals and objectives, an organization can better define what it does and how it delivers value to different clients and audiences. Some of the value propositions common across MVHS included the following:

1. We evaluate complex technology solutions objectively for clients.
2. We develop "simple and compelling" e-learning solutions with partners.
3. We work with clients to solve problems and challenges they face. We identify "quick wins"—cutting through complex processes and procedures.
4. We identify "best-in-class" products and services that create turn-key e-learning solutions for governmental, business, and educational clients.
5. We aggregate products and services across the state to create the most cost-effective solutions for constituents.
6. We advance lifelong, career-long educational and professional development and learning for clients.
7. We identify ways to help prepare educators, trainers, employees, and students for the workforce of tomorrow—today.

At the Michigan Virtual High School, the initial branding strategy for the first year involved billboards and mass media, including online and radio spot announcements, to increase overall public awareness. In subsequent years, we shifted the resource mix more toward a direct sales approach, with supporting communication to get closer to the customer. A "simple and compelling" message was delivered to the key target audience (school building principals and administrators), and an e-mail and fax communication campaign was directed toward school principals, along with flexible supporting collateral presentation materials.

In the first year of the new offering launch (moving from a free to a fee-based service) the customer base increased from approximately 87 school districts to over 200. This was significant, given that school administrators were now obliged to pay (although just a portion of the total cost of services) for what had originally been available at no cost. The transition from a free to fee-based model speaks to the fact that free services online need to be balanced against broader public policy issues of student access. But this model provides a basis for creating additional funding mechanisms for the Michigan Virtual High School.

Marketing Communication and Direct Marketing

A newsletter that is both online and provided in hard copy can organize marketing communication by customer audience and serve as the cornerstone of a "push" communication to feed constituents continuous information on products, services, and initiatives. Additional marketing communication (e.g., targeted e-mail communication, direct mail, collateral support for marketing events, conferences, and sales calls) can also be used to support a coordinated and effective communication strategy with clients.

At the Michigan Virtual High School, we have learned that our customers desire frequent communication: because our offering is complex, myriad reinforcements surrounding program offerings are needed in order to communicate to various school staff as they become more involved in implementing our programs.

Direct Selling and Marketing Events

Direct sales activity is extremely effective when (a) products or services are available at some cost to the customer and (b) customer feedback is critical to the organization in terms of shaping future programs and offerings. Understanding the sales calendar/sales cycle is critical (e.g., one can't visit schools in July requesting a purchase of services for the fall). Customer satisfaction and service can also be part of the sales process. Many e-learning products and services require direct, face-to-face customer contact, and this is best delivered as part of a direct sales approach.

Public Relations and Cause-Related Marketing

An effective public relations approach requires proactive communication, which is an integral part of the strategic marketing plan. In the absence of a strong plan that is broadly supported across the organization, there is a tendency for communication to become chaotic and reactive; in the case of problem events, the organization may become reactive and defensive. Lack of a strong marketing plan can also produce inaction, because there is not clear consensus on how to communicate externally. In order to keep the organization "on message," it is critical for marketing staff to maintain a high degree of positive interaction with staff in order to continually reinforce key messages that need to be communicated externally.

Cause-related marketing (e.g., supporting community events and causes) that supports the organization's key objectives is a natural outgrowth of dialogue between the organization and its customers. In sum, the value of a proactive public relations approach is that it gets key customers amplifying the organization's value proposition externally.

SELECTING THE RIGHT ADVERTISING AGENCY

Selecting an ad agency for an enterprise is tantamount to selecting a partner to assist in defining its branding and imaging strategy. Oftentimes, the overall market strategy will help determine the size, type, and specific agency that is right for the organization. In the course of over a dozen agency reviews, I have seen organizations make some common mistakes worth identifying here.

The most common mistake is the tendency that many marketers have of conducting the agency selection process without internal participation across key departments. It is critical to bring nonmarketing staff within the organization into an understanding of the overall marketing direction and the agency's role in it. All too often, agency reviews and changes occur because the marketing direction doesn't resonate with specific customer audiences, or fails to keep the organization "on message" with its customers. Sales departments, in particular, are excellent organizational reservoirs of customer insight and perspective; failing to tap into these sufficiently can prevent an organization from keeping its program aligned with its customers.

Another common mistake is changing advertising agencies too frequently. This usually occurs when the agency is not properly managed internally, and the creative message and direction veer from the overall strategy for the enterprise. While it is always important to maintain a fresh and customer-driven approach, an agency with institutional memory in good standing can provide vital assistance and support as a partner in refining the message, and even changing or altering direction. Chances are if an organization has had multiple agencies in a short period of time, it is time to assess the marketing group's overall strategy and plan to ensure they have properly and comprehensively identified the organization's key goals, value proposition, and priorities.

Finally, it is important to identify current and anticipated organizational competencies in order to manage resources effectively, and limit redundancies with the agency. This is especially true in small or start-up organizations. If plans call for utilizing a host of direct mail and targeted marketing communication, a boutique agency specializing in graphics and communication may be far more suitable than a large organization that cannot provide personalized attention and service.

A list of questions for the agency selection process can eliminate a large pool of potential agencies from consideration, and assist in addressing some of the more strategic marketing issues the organization faces:

1. What steps does your agency take to ensure your work is "on message" and resonates with the customer? What specific client experiences enhance your agency's understanding of our core audience?

2. How do your business processes build knowledge and confidence among decision makers in our organization (many of whom do

not have a marketing background) to ensure that our organization continuously enhances its relationship with customers?

3. A *brand* is a term that signifies an organization's goods and services and differentiates them from what others offer. Building a brand can be tough because it takes three things organizations are often unwilling to provide—extensive resources, money, and time. What are some of the most effective "quick and dirty" and inexpensive ways to build the organization's brand?

4. Many companies face the same challenges—lots of distinct messages that can be confusing to the customer. What do you recommend to support the core brand and other brands within business units?

5. What is the biggest client challenge you faced? How did you handle it? How did it change the way your firm operates?

6. Sometimes key decision makers get involved in creative decisions and overrule the agency (and the organization's own staff). These decisions often reflect subjective bias and may not be valid. When this happens (and every organization experiences this), what have you found to be the most effective way to work through these circumstances?

7. Although we are an Internet-based organization, many of our customers are not very tech-savvy. What kinds of Web-enabled strategies work to assist customers in accessing information about our organization and our services from our Web site?

8. Many ad agencies speak aggressively about their return on investment, or ROI, and their results. What is the best example of the cheapest and quickest campaign that produced above-expected results?

9. Every organization works with limited resources. When times get tough, marketing is often cut. What are some examples of strategies and programs that were effective even during lean times. How would you utilize the full mix of marketing elements with our organization (e.g., event marketing, media, PR/media relations, print, Web marketing, Web site/graphics/design)?

10. Based on your understanding of our account, where do you see the most promising opportunities for our organization?

VENDOR-SPONSORED MARKETING

In addition to an agency or marketing service provider, what can your partners do to help market your program? This is an often-overlooked area for leveraging resources. Marketing materials and support from e-learning product vendors can be identified in initial negotiations to include support of organization-sponsored activities (e.g., booth exhibits, premiums, collateral materials, training support).

RESOURCE ALLOCATION AND PLANNING

Many organizations start out focused on delivering a particular product or service. It is only in the next phase of their growth that they begin a transition toward a more customer-focused enterprise. This can happen as an outcome of a strategic planning process, or it can be provoked, in whole or in part, by the demands of growth and internal competition for an organization's limited resources. The organization then begins to "find its way to the customer."

As more resources within the organization are allocated to the marketing and sales efforts, an understanding of the budgeting process is critical. Marketing activities require extensive planning and development up front, sometimes before it is possible to commit specific budget dollars.

At the Michigan Virtual High School, marketing communications were targeted to school administrators and principals, and limited with parents and students. Why? Because there was a recognition that the customer—namely, the school district—needed to be persuaded by the value proposition first. School support might, in fact, be jeopardized by prematurely raising interest and expectations among parents before administrators had a chance to evaluate the offering for their students.

The key in allocating resources effectively is, again, to "plan the work, and work the plan." If a strategic marketing plan is developed and then rarely used to drive goals and activities, it is nothing more than a static document, at risk of becoming obsolete quickly. An effective marketing plan is one that is regularly and consistently communicated throughout the organization so that internal stakeholders as well as external customers can readily identify consistency in message, direction, and outcomes.

MARKETING'S GUIDING PRINCIPLES:
MAKING THE MESSAGE MATTER

Effective marketing can enhance an organization's throughput and align broad program goals and initiatives. Marketing is not a panacea; it cannot cover the ills of poorly conceived product development schemes, faulty service or delivery models, or poor customer service. But marketing can, and does, offer organizations the opportunity to assess their own goals, focus efforts with the benefit of customer insight, and leverage limited resources toward greatest advantage.

Attention to marketing considerations at the outset is a sure way to support an organization's K–12 virtual efforts and translate that connection into a long-term, sustained, and productive relationship with constituents.

As a virtual school begins to assess its marketing needs, it should ask whether the enterprise addresses the following "mission critical" competencies, and should include them in the program marketing mix. If not, take heed. The following checklist is a great starting place to ensure that a virtual school optimizes enterprise marketing efforts and makes the message matter for its audience.

MARKETING TOP 10 CHECKLIST FOR THE VIRTUAL SCHOOL ORGANIZATION

1. Is the organization's marketing program aligned with its overall strategic planning process?
2. Does the organization's marketing planning process provide a "living document" to facilitate ongoing marketing practice into program design and delivery?
3. Has the organization reviewed the overall balance of marketing-mix elements that can be deployed based on its goals, objectives, and available resources?
4. Have key stakeholders across the organization been engaged in a comprehensive review and evaluation process for use with the advertising agency?
5. Does the organization's marketing program begin (rather than end) with the customer? Does it include structured ways to identify specific needs before translating them into products, services and solutions? Is the program structured to revise program elements based on continuous customer feedback? Marketing creates a vital, ongoing "communication bridge" to the customer. Is this built into the program design?
6. The more an organization's structure and culture center on the customer, the greater the likelihood that the marketing program is integral to building and supporting a loyal base of long-term satisfied customers. Does the organization's technology system gather and build institutional knowledge of the customer? Equally important, is this information and understanding translated into innovative and improved products and services based on customer insight?

7. Marketing can often be the glue that connects different enterprise activities and assists everyone to better understand how to serve constituents. Is the organization working together effectively with key stakeholders within and outside the organization who can utilize customer insights to build upon and improve programs?

8. Marketing helps everyone understand what is needed and what are the costs of serving the organization's constituents. An integrated marketing program also helps identify when the customer will see it, what it cost, how it worked, and what needs to change based on the results. Does the organization understand what marketing activities are being conducted and what those marketing activities are delivering to bottom-line revenue?

9. Effective marketing planning requires a timeline for developing promotional activities with specific deliverables and dates, as well as persons responsible. Is the organization on task with a marketing calendar that is clearly communicated and aligned with its customers' schedules?

10. Structured feedback and assessment of marketing goals and outcomes from customers help build on the success of the program and allow for changes based on specific needs. Is the organization regularly communicating results to support continuous improvement and delivery? Does it know what's working and how to improve what is not?

PART II

Case Studies

Florida Virtual School:
A Choice for All Students

Bruce Friend & Sharon Johnston

FLORIDA VIRTUAL SCHOOL (FLVS), an innovative educational opportunity, breaks the mold of traditional education. Educators involved in creating this "out-of-the-box" learning environment exhibit extraordinary dedication to the success of students. Because of the uniqueness of the online school and work environment, Florida Virtual School (http://www.flvs.net) does not follow the traditional educational norms and practices. The public school's virtual environment offers an "any time, any place, any path, any pace" choice for all learners; students choose the time convenient for them to "attend class." According to research, student choice accounts for the majority of high school students enrolling in online courses (Roblyer, 1999). Free to Florida students, FLVS enrollments consist of public school, homeschool, and private school students, including athletes, performers, and students with scheduling conflicts or medical problems. The primary reasons for the creation of FLVS were to give students choices in how, when, and where they learn; to increase student achievement; and to ensure that all students in Florida have equal access to all courses, including honors-level and Advanced Placement courses.

FUNDING

From 1996 until 2003, the Florida legislature supported FLVS through a direct line-item budget allocation for research and development. Initially named Florida High School in 1996, the project was funded under a $200,000 state grant. Renamed Florida Online High School in 1998 and Florida Virtual School in 2000, the funding remained under the category of research and development. Over the last 3 years, FLVS has been in the midst of a major evolutionary step in its development as a unique public educational institution and in its task to devise a funding model. The 2000 Florida legislature established FLVS as an independent educational entity with a separate governing board appointed by the governor. In most respects, FLVS now has a comparable legal status to the 67 school districts that make up Florida's public school system. In 2003 Florida law decreed that FLVS funding would become performance based, meaning that FLVS will receive full-time equivalency (FTE) funds for each student who successfully completes a course. FLVS is the only school in Florida to be funded solely on student performance (Florida Virtual School, 2004).

PHENOMENAL GROWTH

When it launched courses in 1997, FLVS enrolled only 157 students. Each year the administration has had to cap student enrollments because of limited budget and bandwidth. Demand has definitely exceeded capacity. In the 2002–03 school year, FLVS served more than 12,000 student enrollments and attained a 95% completion rate. For the 2003–04 school year, it is estimated that FLVS will serve 18,000 enrollments in over 70 online courses.

STRATEGIC PLANNING

A board of trustees, appointed by the governor, approves policies and collaborates with staff in establishing, reviewing, and updating the strategic plan. Involved in the planning are members from the homeschool community, K–12 public education, postsecondary education, parents, students, and business partners.

MISSION AND CORE BELIEFS

Over the last 8 years, the FLVS Mission Statement has changed four times, but the Core Beliefs have remained unchanged:

FLVS MISSION STATEMENT, 2004

The mission of Florida Virtual School is to provide students with high-quality, technology-based educational opportunities to gain the knowledge and skills necessary to succeed in the twenty-first century.

FLVS CORE BELIEFS

- Learning occurs through the development and delivery of dynamic, engaging, and transdisciplinary curricula.
- Students learn best through actively participating and applying knowledge to relevant situations and issues.
- Students learn best when they, their instructors, family, peers, and community members interact as facilitators of learning and share responsibility for student success.
- Instruction should accommodate students' varied learning styles and intelligence types to assist and encourage the path and pace by which they learn best.
- Students must be provided with appropriate support services that link academic, personal, social, and career goals.
- Assessment should measure student knowledge, guide student development, and allow meaningful evaluation of the processes as well as the products of education.

INITIAL GOALS

Florida Virtual School came into being in 1996 as a grant-funded research project. Four goals were defined for the initial project:

- Redefining and continuously revising curriculum, instruction, and assessment at the high school level to reflect current best practices.
- Providing a rapid, timely, and readily available delivery system for educational reform, teacher in-service, and staff development programs.
- Developing the pupil skills and providing the resources to view learning as a lifelong process.
- Preparing students to take advantage of distance learning courses through the State University System.

Today, Florida Virtual School is an incorporated, nonprofit school providing middle and high school curriculum to students in all 67 Florida counties, as well as to students throughout the United States and the world. Much has changed since 1996, but the four goals specified in the original grant application remain as vital and important today as they did then. The goals, essential for any successful K–12 enterprise, are designed to put the learner at the center of instruction.

VIRTUAL SCHOOL EVOLUTION

Educational leaders across the nation are being challenged as never before to create opportunities to meet the varied needs of students. School districts are beginning to implement online education as a part of the solution to meet challenges such as providing educational choice, promoting the use of technology in learning, dealing with large increases or decreases in student enrollment, and producing students who have the knowledge and skills to immediately succeed in their postsecondary pursuits or the workforce.

When FLVS launched its first courses in spring 1997, only a few virtual schools existed across the nation. According to research by the Peak Group (2002), there were 88 virtual schools in the United States serving nearly 180,000 enrollments in 2002, and it is anticipated that in the year 2004, more than one million students will take an online course. Currently, FLVS is reported as being "the largest and most well-established state-supported virtual school in the nation" (Doherty, 2002, p. 19).

Today, the Internet offers students options in how, when, and where they demonstrate state competencies. In his comprehensive review of online learning, *A Classroom of One* (2003), Gene Maeroff writes:

> Developments in online learning in just a little more than ten years force one to conclude that this is a sea change, not a fad. By the end of the twenty-first century's first decade, e-learning will be an embedded feature of education, widely available and no longer an object of controversy. (p. 2)

High-quality instruction will never be a fad or folly. Similarly, high-quality online instruction that is delivered "any time, any place, any path, any pace" will have an important place in the delivery of education in the twenty-first century.

GLOBAL SERVICES

To address marketing needs, FLVS has established a Global Services Department to promote the organization's unique virtual learning opportunities to Florida students and others across the nation and throughout the world. Global Services is comprised of a team of highly experienced educators and business professionals who publicize FLVS products and services and build relationships with decision makers who are seeking innovative educational solutions for their constituencies. To share FLVS expertise with professionals seeking information and guidance on how to develop a virtual school, Global Services hosts a 2-day Virtual Leadership Workshop. To assist virtual school ventures, Global Services markets the Virtual School Management System, a tool developed specifically for day-to-day classroom operations and data tracking along with FLVS courses. Developed with DreamWeaver in HTML, courses are easily transferred and maintained in any learning management system. The revenue from these products provides funds for enhancing and increasing educational offerings for Florida students. For example, a portion of the revenues generated from leasing courses supports the updating of courses by adding interactivities and simulations. By sharing its expertise in virtual learning and its curriculum across the world, FLVS has emerged as a global leader in the development, delivery, and instruction of Web-based courses that have repeatedly received the U.S. Distance Learning Association's Award for Excellence.

ORGANIZATIONAL STRUCTURE

A fully online school, FLVS differs from other schools in that it does not have traditional physical facilities. FLVS is virtual in the sense that there is no FLVS building; its students and teachers can be anywhere in the state or the world. Although the administrative functions of FLVS are primarily housed in Orlando, many of the teachers and support staff are located throughout the state. FLVS's online educational delivery system transcends traditional education programs and offers an unprecedented degree of access and flexibility in serving the unique needs of students throughout the state of Florida and beyond. For example, students in West Virginia enroll in computer science, Spanish, Latin, and Advanced Placement courses that are not always offered in their rural areas. Online delivery provides equal access and choices for learners wherever they reside.

Instruction

Florida Virtual School is staffed with highly qualified, Florida-certified instructors who are well versed in Florida standards and expected performance outcomes. Currently, 20 staff members have attained National Board Certification. FLVS's exemplary teachers are trained in online instructional strategies and serve as primary educators in the online teaching and learning process. An important lesson learned, though, is that good teachers in the face-to-face classroom may not succeed at online teaching. In the online classroom at FLVS, the teacher must enjoy talking to students and parents on the telephone, teaching students one on one, and modifying instruction to meet individual student needs and interests.

Communication

At FLVS, teaching is not just about the curriculum; it is about connecting with students and parents. FLVS has designed its courses and instruction to maximize the student-teacher-parent relationship. In our experience with thousands of students, parents, and educators, we know that the secret to successful virtual education is a high level of communication powered by exemplary instructors. Regular contact with students occurs through several means:

- Welcome call and monthly calls
- Monthly progress reports
- Interaction via e-mail, phone, and course chat room
- Academic competitions
- Extracurricular clubs and field trips
- Student newspaper, *News-in-a-Click* (at FLVS Web site)
- Administrative updates and reminders via e-mails to students and parents

FLVS instructors are available to students via cell phone, pager, e-mail, chat rooms, and instant messaging throughout the day, night, and weekends. School policy dictates that instructors respond to student or parent e-mails or voice messages within 24 hours. Students at first are surprised that the teacher is calling home, but soon they become quite accustomed to the calls. We have created a virtual environment that gives students an opportunity to receive one-on-one assistance in the learning process. Cognitive scientist Roger Schank (1999), in a keynote address to the National Education Computer Conference, stated, "Technology enhances one-on-one opportunities, eliminates embarrassment of failure in a group, provides chances to experiment, can create realistic situations, and allows for individual differences in learning styles." A lesson learned about communication is rather ironic. Students report that often in their large, crowded traditional high school classes they are often just a number, but online learning at FLVS is personalized. The individualized teaching and learning model that Schank described and that FLVS supports ensures that no child is left behind.

ACCOUNTABILITY

Commensurate with the increased course offerings and student enroll-ments, FLVS has expanded its professional staff from 6 teachers in the first school year to a staff of 85 full-time teachers and 105 part-time teachers to serve 18,000 course enrollments. All FLVS teachers are held accountable for their students' performance. The administrative team views and con-tinually analyzes the monthly progress reports sent out to students, teacher phone call logs, and course completion rates. From the monthly progress reports, administrators and teachers determine if students are performing at an acceptable level academically and in meeting suggested pace require-ments. When problem areas are detected, the administrators and support staff members contact the teacher to create an action plan for resolution. Handling the increase in enrollment and staff successfully requires a man-agement plan that includes specific accountability measures.

STUDENT SERVICES

FLVS provides tremendous levels of student and parent support, from the beginning process of information gathering in registration to having the final grade sent to the school and/or home. FLVS even provides an online tutoring service to assist math students. Math teachers share the access information with all their students.

Online Resources

At the FLVS Web site, students and parents access valuable information under the Student Services tab. For example, updates and information helpful in planning the high school career and beyond are available with just a click. Listed below are a few of the search categories, each providing Web sites for students and parents to use in researching career and college possibilities:

- High school planning
- Career planning tools
- Postsecondary planning resources
- Information on technical schools, 2-year community colleges, 4-year colleges
- Tests, tests, tests (Standardized test tips and schedules)
- Financial aid and scholarship resources

Also at the Web site, FLVS offers a 21-page parent guide outlining the FLVS student progression plan, core curriculum recommendations, the FLVS grading system, academic integrity, and other essential information. To assist students in selecting courses, the entire curriculum guide is accessible at the Web site. To acquaint parents with the virtual environment, the flyer shown in Figure 7.1 is available in guidance offices located in all 67 Florida districts, as well as on the Web site.

www.flvs.net

Florida **Virtual** School – FLVS
"FLVS Parent Tips & Suggestions"

Dear Parents,

Thank you for choosing FLVS. As a parent, you are a very important member of your child's e-learning team.

To assist us in providing a quality education to your child, please consider the following suggestions.

- **Access**. Know your student's username and password so you can access the course(s).

- **Progress.** Check your student's online grade book at least once a week to see how many assignments have been submitted and what grades were received for that week.

"*Florida Virtual School has been and continues to be a most rewarding experience. I am very pleased with the instructional staff. I have actually found myself MORE involved with my daughter's education.*" **FLVS Parent**

- **e-Updates.** Establish an email account and enter the address in your student's online profile to receive monthly progress reports.

- **Communication.** Read the comments made by teachers on the various assignments by accessing your student's outbox.

- **Outreach.** Contact the instructor or an FLVS guidance counselor for questions or concerns.

- **Experience.** Provide a positive working environment where your student can concentrate and has access to the Internet, a telephone, and a printer.

If you have any questions you can call Florida Virtual School at (407) 317-3326 or email us at info@flvs.net. If you experience technical difficulties with the FLVS website, email us at help@flvs.net.

Florida

VirtualSchool   any time, any place, any path, any pace™

Figure 7.1. Florida Virtual School's introductory flyer and Web page for parents.

Guidance Department

A crucial element in the instructional segment of student services is the guidance department. FLVS employs guidance counselors and e-learning managers to advise students and parents in selecting the appropriate courses, to monitor progress reports and final grades, to support students in the virtual environment, and to assist counselors in traditional schools with student placement and other issues. Students and parents visit the guidance area at the FLVS Web site to find the guidance counselor and e-learning managers who serve their area of the state. What does a virtual guidance counselor do? Here are the primary guidance counselor responsibilities:

- Provides information to public and nonpublic schools and home-school organizations regarding FLVS courses, instructional approach, and administrative procedures
- Consults with e-learning managers to increase student enrollment
- Collaborates with the Curriculum Team to address ongoing curriculum development and enhancement
- Serves as the primary contact between parents and Florida Virtual School
- Provides direct consultation and guidance to students and parents on matters relating to courses, procedures, learning strategies, and college selection
- Provides advice and consultation to teachers of students with special needs
- Provides information on graduation requirements to administration and faculty
- Assists in training support staff
- Assigns students to teachers and maintains appropriate student-teacher ratios
- Serves as a liaison with the Florida Department of Education Office for Home Education and with nonpublic schools

The guidance counselors serve as the primary contact between parents and Florida Virtual School. E-learning managers serve as the primary contact between schools and FLVS. Unless students require teacher input or technological assistance, it is recommended by FLVS staff that all questions be funneled through the guidance counselors or e-learning managers. Consequently, the guidance counselors and e-learning managers, who work from home, spend much time on the phone or in e-mail answering questions for parents and students. Since guidance counselors talk with parents frequently, they hear and pass on compliments for a job well done to the staff. Guidance counselors share heartwarming anecdotes such as the story of the young man who decided to turn his life around in his senior year. FLVS teachers worked patiently with him as he took multiple courses online along with the six courses at his traditional school, so he could graduate with his class. Online guidance counselors and e-learning managers are essential for ensuring student success.

CURRICULUM AND INSTRUCTION

Current FLVS course offerings include a variety of regular and honors-level high school credit courses covering all curriculum areas, high-stakes test preparation courses, 11 Advanced Placement courses, and middle school courses. In addition, through the creation of a unique partnership with eight school districts, FLVS has developed eight courses specifically targeted for adult high school students as well as the state's first fully online GED preparation course.

Course Development

Teams of FLVS instructional and technical staff develop courses. Instructors are trained in online learning theory and pedagogy, Gagne's Nine Events of Instruction (discussed below), Bloom's taxonomy levels 4, 5, and 6 (analysis, synthesis, evaluation), and vertical teaming across levels of courses. Each course is developed from the Sunshine State Standards and each lesson is aligned with national standards. Courses undergo a rigorous peer review process, incorporating formative review by subject matter experts and educators from around the country before they are released for student use. FLVS's subject matter experts who are involved in creating a course know that they "must construct instructional content and processes within the course presentation and assignments that anticipate the differential learning requirements of the class members and embed the creative responses in the course material itself" (Schnitz & Azbell, 2004). To engage students, FLVS developers know to create production-oriented activities that give students choices in how they demonstrate their understanding of concepts.

Standards-Based Goals

Real success needs something real by which to measure it. Mastery learning and a system that allows each student to strive for defined goals, is the path to those goals. This path may differ with each student, but the standard for excellence is never in doubt.

Defining goals and outcomes begins with understanding the standards developed by the state Department of Education. The first step in creating a virtual course at FLVS is to consult the Sunshine State Standards for that course. FLVS developers know that the correspondence between the standards and student performance outcomes must be clear to educators who review the courses and also for students and parents. So that courses may be provided to other states, FLVS also aligns course activities to national standards.

Relevancy

Engaging students by connecting real-world applications to their learning is accomplished by the use of motifs or metaphoric constructs. In the American government course, for example, students take a virtual tour of Washington, D.C. In the process, they become politically active and learn how to access the governmental system. Projects include writing letters to senators, researching interest groups, and creating a persuasive product to support a political issue. In this kind of instruction, learning activities encourage students to make connections as they discover new concepts.

As part of our earliest thinking at FLVS, we wanted to respect and challenge our students' ability to think and to make connections. That has remained a consistent theme throughout all of our development. Designed into every course is a minimum of 60% of Bloom's levels 4, 5 and 6—analysis, synthesis, and evaluation. By integrating higher order thinking and successful workplace skills throughout the curriculum, we offer students opportunities to be engaged in problem-solving activities with real-world applications.

In the ninth-grade English course, for example, students analyze the effectiveness of advertisements to discover what people buy and what strategies cause them to buy. After researching products at virtual sites provided by the teacher, students create a chart to determine the target audience, the type of delivery, and the effectiveness of the advertisement. Finally, students create their own product and an accompanying marketing strategy.

To involve the students in the learning process, they are given choices on what resources to consult and how to demonstrate learning. For example, in AP Literature and Composition, the motif casts students as members of a dinner party. In this role students enjoy a menu of appetizers (short stories and poems), examine entrees (often literary works they choose), engage in table talk, and have a choice of whether or not to take dessert (creative projects that are optional). The instructor models for students how to design a dinner party, and then toward the end of the course, students become creators and make choices in designing their own themed dinner party.

What students learn is in large part a matter of the way their curriculum is designed. If teachers look for nothing more than memorized responses, they are likely to receive little more than that. However, when teachers encourage their students to make discoveries, to make connections, and to make choices, they and their students are likely to enjoy the learning process.

Gagne's Nine Events of Instruction

As the structure for creating a curriculum that is both engaging and student centered, the FLVS staff selected Robert Gagne's Nine Events of Instruction (Gagne, Briggs, & Wagner, 1992) as a model for development. Gagne's events of instruction, well known in educational research, provide clear definition for the complementary roles of teacher and student:

1. Gaining learners' attention
2. Informing learners of the objectives
3. Stimulating learners' recall of prior knowledge
4. Presenting the stimulus to the learner
5. Providing guidance to the learner
6. Eliciting performance from the learner
7. Providing feedback to the learner
8. Assessing the performance of the learner
9. Enhancing the learners' retention of the information and transfer of the information to other ideas and contexts

By using Gagne's Nine Events of Instruction as a model, FLVS course developers have designed dynamic curricula (see the appendix to this chapter for an example) that allow students to problem solve and create meaning. Fortunately, the Internet is now sufficiently advanced to support this kind of constructivist, student-centered curriculum. According to educator Bernie Dodge (1996), "A constructivist use of technology presents information to the learner in multiple forms from multiple sources and invites the learner to make sense of it" (p. 225). This is obviously a far cry from "push and click," wherein only one source of information and one correct answer can occur.

HIGHLY FACILITATED STUDENT-TEACHER INTERACTIONS

Technology has made it possible for one instructor to "teach" a large number of students at one time. On the surface, this might seem like an ideal solution when money is in short supply. It costs relatively little to allow the computer to present information, record test scores, and record time on task. From the beginning, Florida Virtual School committed to building a virtual environment that allows teachers to teach, and to coach students to success. Students turn in assignments, and the teacher gives written feedback in the electronic course room or phones to discuss ways the students can improve performance. Student-teacher ratio must be kept at a level that fosters this type of student-teacher interaction.

Highly facilitated refers to the degree to which instructors interact with learners. Distance-learning research indicates that this instructor-learner interaction is the most important ingredient in student success. Except for club field trips and special events, students at Florida Virtual School rarely see their teachers face-to-face. That does not mean, however, that students and teachers do not get to know each other. Using e-mail, frequent phone conversations, threaded discussions and synchronous chats, students are closely connected to their teachers. Since most of these contacts are one on one, many online students actually receive more individualized attention than is possible in traditional classrooms in which many students compete for attention.

For an effective one-on-one learning environment, teachers are chosen for their ability to make individual connections with students. A good online teacher is a motivator, a guide, and a listener. On the other hand, a teacher who prefers a large audience is unlikely to find fulfillment while working in a one-on-one environment. "Highly facilitated" also means highly responsive. Florida Virtual School policy requires teachers to answer student inquiries within 24 hours. In an environment that is characterized as "anytime," these inquiries can come any day of the week. Consequently, online teachers must have a disciplined approach to keeping the lines of communication open.

In a highly facilitated virtual course, the goal is not to "get through" the material. The goal is to assist students in connecting the learning and creating meaning. FLVS educators confirm that student-teacher interaction is the most important ingredient in achieving student success.

At FLVS, this interaction starts even before the student is formally activated. A welcome phone call from the teacher greets the student, ensuring that there are no circumstances that might prevent successful course completion. This call also begins the process of building a rapport that will continue throughout the course.

Maintaining continuous communication throughout the course is an important aspect of every FLVS course. Throughout the semester, teachers and students stay in contact by phone, e-mail, threaded discussions, courseroom activities, synchronous chats, and club field trips. Teachers also talk with parents, partnering with them to encourage and assist their students.

How valuable is the connection between teacher and student? Many online students appreciate the opportunity to have individual questions and concerns addressed when they arise. In an online setting, they may also feel less constrained in discussing coursework difficulties than they would in an open classroom with their peers present. In a "highly facilitated" online environment, the ultimate goal is to provide the kind of individual attention that allows no student to fall between the cracks.

Good teachers guide their students, encourage their students, and care about their students. All of these things require that teachers and students have effective channels for communication whether they are in a traditional or virtual classroom.

SERVING THE UNDERSERVED POPULATION

A reward of virtual education is filling learning gaps for students. For example, with FLVS, students in rural schools with small populations have access to the same curriculum as any large school. A student who wants a medical career but lives in rural Cedar Key with a seven-member senior class has the same opportunity as a student in a Miami school to take Advanced Placement biology. Making sure that *all* Florida students know about the choices provided by FLVS requires an intentional marketing campaign. To reach the underserved population, Florida Virtual School hired a staff member, an e-learning manager, specifically to connect with minority groups to promote access for minority and disadvantaged students. By working with One Florida, a state initiative that unites Floridians behind a shared vision of opportunity and diversity, FLVS is involved in projects that promote educational and technological equity throughout the state. A major challenge has been to find ways to provide equal access as well as connectivity to those in need, especially in locating or creating local community centers or hubs that can provide Internet access for students. Despite all efforts, the demand for computers and connectivity outweighs the supply. Calls come in each day with requests for connectivity to the Internet, computers (new or old), and computer peripherals (e.g., printers, scanners).

Leveling the Playing Field

Another key organization that has assisted FLVS in serving the underserved is the Florida Learning Alliance (FLA), created in 1998 by the three regional consortia that represent 34 small and rural school districts and FLVS. The mission of FLA is to increase academic achievement for students in rural and small school districts through distance learning and other innovative educational strategies. FLVS teamed with the three regional consortia—Heartland Education Consortium, North East Florida Educational Consortium, and Panhandle Area Educational Consortium—to submit and receive a U.S. Department of Education Technology Innovation Challenge Grant. With grant funds, high-end technology has been provided in the rural schools, giving many students access to FLVS courses. Through the dedicated efforts of the FLA staff, students and educators in rural areas receive information on FLVS registration. FLA publicity and consortia activities are largely responsible for the dramatic increase in FLVS student population in underserved areas.

Providing More AP Courses

To serve all Florida students with quality AP courses, FLVS collaborated with the College Board in another One Florida project. FLVS, the College Board, and the Florida Department of Education submitted a proposal for an AP Incentive Grant, which was funded in 2001. The AP Incentive Grant is a federal grant given to states to support AP exam fee reductions and professional development for teachers so students will have expanded access to AP courses. FLVS teachers work in partnership with teachers in schools with underserved populations that have no Advanced Placement courses. The schools identify teachers who may want to teach AP to participate in FLVS summer workshops and College Board Advanced Placement Summer Institutes to learn about curriculum online and about AP best practices. Throughout the school year, these teachers work with the FLVS teacher in offering the AP curriculum online to students at their schools. Students and teachers are winners in this grant project—students have access to AP courses, and teachers see the activities and assessments in the online classroom and will be prepared to teach the AP course or to support students in online AP courses in the future. As a result of the AP Incentive Grant project and other efforts, in the 2002–03 school year, 39% of the students in AP courses represented minorities. To assist students taking these rigorous courses, FLVS has created online AP exam reviews that students will access 4 to 6 weeks before the national exam. In an agreement with the College Board, FLVS will be incorporating past AP exam materials in the reviews, so students will have practice with authentic test resources.

Equal Access

In addition to working with organizations and community groups throughout Florida, FLVS has worked internally to serve the underserved population. By establishing a priority registration process that allows minority students top priority in registering for courses, FLVS has witnessed the minority population increase to 21%. To reach into the community, FLVS teamed with colleagues in Work Force Education to submit and receive a Front Porch Grant that targets a specific community center in the heart of Orlando. In February 2003, FLVS staff hosted a technology workshop for the leaders of the center. One FLVS teacher will work with the students and parents at this center, and the students will be enrolled in the FLVS critical thinking course for the Florida Comprehensive Achievement Test, Florida's high-stakes test that students must pass to graduate. A testimony of FLVS's success in serving all students is found in the following student comment.

A FLVS STUDENT SPEAKS

My name is Shalissa Brown, and I am an African American young lady who is currently a senior in an FLVS course. Regardless of race and poverty, online learning has given students the chance to challenge themselves, try something new, obtain a higher level of freedom, earn a college credit early, and display intelligence and potential. Although minority students facing poverty may have a little more difficulty in obtaining these benefits, we are not at all discouraged from reaching our goals. In fact, our disadvantages help us to reach higher and stretch further for the advantages.

Four of the students that took the FLVS AP Microeconomics course with me lived with a single mother. Three of them were black. All four students' fathers had left their families and only one of the black students had no sibling(s). Yes, none of us had the money to buy three computers, pay $700 a month for a car, or go to the mall every week, but we all at least had the chance to take a free accelerated course online. Online learning opens a door to the future and closes a door of the past.

As this student's statement shows, virtual learning equalizes the learning opportunities for students. Both talented and disadvantaged students can benefit from the flexibility and choice of virtual education as well as students from varied socioeconomic backgrounds and ethnicities (Shaw, 2000). Finding ways to ensure that all students have access to the choices that virtual learning provides is a mighty challenge, yet a rewarding endeavor for FLVS.

APPENDIX: APPLICATION OF GAGNE'S MODEL

To show how Gagne's Nine Events of Instruction guide our curriculum development, illustrations from the geometry course will be highlighted.

Event 1
Gaining Learners' Attention

Consider how the geometry course gains student attention with an apt architectural motif. On the opening page of the course, students see this graphic:

Welcome to Architects of Tomorrow!

To access the different modules, use the jump menus below.

Throughout the course, students continue to see geometry through an architectural lens as they become architects. The motif captures their attention and allows the students to make connections with the world around them. Moreover, the course taps students' attention by providing the software, Geometer's Sketchpad, so that students can create and manipulate images.

Event 2
Informing Learners of the Objectives

To inform students of objectives, the course developers ("content engineers") list the objectives at the beginning of each lesson. Giving students the purpose of the lesson is essential, so the course makes a point of stating the objectives.

Event 3
Stimulating Learners' Recall of Prior Knowledge

One example of triggering recall of prior learning is the following lesson, in which algebraic connections and items from the student's world are used to introduce geometric planes:

PLANES

In algebra you used a coordinate plane. This plane contained points and lines.

1. In geometry, a plane is a flat surface that extends indefinitely in all directions.
2. A plane can be named by a capital script letter or by three noncollinear points in the plane.
3. If points are coplanar, they lie on the same plane.
4. A plane contains an infinite number of points.

Examples of geometric planes: a sheet of paper, a piece of cloth, the top of your desk, a wall in your house.

Event 4
Presenting the Stimulus to the Learner

The stimulus is easily noticed in this assignment:

Visit the suggested Web sites given below to find articles on the history of geometry. Choose one article that interests you. Write five questions that can be answered by reading your article of choice. Put your questions, the answers to the questions, and the URL of your chosen article in your notebook. You will be asked to make this assignment part of your Math Trail, introduced in Lesson 1.21.

SUGGESTED WEB SITES

http://library.thinkquest.org/C006354/history.html?tqskip1=1&tq
time=0516
http://www.district30.k12.il.us/collaboratory/hansen/history/
history.html
http://netdial.caribe.net/~csantini/page29.html
http://www.faculty.fairfield.edu/jmac/rs/bridges.htm
http://www.mathgym.com.au/history/pythagoras/pythgeom.htm

In the geometry course, as well as in other courses, Web sites such as those used in the assignment above can serve as a stimulus for introducing or reinforcing a concept. Additionally, videos and sound files, software with animation or interactivity, stories, and other curriculum resources create the stimulus for learning in the virtual curriculum.

Event 5
Providing Guidance to the Learner

To provide learning guidance, the virtual course utilizes many tools, such as pictures, diagrams, tutorials, teacher feedback, models, flowcharts, rubrics, and so on. Note how this simple picture guides the learner in geometry:

GEOMETRIC MODELS

Below is a geometric model of a leaf. A geometric model is a geometric figure that represents a real-life object. A good model shows all of the characteristics of the figure or object it represents.

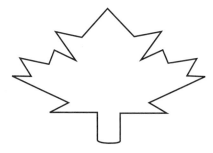

One important characteristic of the model above is that one half of it is a mirror image of the other half. If you draw a vertical line at the center, the leaf is divided into two equal parts. The leaf has reflection symmetry, and the line is called a line of symmetry.

Event 6
Eliciting Performance from the Learner

One of the most successful ways to elicit performance from students is to allow them to remediate their work by resubmitting assignments until they reach an acceptable level of quality. Students may be prompted during remediation, for example, by returning a chart the student did not complete, with some of the information filled in. This may encourage a student to find the information to completely fill in the chart. Another way to elicit performance is to ask provocative questions throughout the course, especially in the threaded discussion section of the course. For example, in the beginning of the geometry course this question is posed:

> Throughout the world manhole covers are round. Why do you think they were designed in that shape?

Event 7
Providing Feedback to the Learner

Key to student learning is feedback. Virtual school teachers need to take the time to talk to students on the phone or in the chat room or to give written feedback within online FLVS course components such as the courseroom, discussion, and assessment areas to ensure that students understand concepts. Having students submit work, receive feedback, and resubmit the assignment gives the learner time to process the feedback and, if needed, call the teacher for clarification before resubmitting the assignment.

Event 8
Assessing the Performance of the Learner

Performance is assessed throughout the courses in a myriad of ways: pretests, quizzes, tests, self-assessments, reflective exercises, demonstrations, discoveries, action plans and reflections on previous action plans, portfolios, and so on. In FLVS courses, students have the option of submitting assignments for review. Teachers give feedback. Students then revise and resubmit assignments for grading. The goal of these formative and summative assessments and mastery of learning approach is to allow each student every opportunity to achieve course objectives. At FLVS, we believe that every student has the potential to earn an A. For some students, achieving an A may require considerably more work than it might for others. But all course objectives are clearly stated, and the course structure provides ample opportunities for mastery. If, as educators, we truly believe that all students can learn, we must be willing—and even glad—to see the bell curve replaced by an uphill slope.

Event 9
Enhancing the Learners' Retention of the Information and Transfer of the Information to Other Ideas and Contexts

Enhancement of retention and transfer loops throughout the courses in the motifs, assignments with rubrics, models, Webquests—and in opportunities for students to engage in metacognitive reflection on what they have learned, how they have learned, and how well they have mastered a concept. Note how this reflective exercise in the geometry course impacts learning:

> Look closely at the kite on this page; think carefully about kites you've seen in the past. What do you think about the symmetry of kites? Using the labels on the kite above, write conjectures about the symmetry of a kite. Note any angles or segments that might be congruent to each other or bisected.

The Virtual High School: Collaboration and Online Professional Development

Liz Pape, Ruth Adams, & Carol Ribeiro

THE VIRTUAL HIGH SCHOOL (VHS) is built on a simple collaborative concept. Each school in the collaborative selects one or two innovative and technologically adept faculty members to teach over the Internet. These teachers receive training in how to teach VHS online courses (NetCourses) in ways that are student centered, maximize the use of Internet-based resources, and utilize the flexibility and unique nature of the medium. In exchange for each teacher released by the school to teach one NetCourse, the school is able to register 25 students each semester to take NetCourses offered by any of the participating schools. Because the teachers for these 25 students may be in 25 different schools, each school designates a site coordinator to act as a guidance counselor and technical advisor for students in that school who are taking NetCourses. This collaborative concept makes VHS unique among online education providers.

THE INITIAL CHALLENGE

The initial goal of the Virtual High School (http://www.govhs.org), which began as a project funded by a U.S. Department of Education Technology Innovation Challenge Grant, was to create a national consortium of schools offering online high school courses. The vision of the principal investigators, Robert Tinker of the Concord Consortium, and Sheldon Berman, superintendent of Hudson (Massachusetts) Public Schools, as stated in their successful 1996 Technology Innovation Challenge Grant proposal, was to "create an online community of learners, to harness the power of the Internet to increase a school's curricular offerings, and to enable students to gain advanced technology skills" (Tinker & Berman, 1996).

Over the 5 years of the Virtual High School grant, the project grew from the initial 28 course offerings in 1997–98 to 156 offered during the 2000–01 school year. Member schools grew from 28 to 232, located in 26 states and 11 countries. VHS continues to refine its unique scalable model of K–12 online education through its work in defining online standards, online collaboration and community building, and professional development for online teachers.

THE OUTCOME

During the past 2 years, the Virtual High School, now VHS, Inc., has operated as a nonprofit education provider. Member schools pay an annual membership fee to be part of the VHS cooperative and VHS supplies those schools with the administrative, technical, training, and management services required for a collaborative of high schools to cooperatively offer online courses.

During its development, growth, and transition to a self-sustaining nonprofit, VHS addressed the challenges of technology, funding, curriculum, student services, professional development, access and equity, assessment, policy and administration, and marketing and public relations issues. The goal of this case study is to share how the Virtual High School met these challenges and implemented solutions in each of these areas. The challenge of professional development will be discussed first and in greater depth, because VHS's successful creation of a professional development model was critical to its success in delivering quality online courses to students. These solutions are presented as a model for those currently delivering or planning to deliver online courses, or those establishing a virtual school.

THE SUPPORTING PROCESSES:
ONLINE PROFESSIONAL DEVELOPMENT

As the Virtual High School was the first national effort to create high school courses to be delivered entirely online, the recruitment, training, and supervision of this "new breed" of teacher presented the greatest challenge. VHS was designed to be a collaborative of existing schools, which meant all prospective VHS teachers would be existing faculty members of the member schools; teachers would not be hired directly by VHS but would remain under the authority of their individual school districts. Therefore, although VHS could and did establish a rigorous application process in an attempt to train only the most qualified applicants, the ultimate decision as to which faculty member would be eligible to teach online was left to the administration of the member schools. The Virtual High School recognized from the onset that, in order for online course delivery to be effective, a professional development model had to be created to ensure proper training of teachers "at a distance." Although all VHS faculty members are certified in their content area, they are from different states and have varied backgrounds. To ensure quality control of course design and delivery, it was imperative that all VHS faculty be held to the same online course design and delivery standards. In many ways, VHS needed to establish—years before the concept of national certification existed—a method to ensure that all members of its faculty met the same exacting standards. The challenges in creating such a professional development model included the following:

1. Existing data on online pedagogy and delivery had to be researched and the most effective methods incorporated into the model.
2. VHS had to determine the qualities necessary for effective online teaching, and then recruit teachers who were willing to make the time commitment necessary to learn to teach effectively online.
3. As the courses were to be delivered in a new medium (online rather than face-to-face), the professional development also needed to be delivered in the new medium—to "model the model" so that educators could experience for themselves the medium and the methods that they would then be expected to employ.
4. Exacting standards for course development and delivery needed to be established.
5. Evaluation criteria needed to be established so that courses would be developed on time and according to the established standards.
6. Mentors needed to be identified to guide teachers in training through every step of the professional development process.
7. A system needed to be in place to monitor and mentor teachers during their first semester of delivery, and then a process needed to be established to continue monitoring the quality and quantity of the responsiveness of the online teachers.

8. Ongoing professional development modules needed to be developed so that online teachers could be trained in new methods as they emerged.

9. There needed to be a system in place to monitor the incorporation of these new methods into existing courses.

STANDARDS

It was the intent of the grant that the Virtual High School be designed as a scalable model that could, theoretically, become part of the course offerings of every high school in America. VHS recognized from the beginning that the training of its teachers needed to be designed to serve as a national standard and not one which would meet only the specific needs of one district, one state, or one geographical region. In 1996 when VHS started, no standards yet existed for online course design and delivery. Today, the standards established by VHS have become the basis for the proposed national standards for online professional development and online course design and delivery, as proposed jointly by VHS and the National Education Association, along with other organizations, including the American Association of School Administrators and the National Association of State Boards of Education, in the 2002 publication *Guide to Online High School Courses* (NEA, 2002).

DESIGN FEATURES

Teacher as Designer

Unlike other online providers who employ course designers to create online material, the Virtual High School believed that teachers want and need to be involved in the entire course design process. Thus VHS established professional development programs that empower teachers (with the help of mentoring by "master teachers") to design semester-long online classes from scratch. Due to the unique 24/7 nature of online education, and the geographic distribution of VHS teachers and member schools, it was obvious that traditional methods of professional development were not an option for the Virtual High School. The professional development program for VHS needed to be conducted entirely online—in the medium in which the teachers were to deliver their courses. VHS employs a "model the model" format, using collaborative, metacognitive discussions. Professional development participants discuss what does and doesn't work effectively online, and reflect on the nature of the new medium they are experiencing as students during their training and will later employ as instructors during delivery of their courses. For example, professional development participants engage in self-selected study groups, team projects, and facilitated discussions, which allow them to have a clear understanding of exactly what it is like to be a "student" in a course which is so designed, and which allows them to experience the same difficulties that their students may encounter when they, as teachers, assign such activities. Then, through detailed analysis and sharing of the process, these same participants are required to offer strategies to each other to help ensure student success on similar activities, for example, the need for specific expectations and rubrics before the activity begins and the need for periodic updates and feedback through the process.

Design Considerations

Beyond the format, the larger question was exactly what pedagogy to advocate in the courses and how best to train teachers to effectively deliver that pedagogy while fully utilizing the power of the medium. Thus the VHS NetCourse Evaluation Board was established in 1998 to help determine curriculum, design, and delivery standards that should be incorporated into all VHS NetCourses. After careful research and consideration, and based on lessons learned in the first few years of online course delivery, VHS developed the following course design standards, which were incorporated into its teacher preparation program and are evident in all VHS classes.

1. *Instructor-led teaching.* Unlike postsecondary courses, which have utilized online instruction for years, most high school students do not possess the self-discipline to successfully stay on task and organize their time in order to be effective in a virtual environment. VHS's online pedagogy standards call for clear and consistent teacher presence as part of the online course delivery.
2. *Student-centered teaching.* VHS's design and delivery standards call for an instructional style in which instructors serve as facilitators and educational coaches, designing challenging activities and providing effective guidance and quality feedback.
3. *Collaborative activities.* In order to foster an online community of learners, all VHS courses contain small-group activities and team projects where students must collaborate.
4. *Asynchronous scheduling.* To accommodate student schedules and provide optimal flexibility over time zones, all VHS courses are

scheduled—that is, students must complete established activities within a given timeframe—but are asynchronous so that students can access and work on their courses 24/7.

5. *Fostering twenty-first-century learning skills.* Online courses are designed to fully utilize the medium to develop effective online communication and interpersonal skills as well as collaboration and team-building skills and to require students to use inventive thinking skills, such as creativity, problem solving, and critical thinking.

6. *Format and instructions.* Given the asynchronous and largely text-based nature of online communication, courses are designed to minimize student confusion through use of specific directions and to have an aesthetically pleasing presentation.

7. *Expectations and assessments.* As in quality face-to-face courses, these online courses have clearly established expectations for students with specific grading rubrics. Activities and assessments are varied to meet the learning styles of all students.

8. *Utilizing the latest "best practices" recognized as effective.* VHS uses the backward design model of course creation recommended by the Association for Supervision and Curriculum Development (ASCD), as explained in *Understanding by Design* (2001) by Grant Wiggins and Jay McTighe.

Online Community of Learners

Based upon a belief that teachers need to experience for themselves effective online collaboration in order to design student-centered and collaborative classes effectively, the VHS model of teacher development emphasizes collaboration and the building of an online community of learners. The use of small-group projects, team assignments, and a non-course-specific "water cooler" where participants can discuss subjects not related to the course all help contribute to the sense of community. By requiring a certain number of thoughtful posts responding to the contributions of others in threaded discussions, VHS assures the development of horizontal discussion—back and forth between many participants—rather than only vertical, teacher-to-student discussion. This is evident in the following posting by Tom Anderson, a VHS professional development participant, comparing his VHS professional development training, stressing community-building and collaboration, to a more typical online course on the college level:

Last week my son and I were talking about our online course experiences. He's taken three or four online courses, and this . . . is my first.

As we exchanged our anecdotes and talked about how the courses were taught, I did consciously note some differences . . . when I read the article that our very own VHS people wrote, it all made sense. The difference between his online course experiences and my experience in this course was (and is) that sense of community. Only one of his courses included group work, and pretty much, his classes were largely student-instructor interaction. I'm convinced that the key to creating a meaningful NetCourse experience is that sense of community that the writers highlighted so well.

Through its 7 years of providing online professional development, VHS has learned a few things about the importance of community in online learning:

- One feature that differentiates the online learning of high school students from that of students in higher education is the need to feel part of a community of learners. Research (e.g., Na Ubon, 2003) shows that building community in any classroom is important, but nowhere is it more crucial than in the virtual classroom.
- By definition, virtual learning is *distant*, but it should not be *isolating*.
- By creating environments where participants are comfortable, the stage is set to work together toward a common goal.

Design Feedback

During the 22-week Teachers Learning Conference, teachers work with each other to provide quality feedback on the activities designed by their colleagues. They become students in each other's classes, performing the activities as designed and then giving feedback to the designing teacher on the clarity of instructions and the effectiveness of the lessons. In January 2003, VHS teacher, Anne McKernan described this part of her VHS professional development experience in a presentation to prospective VHS teachers:

> During training we would become students in each other's classes, giving feedback to our colleagues on each other's lessons. Were the directions clear enough? Was the assignment understandable? How might I modify the activity to make it more effective? I really learned a great deal from the other teachers taking the online training with me, as well as from my one-on-one mentor during the entire process of course creation.

Some Benefits of Professional Development on Design

At the end of collaborative projects, professional development participants focus on the process they have gone through so that they can understand what students will experience and also try and fix things that went wrong by offering alternatives. As Richard Clevenstine stated in 1999 toward the conclusion of his online professional development training,

> While I am only a teacher in training for the VHS and presently writing my course for next year, I want everyone to know that this year has been the best professional development year for me in 27 years of teaching. I not only feel part of a new wave of education but I feel that I have refallen in love with my subject—biology. By developing my course, I have had the opportunity to introspectively analyze what I am teaching, why I teach in the way I do, and how I can change and improve my communication with students. I am deeply grateful for the opportunity afforded me by the VHS at this point in my career.

CONTINUOUS IMPROVEMENT THROUGH ONGOING PROFESSIONAL GROWTH

In order to meet the continuous advances in the field of online teaching and learning, VHS has developed processes to ensure that courses and teachers meet changing design and delivery standards. Teachers who belong to the VHS collaborative receive ongoing professional development to learn how to use the latest tools and techniques and incorporate best practices.

The current delivery standards of VHS include the following:

1. *Appropriate communication.* Online teachers need to learn to develop an appropriate online "voice" as students do not have the advantage of facial expressions or body language.
2. *Appropriate and timely feedback.* Teachers must appropriately address specific student concerns within 24 hours of posting and complete the grading and feedback on assignments in a timely manner.
3. *Facilitated discussions.* Teachers need to be effective online facilitators and practice this skill while in training. In delivery, faculty mentors monitor facilitation and provide feedback to the instructor.
4. *Facilitation of teamwork and multimedia projects.* Given the nature of distance learning, the barriers to effective group-work are

multiplied. Since teachers must effectively utilize small-group activities periodically in their courses, helpful hints on how to effectively facilitate such work are provided by the faculty mentor.
5. *Adaptation of curriculum as appropriate / Adjustment of materials to meet
   individual student needs.* As in a face-to-face course, curriculum
   sometimes needs to be adapted to maximize effective learning,
   given the varied background and skills of classroom students.

Using the professional growth model, VHS has developed a course
evaluation and professional growth procedure reflective of those found in
a bricks-and-mortar school. All VHS teachers must go through a process
of self-evaluation, peer mentoring, and then a formal evaluation of their
course according to the continually improved standards of excellence that
VHS has established. Teachers then refer to professional development
modules that help them adjust and enhance their courses according to the
evolving standards set by VHS.

The importance of professional development and the success of the
VHS model have been internationally recognized. The international jury
announcing the selection of the Virtual High School as the winner of the
Stockholm Challenge Award in Education cited the quality of professional
development through course design and delivery as a key factor in its selection: "It is changing the way teachers think about teaching" ("Winners,"
2001). This independent analysis further stressed the importance of quality professional development to the success of online learning.

STUDENT ASSESSMENTS

VHS teachers design assessments as they design the NetCourse. Course
design standards around assessment focus on designing a variety of assessments to meet individual student needs and learning styles, with an
emphasis on authentic assessments over more traditional tests and quizzes. Assessments may include research assignments, weekly journal en-
tries, discussions and postings in the online course room, team projects,
tests and quizzes, and papers. Shorter term assignments, discussions, and
postings can be used to keep students engaged in the online course on a
daily basis. Students need to check into the online course frequently to post
assignments and discussions in order to receive grades for such shorter term
assignments. Online assessments like tests and quizzes can be used for
students to show mastery of content and give students immediate feedback on results. Longer term projects, papers, and team activities often need
to be broken into smaller sections so that teachers can replace face-to-face

reminders with required check-ins on progress to date. Assessments vary between NetCourses and are determined by each individual teacher based on course content and learning objectives.

STUDENT SERVICES

Students who are accustomed to learning in face-to-face classroom settings do not necessarily know intuitively how to learn in an online environment. They may not have the independent learning skills needed to manage their learning without constant teacher presence serving as a reminder of what needs to be done. They may not have time management skills needed to accomplish a list of assignments that may at first look overwhelming. The more services and support provided, the higher are the chances for successful online learning experiences for students.

VHS courses are offered to students as part of their school day at their high school. A VHS site coordinator offers on-site support to the student in both the online learning experience and learning in a technology-rich environment. Like VHS teachers, VHS site coordinators are trained online as students in an online learning environment, giving them an opportunity to experience the online learning environment and technology first-hand. VHS also provides additional student services such as technical help-desk support and online grading and registration systems, which enable students to receive grades based upon their school's grading schedule and allow schools to maintain site-based control of student enrollments.

THE VIRTUAL HIGH SCHOOL'S CURRICULUM

Believing strongly that online learning, when appropriately structured and supported, can work for students of all abilities, VHS has developed courses to meet the interest and abilities of a wide range of students. Course design standards focus on cooperative and project-based learning and performance-based assessment. Course delivery is asynchronous—any time and any place. Offerings range from Advanced Placement and International Baccalaureate courses to basic courses for credit recovery. Course academic levels and prerequisites are clearly labeled in the VHS course catalog. To utilize course offerings, VHS promotes a site-based management system. Member schools make the decision about the extent of their participation in VHS, which courses in the extensive VHS course catalog they offer, when they schedule their students into their VHS courses, and how many students they enroll in VHS.

ACCESS AND EQUITY

Students take VHS courses as a part of their school day, and schools provide the necessary computers, Internet access, and on-site mentor support (through the VHS site coordinator). Students can use any available computer that has Internet access—at home or at a town library or an after-hours school computer—to access their online courses and do their homework. VHS courses do not require unique software; courses are accessible through an Internet browser. The Virtual High School requires all courses to have a variety of both online and off-line course activities so students do not need to be in front of a computer for all parts of their VHS coursework. For example, literature courses often require reading and composition, science courses may require fieldwork, and social studies courses may have students conduct face-to-face interviews of city or town managers or Holocaust survivors.

Teachers design VHS courses to be taught asynchronously so that students from a variety of time zones can participate collaboratively. Students not only have the ability to communicate with one another across barriers of time and place, but also have equal opportunity to reflect upon and then discuss the topic. Asynchronous course delivery also gives school administrators the flexibility they need to maximize a student's course schedule, fitting VHS into a student's available periods after all the face-to-face classes have been scheduled.

POLICY AND ADMINISTRATION

VHS has developed, enforced, and revised policies on areas affecting how students, teachers, site coordinators, parents, and schools participate in VHS, including student and teacher attendance, grading, discipline, students with special needs, and teacher probation. VHS policies are used to guide the Virtual High School operations and provide the administrative structure necessary for integration of VHS courses into member high schools. All policies are clearly communicated to students and faculty through the use of an online handbook, which is located in the password-protected school side of the VHS Web site.

TECHNOLOGY

VHS focused on furthering its expertise in online education during the development of its day-to-day operations. Instead of building expertise on the management of a 24/7 data center, VHS outsourced the technical services necessary to support its online professional development and student course delivery. Managing its vendors and building a strong working relationship with them enabled VHS to use its small technical staff to work on the integration of technology with its online pedagogy, and to build the necessary infrastructure needed to support its unique course delivery needs.

MARKETING AND PUBLIC RELATIONS

For VHS, communication has been a critical component in its ongoing marketing and public relations efforts. Over the past 7 years VHS staff have given presentations at many national and international conferences, sharing their K–12 online course experience with educators from all over the globe. In 1996, when the VHS grant was awarded, there was little research available about K–12 online learning. As part of the grant evaluation, Stanford Research International (SRI) was tasked with providing data not only on program evaluation, but also on the efficacy of online teaching and learning. SRI (1998, 1999, 2000) published reports after each of the first three years; the last of these, for 1999–2000, was the first research study that compared online and face-to-face courses in K–12 education.

VHS's recent marketing efforts have focused on its viability as a non-profit organization and its partnerships with schools. VHS's mission and beliefs, as well as financial reports, were published online at the VHS Web site in the first annual report in December 2002 and as modified at the September 2003 meeting of its board of directors. VHS's beliefs focus on the VHS educational philosophy:

- VHS believes that student-centered online courses can be designed and delivered to students to promote a high-quality collaborative learning environment in which student exchange and interaction is a valued component of the instructional process.
- VHS believes that barriers of time and place and lack of qualified faculty need not limit educational opportunity. Rather, VHS believes that high-quality education is possible today for all students in all locations. Online education offers any school with Internet connectivity a wealth of trained, experienced faculty members qualified to teach a wide array of courses designed to meet the needs of all students. An innovative, standards-based curriculum delivered online offers diverse, exciting learning choices for students, and the opportunity and skills to participate in a national and global community.

- VHS believes that online teaching should augment rather than replace traditional classroom teaching. The Virtual High School's online courses are a proven, flexible solution for schools needing an expanded curriculum, teachers seeking new horizons, parents wanting more involvement with their children's education, and a society grappling with ways to offer opportunity to all of its citizens.
- VHS believes that putting value and service first best advances the goals of education. When schools work together in a collaborative network such as the Virtual High School, they become part of an abundant and generous educational community that promotes the affordable sharing of professional resources.

FUNDING

For the first five years of the Virtual High School, the U.S. Department of Education under its Technology Innovation Challenge Grant Program provided funding. The primary task during those years was to meet the goals of the grant proposal—to provide high-quality online courses to high school students and to provide professional development to teachers to prepare them for teaching in the online environment. During that time, SRI International was responsible for evaluating the program against its goals, and the results of those evaluations were published on the VHS Web site. During the 3rd year of the grant, a business plan was developed, defining levels of expenditures and revenue sources necessary to continue VHS postgrant funding for the first five years of independent operations. From that plan, projections were then made to determine how many schools needed to participate during those transition years. In the middle of the 4th year of the grant, VHS began the process of communicating with its member schools by describing plans for continuing as a nonprofit, describing membership options and fee structures for schools, and setting deadlines by which schools needed to indicate their plans for participation. An 18-month budget cycle was built into the business plan to give schools adequate time to incorporate their membership fees into their school budgeting process.

Over two thirds of the VHS grant schools transitioned to VHS during its first year as a nonprofit. Those who did not renew their membership in VHS did so because of an inability to afford the annual membership fee, not because of dissatisfaction with the VHS program.

VHS currently operates as a self-sustaining nonprofit, depending upon two primary sources of revenue: professional development tuition and membership fees. Membership fees are based upon the number of courses a school offers, and are on a sliding scale. Professional development tuition is for teacher training and site coordinator training.

LESSONS LEARNED

VHS is presently in its 7th year of online course delivery. During those years, VHS has delivered nearly 1,400 course sections to over 15,000 students. Nearly 700 teachers have participated in VHS's online professional development. Through this 7-year process, VHS has learned many important lessons:

- We have learned to remain focused on education.
- We have learned to first define our educational values and beliefs, and then translate those to an effective online pedagogy.
- We have learned that online education is about high-quality education, and that online is simply the delivery mechanism.
- We have learned that by reviewing and refining our values and beliefs, we can make technical decisions based upon our educational needs, and not be pulled into the "bells and whistles."
- We have learned that standards are essential; they are the measure of our own performance as well as the yardstick against which we measure courses, teachers, and students.
- We have learned that students and teachers succeed when given training, infrastructure, and support.
- We have learned that online learning, when appropriately structured and supported, can work for students of all abilities.
- We have learned to develop our skills around education and to outsource the rest.
- We have learned that communication is critical. Although things don't always work out as planned, if plans are communicated clearly and in advance, recovery from errors is possible through the support of teachers, students, and the wider community.
- We have learned to listen to students, teachers, administrators, and the public, through feedback mechanisms on our Web site, through annual surveys, and through face-to-face meetings.
- We have learned that online education is a valuable tool for fostering collaboration and global citizenry skills, and we need to continue to work to make it possible.
- We have learned that when collaboration exists between local schools and online education providers, online courses are an enhancement to, not a replacement for, face-to-face instruction.

- We have learned that sometimes these lessons crept up on us, sometimes they took us years to understand, and, thankfully, only a few times were they accompanied by major upheaval.

These lessons were valuable and gave us the confidence to grow in our beliefs around the possibilities of online education, and to grow more skilled at the design and delivery of effective online courses.

CONCLUSIONS

VHS has maintained its viability during the transition from grant to self-sustaining nonprofit by remaining focused on high-quality education. It has used the tools of the Internet and its learning platform to facilitate its educational vision of online collaborative learning for students and teachers. By working to advance online education, through its work on developing nationally adopted standards for online courses and advancing skills and professional development for teachers teaching online, and by building an infrastructure to support students and schools participating in VHS's online courses, VHS has not only assured its own success, it has fostered the development of national, state, regional, and local online learning initiatives. Where VHS leads, others follow.

9

K12, Inc., and the Colorado Virtual Academy: A Virtual Charter School

Jason D. Baker, Cathy Bouras, Susan M. Hartwig, & Earlene R. McNair

SINCE THE ADVENT of charter schools in the early 1990s, the school choice movement has grown significantly. A charter school is a public institution that is created with a contract or charter "specifying how it will operate and what it must do in order to receive public funds for a set period of time" (U.S. Department of Education, 1997, p. 1). The charter identifies the specifications that will be used to hold the school accountable for student performance and fulfilling the mission of the institution. In contrast to private schools and home-based instruction, charter schools are public schools and are therefore tuition-free options for qualified students.

With the advent of the Internet and online distance education, it is not surprising that entrepreneurial educators have considered ways to provide K–12 education using this new technology. One emerging approach is the virtual charter school. As with other charter schools, a virtual charter school is a public institution that is guided by a charter and offers a tuition-free educational option; however, virtual charter schools are unique because they deliver educational programs over the Internet. Approximately 50 virtual charter schools are currently scattered across the United States with more planned in the near future (Kafer, 2003).

Unlike traditional charter schools, which are locally based, virtual charter schools can be run from anywhere, thereby opening the market to educational companies interested in entering the primary and secondary market. The largest of these companies is K12, Inc., a for-profit company founded in 1999 by former U.S. secretary of education William Bennett. K12, Inc. (http://www.k12.com), often simply called K12, currently provides an educational program for kindergarten through eighth-grade virtual charter school students in California, Colorado, Florida, Idaho, Minnesota, Ohio, Arkansas, Wisconsin, and Pennsylvania. It has immediate plans to expand the program to include grades 9–12 and to extend their charter program into additional states. K12 also licenses its curriculum to parents interested in using it for homeschooling as well as to those interested in starting virtual private schools.

This chapter will examine the K12-affiliated Colorado Virtual Academy (COVA) as a lens into this new type of institution: the virtual charter school.

CHALLENGES

The No Child Left Behind Act (NCLB, 2002) adds teeth to a national call for accountability and school reform. Signed into law by President George W. Bush in January 2002, this law calls for states to publicly identify schools that have failed to make adequate yearly progress toward obtaining state-identified learner standards for 2 years in a row. Last year, children in 2,652 schools nationwide were afforded the opportunity under this law to transfer to a better performing traditional or nontraditional school (Kafer, 2003).

The first charter school in the United States opened in 1992, and currently there are approximately 2,700 charter schools in operation, a number that rose by 14% in the last year. According to the Heritage Foundation, all 50 states have legalized homeschooling, 40 states and the District of Columbia have enacted charter school laws, and 6 states provide state- or district-funded scholarships that students can use to attend private schools (Kafer, 2003). Virtual charter schools take an innovative approach to answering the call for school choice and NCLB legislation by providing an alternative to the traditional bricks-and-mortar public school program. This entire movement is a product of the growing concern that the public school system is not meeting the needs of the society. Reports such as *Challenge and Opportunity: The Impact of Charter Schools on School Districts* (Ericson, Silverman, Bernam, Nelson, & Solomon, 2001) support charter school advocates and educational theorists who purport that by providing an educational choice, systematic change in the current public education system will ensue, providing more educational options and models and producing competitive market forces (Ericson et. al, 2001).

There are a number of challenges facing virtual charter schools in general and the K12-affiliated virtual charter schools in particular. Like other educational efforts, these schools face the challenge of effectively educating a diverse population of students within a limited budget. Furthermore, since virtual charter schools deliver education online, they must deal with additional equipment costs, technological limitations and troubleshooting, and increased parental involvement and responsibility. Finally, as a for-profit company delivering a new model of instruction, K12 must convince parents, educators, and legislators that they're offering a high-quality program worthy of taxpayer support.

STAKEHOLDERS

K12-affiliated virtual charter schools currently serve students from kindergarten through eighth grade. Generally children living in the participating school districts and occasionally in neighboring districts are permitted to enroll in the program. The academies are equipped to serve regular and special needs students in accordance with federal and state regulations and guidelines for free and appropriate public education. A parent, caregiver, or other appointed adult is responsible for facilitating lessons, supervising student learning, maintaining attendance records, and monitoring student work while the child is enrolled in the virtual charter school.

Parents (or other responsible adults) work with teachers in what K12 calls a "team-teaching" approach. K12 virtual charter school teachers serve primarily as consultants rather than direct instructors and classroom managers as in the traditional classroom. They oversee the instructional process and offer support to the parents through regular contact with home instructors and monitoring of student progress through the student learning system. It is the teacher's responsibility to intervene when necessary to assist students who are experiencing difficulties. K12 virtual charter school teachers work collaboratively to evaluate and improve the instructional program.

In addition to the teachers, parents, and students involved in the K12 virtual charter schools, the legislature and larger population also have a vested interest in these initiatives. After all, the legislators are generally the ones who pass the charter legislation in the first place, and since virtual charter schools are public schools, they are funded through the tax dollars of state citizens just as other K–12 schools are. The concerns of this larger group of stakeholders are perhaps best expressed by opponents to the school choice movement. A motion filed by the Ohio Federation of Teachers (OFT) explains the root of the controversy:

The community school law also violates . . . the Ohio Constitution, by co-mingling taxpayer funds with the funds of privately owned corporations, allowing community schools to borrow based upon the anticipated flow of taxpayer dollars, and providing state guarantees of loans taken out by private corporations.

A separate motion has been filed challenging so-called "cyber" schools. . . . Treating cyber schools as if they are schools with classrooms allows their for-profit backers to earn windfall profits because the overhead expenses related to cyber schools are so much lower than legitimate public schools with real classrooms (OFT, 2002, para. 6, 8).

EDUCATIONAL MANAGEMENT

In 1993 the Colorado General Assembly approved the Colorado Charter Schools Act, which expanded Colorado's public school choices by offering parents, teachers, and the community innovative ways of educating children. This law allowed the creation of charter schools, which are not entirely autonomous, but rather are public schools. Through this act, the Academy of Charter Schools (ACS), a K–12 public charter school, was established as a Core Knowledge School. Based on research conducted by E. D. Hirsch, a Core Knowledge School program utilizes a core, grade-by-grade curriculum for a strong foundation, which is designed to foster academic success because each academic year builds upon the foundation of the previous year (Core Knowledge Foundation, 2004). To expand its public school services, the Academy of Charter Schools (http://www.academyofcharterschools.homestead.com), located in the Adams County School District No. 12, established the Colorado Virtual Academy (COVA) in 2001.

Although COVA is sponsored by ACS, a bricks-and-mortar public charter school, and does not have a separate public school charter, it does function as ACS's online public charter school program. ACS continues to serve as the administrator of the Colorado state funds for COVA, which has grown during its first two years of operation.

During its first year, Colorado Virtual Academy accepted 400 students. By 2003–04, enrollment had tripled to 1,200 students. Of these 1,200 students, approximately 33% were involved in either a home or private school, while approximately 66% were exclusively traditional school students. Interestingly enough, the fastest growing population is its special education students. COVA employs a special education director and three special education teachers to meet the individualized needs of the child, including Individualized Education Program (IEP) modifications. Furthermore, COVA designs its programs to comply with Title VII of the Civil

Rights Act of 1964, Title IX of the Educational Amendment of 1972, Section 504 of the Rehabilitation Act, the Americans with Disabilities Act, the Individuals with Disabilities Education Act, and applicable Colorado laws. Upon parental request, special education COVA teachers can make home visits to offer instructional strategies based on student-parent observations or to model parental behavior, as it relates to the curriculum. COVA also contracts with other providers to provide these students with related services, such as speech and language therapy, occupational therapy, physical therapy, and so forth. In addition to the special education director and teachers, COVA employs a program director, an assistant program director, and four teachers.

To build their initial staff, COVA and K12, Inc., aggressively marketed the program to the educational community. COVA published materials through the Colorado Department of Education and advertised in the League of Charter Schools, and K12 developed a COVA Web site (http://www.covcs.org). As a result of their marketing efforts, COVA received a large number of applications and hired seven teachers through a rigorous interview and application process. These seven certified teachers varied in their backgrounds; teaching experience ranged from 3 to over 26 years, including public school, private, and homeschool teaching experience.

In addition to the teaching responsibilities, COVA also partnered with K12 to provide a variety of educational support services. In this collaborative partnership, COVA assumes responsibility for the project's administration, including budget planning and management; developing a strategic plan; managing the application, enrollment, and withdrawal process; and staff development, such as computer skill development, organizational skill development, and online test preparation. K12 is responsible for the program's operational management, including developing, delivering, and upgrading the program's curriculum; managing student records and academic achievement data; providing tools and training for the program; sustaining the COVA Web site; and maintaining a toll-free call center for parents.

EDUCATIONAL PROCESSES

So how exactly does a K12 virtual charter school work with a student? Any student living in Colorado may apply, but COVA's application states that applicants may be subject to certain geographic or prior school enrollment constraints. Each student submits an application to the program. COVA then provides each eligible student with a textbook and instructional materials, computer, printer, and reimbursement for Internet connection.

However, the parents or a legal guardian are responsible for establishing their own Internet connection and supplying their own printer ink and paper. Although the parents normally receive technical assistance from COVA and K12 via the telephone or the Internet, on rare occasions COVA has sent someone out to a student's home to troubleshoot their computer system or to offer technical support. Since these computer systems are owned by COVA, they are considered instructional property and must be returned in the event of student withdrawal.

Once the student is selected, the student and parent receive orientation and training for the program. COVA also gives students a language arts and math assessment test developed by K12 to place the students in their appropriate level. Although a child's entry point into the curriculum is determined by an initial assessment, students can then progress through the curriculum at their own pace. If they are struggling with a concept or skill they can spend additional time on each lesson or are assigned additional lessons to ensure comprehension. Once mastery is demonstrated, students move forward in the curriculum, investigate topics in greater depth, or take advantage of challenge problems. Students are required to complete 90% of the lessons assigned by the teacher for promotion to the next level. Throughout this process, the parents are required to document the accomplishments and the time spent on task to ensure that each student meets the state requirement of 968 hours of elementary education per year.

Because K12 curriculum does incorporate a significant amount of off-line work—K12 estimates that 70–80% of kindergarten through fifth-grade work is off-line—there are opportunities for students to draw, explore, use workbooks and textbooks, math manipulatives, music CDs, and other resources, as well as participate in various off-line activities. In the future, COVA plans to use additional communication tools, such as newsletters, message boards, and the COVA Web site to offer suggestions about age-appropriate activities, identify interesting places for children's field trips, and facilitate events and gatherings. In addition to looking at the inner workings of COVA, it is also important to look at COVA's curriculum.

The curriculum for the COVA is supplied by K12, Inc., and is based on the Core Knowledge approach developed by E. D. Hirsch, an English professor at the University of Virginia. The curriculum emphasizes phonics-based reading and uses a Great Books approach in literature. In social studies, Western culture and history is emphasized. K12 divides the kindergarten through fifth-grade curriculum into six subjects: language arts, math, science, history, art, and music. For each course, K12 has developed online lessons, worksheets, and teacher guides, all of which can be downloaded from the Internet. Additionally, K12 distributes textbooks, CDs, manipulatives, and other traditional materials to accompany its online curriculum. Furthermore, K12 makes lesson resources available to parents and teachers, such as lesson-oriented learning objectives, user-friendly procedures and hands-on activities, creative ideas, materials, key definitions, teaching strategies, and suggested readings and activities to incorporate into each lesson.

K12 also provides COVA teachers and parents with a variety of planning and progress tools including a planning tool that allows parents to customize their child's daily schedule, a progress tool that provides details regarding the completion of a lesson and lesson mastery with accompanying assessments, and an attendance tool that allows parents to record their child's school attendance time. For each subject, the parents and teachers can access the course overview, the total number of lessons for the grade, including the length and approximate time for each lesson, and lesson materials, including standard and additional curriculum items.

Throughout this program, the teacher is responsible for developing a team instructional approach with the parent. While the teacher is responsible for monitoring course content, ensuring proper delivery of the instructional system, monitoring the student's progress and reporting it to the parent, and assisting students and parents with difficulty with instruction, parents are responsible for guiding the student through their daily lesson whether it involves online or off-line activities, and contacting COVA, teachers, or other parents to resolve problems.

In addition to the resources offered by K12, COVA offers its parents and students other resources related to increasing social interaction. Several local school districts in various Colorado regions have monthly field trips for clusters of students. Other COVA parents formed optional learning co-ops for music and science while others formed group playtime co-ops for their children. Additionally, the COVA Web site maintains an online community forum section that provides information about COVA events, K12 news, and COVA schoolwide information, such as announcements and region-specific information.

PROGRAM EVALUATION

Although participating in social activities is optional, it is mandatory for COVA students to participate in K12 assessments and the Colorado Student Assessment program (CSAP). Students must complete K12 lesson assessments, which assess lesson mastery and readiness for the next lesson, and K12 unit assessments, which assess unit mastery of lessons. In addition, students are required to complete the following Colorado Student

Assessments: Grade 2, CSAP for reading and writing; Grade 3, CSAP for reading and writing; and Grade 5, CSAP for reading, writing, and mathematics. Besides these tests, teachers stay in contact with the parents or responsible adult to review the student's progress and plan for ways to improve students' performance.

Other than assessing its students' progress, the COVA program has not participated in any formal program evaluation; however, the program is being evaluated as part of the public charter school application process, and some stakeholders have offered their comments. According to COVA program director Kin Griffith, since the teachers do not have to develop lesson plans and are not delivering direct instruction, they are enjoying their new role as primarily an "educational consultant," instead of classroom manager (personal communication, May 12, 2003). Thus a COVA teacher quickly identifies a student's weakness, makes immediate recommendations, and supports parents by offering them effective instructional strategies. This is aided by the student's writing competencies, which are still monitored traditionally even though students submit assignments online. In addition, parents' comments from numerous surveys have reported extreme satisfaction with the K12 curriculum's quality, the technical support for the curriculum, teacher support of the curriculum, and the COVA program in general. Parents did indicate that their time commitment investment is an area where they need additional support from COVA, especially for their first-year period of adjustment. As a result, COVA now offers parents time management and organization workshops and ideas on strategies for success.

COMMENTARY

Although still in its infancy, COVA and the K12 virtual charter school model can already be considered a success, at least from a marketing perspective. COVA currently serves over 1,200 students, representing geographic and racial diversity, and has grown steadily since its opening. Considering the newness of this type of instruction, the initial enrollment of 400 is impressive in itself, not to mention the continued growth and expansion of the program. While much of this is likely attributable to the free tuition and effective marketing, the in-state program support and external respectability of K12 also deserve credit. Throughout this process, Colorado's commissioner of education, the superintendent of Adams County School District No. 12, and ACS's administration has been very supportive of COVA and the K12 partnership.

COVA also benefits significantly from the goodwill associated with William Bennett, the K12 founder and spokesman. As a former U.S. secretary of education and author of a number of family and children's books, Bennett lends this new technology-based initiative a sense of old-fashioned educational values. In addition, the K12 team includes a former congressman, multiple Ivy League Ph.D.'s, published authors, experienced educators, and a variety of scholars. Such an array of reputable professionals helps to counteract any perceptions of K12 as a leftover dot-com experiment. The use of a well-known curriculum model, the core knowledge approach, further serves as an enticement for parents unfamiliar with the virtual charter school model.

Assessment is an area that will warrant detailed consideration in the years ahead. Given the patterns demonstrated by small-class-size schools, private schools, and homeschoolers, one would expect that COVA students would generally perform at least as well, if not significantly better, than their public school counterparts. And while this may be the case, it remains to be seen exactly how COVA and K12 will address students who struggle, lag behind, or fail to meet the requirements of the Colorado Student Assessment Program and other measures of achievement. If applications exceed planned enrollment, will COVA simply choose the best performing students or will they attempt to serve the academically challenged as well?

Similarly, should COVA experience an exodus of students in the future (as other schools must have experienced to support COVA's rapid growth), it will be important for COVA to determine the exact causes of such choices. As a charter school, COVA is subject to the same market forces that foster the school choice movement, and it would be interesting to learn why parents choose to transfer their children into COVA as well as why they leave. Detailed surveys, interviews, and focus groups with prospective, current, and former COVA parents would be extremely helpful in this regard. Given the relative newness of COVA and the school choice movement, it's possible that satisfaction and enrollment will run high for many years, simply because COVA offers a choice that didn't otherwise exist. In the long term, however, the educational effectiveness will likely become the dominant factor for parents considering this virtual charter school.

The parental support dynamic is another area in which COVA appears to be succeeding but will likely require continued attention. Existing homeschooling parents will likely find it a relief to hand over curriculum responsibilities to K12 and would find COVA to be quite helpful. Parents without homeschooling or teaching experience may find themselves overwhelmed with the responsibilities associated with teaching children at home, even in partnership with COVA, and may require additional assistance and support. The implementation of time management seminars, regular teacher-parent communication, local events, and other parental support initiatives indicate that COVA recognizes this challenge and is addressing it; however, increased enrollment and grade expansion will only heighten the need for effective formal and informal parental support systems. Similarly, parents who choose COVA will have to address the socialization concerns related to home-based instruction. Again, existing homeschooling families have largely made this a moot point, but COVA may prove attractive to parents who are more accustomed to the school-based environment and haven't considered how to deliberately include community-building activities into their child's education.

As COVA continues to add grade levels, eventually through high school, it will face additional challenges. Middle and high school students will need more sophisticated extracurricular activities, such as intramural sports and drama groups, rather than merely field trips and music co-ops. If parents think that their older child needs the academic challenge of the self-paced K12 curriculum but they still have work responsibilities, it is not unlikely that COVA would enroll some "virtual latch-key students." To ensure that these students stay on task, COVA will need to stipulate parental contact time or else develop new strategies to address many issues currently handled by COVA parents, such as instructional support and academic monitoring. College placement support, from SAT test preparation to college selection, will likely also emerge as a demand as COVA expands into the high school years.

Although COVA appears to be a success, it remains an early model of a virtual charter school; it's just too early to render a definite judgment. The partnership with K12 is clearly a strength and offers tangible benefits to parents and children enrolled in COVA. As the school grows in numbers and scope, it will face many challenges in the future, not the least of which is the future of the school choice movement itself. Regardless, COVA appears poised for long-term success in the market and will likely serve as a model for virtual charter schools to emulate.

Cumberland County Schools Web Academy: A New School District Model

Allan Jordan

S EVERAL BASIC operational models of online teaching and learning have proven successful at the secondary level. One of these models is the virtual high school operated by an individual school district. In this case study I will describe funding, curriculum and instruction, and technology as key themes in the operation of a virtual high school operated by an individual school district. As the principal of Cumberland County Schools Web Academy (www.ccswebacademy.net) ever since it began in 1997, I have experienced all of the growing pains normally involved in creating, supporting, and developing a school district–supported virtual school.

William P. Shipp, a colleague of mine and the assistant executive director of the North Carolina Association of School Administrators, suggests that secondary schools must become assemblers of degrees. Shipp's suggestion is based on his vision that education must change and adjust to current problems, many of which require students to become more mobile. If this is correct, students will bring course credits from increasingly varied places, thereby creating the need to find solutions to the complex issues of correctly and effectively applying credits earned to student transcripts. The logical extension of these problems leads Shipp to the conclusion that online teaching and learning in our secondary schools may help solve some of the current problems. I not only agree, but my anecdotal and quantitative experiences show it to be true.

THE WEB ACADEMY

The belief that this new century requires educators to maximize resources while increasing program flexibility thereby ensuring the greatest number of high-quality opportunities for all students to learn led to the creation of the Cumberland County Schools Web Academy in Fayetteville, North Carolina. The Web Academy was created in the spring of 1997 with the writing of one course. Student enrollment began in the fall of 1997 with 6 students in an advanced English course and enrollment has increased steadily ever since, from 665 after one year to more than 1,600.

The Web Academy shares a campus with Douglas Byrd High School, a traditional high school in Cumberland County. Douglas Byrd has a traditional enrollment of 1,350 students, but of course, the Web Academy students are rarely, if ever, on campus, so the student bodies are never on campus together. The situation is workable, but not ideal: There is no room for growth available on this campus.

Staffing for the Web Academy presents an unusual challenge. In addition to 40–60 trained part-time teachers each semester, there are just 14 full-time personnel, 10 of whom are certified: 1 principal, 8 teachers, and 1 guidance counselor. Although the certified staff have job titles from the mainstream educational framework, all have a complex set of responsibilities far beyond those normally associated with the traditional titles. For example, one full-time teacher is the curriculum and testing coordinator; another teacher is the program director; another is the technology director; still another writes grants and deals with accreditation, while 2 others work full-time with professional development, online courses, and in-house training.

I am classified as a high school principal and the Cumberland County Schools Director for Online Teaching and Learning. My routine duties, however, consist of approximately 25% of the duties normally associated with traditional principalships. I don't know how they compare to those of directors of online teaching and learning because I don't know any of those. The reality of this uniqueness of job responsibilities creates advantages and disadvantages. Among the advantages are that few people understood my job, and what I should be doing, thereby making the accomplishment of certain tasks easier. I operate with more latitude of decision-making authority than most administrators and have less bureaucracy through which to stumble. There is one major disadvantage: Other high school principals distance themselves from me because I am "different," a distinction I am not always able to overcome.

Another critical staffing element involves noncertified personnel. The staffing choices made in this area are as important as those of certified personnel. Without the support of a strong team of bookkeeping, clerical, and administrative assistants, the Web Academy could not function.

Staffing will remain a challenging issue for several reasons, including limited experience with operational design and insufficient operational funding. Limited operational design experience raises questions in the real-world of virtual learning such as what job duties should look like, how much online teaching is enough, and what backgrounds administrators for online programs should have.

Sufficient funding for virtual high schools is often difficult to obtain, thereby complicating short- and long-term training plans. The Web Academy has students enrolled from 76 of the 117 school districts in North Carolina. Enrollment consists of approximately 75% in-county students and 25% out-of-county students. These enrollment percentages help identify a pervasive need within the virtual learning community, specifically, a broad-based, adequate, and fair funding formula that allows for all students to have access to the full spectrum of available online course offerings. In-county students attend at no cost, while out-of-county students are required to pay tuition for each course. Without a fair, state-supported funding formula, this problem is unsolvable.

Another issue is the significant reluctance within education to recognize and support online teaching and learning. This reluctance seems to revolve around the issues of fear of change, lack of confidence in the instructional models utilized by virtual schools, and simply lack of sufficient information. A paradigm shift is needed in how online education is viewed in the world of education. This may be the most complicated problem to solve because it requires changes in human behavior.

Prospects for Future Growth

The Web Academy is uniquely positioned to continue its positive development because several factors lead down a path that ends in a universally recognized need for new solutions to problems that educators are being compelled to face. Whether the problems to be addressed have been moved to the front burner because of federal legislation such as the No Child Left Behind Act, or because of more regional issues such as tightening budgets (local and state), teacher shortages, or realizations of the moral imperative to offer high-quality educational opportunities to all students, online teaching and learning is being recognized by increasing numbers of educators as a viable choice for educational problem solving.

In addition, the Web Academy is well positioned for future growth because of several positive factors within the organization of the Web Academy: strong intellectual capital, internal operational design, instructional design, reputation, and a commitment to success.

Intellectual capital. The concept of intellectual capital is not new, but it is used normally in the world of business and seldom in education. The Web Academy, however, holds that education will benefit from working closer with the business sector. After all, the major goal of education is to produce citizens capable of contributing positively to society, and this includes workplace contributions. Additionally, financial opportunities are available for education-business partnerships, thereby creating stronger relationships between education and business.

Operational design. Since the Web Academy was developed without the benefit of a broad educational experience base from which to draw, intelligent risk taking and brutal results analysis became a way of life. The result of this growth process has been the development of a staff who know that their experiences are critical to the program and that all new ideas, no matter how unusual they may sound, may be considered. The internal operational design is an outgrowth of this process.

Trial and error have been the watchwords here. What are the rules of operation when a virtual school enrolls students from two-thirds of the school districts in North Carolina? How can the maximum opportunities for student success be created and sustained, and what do they look like? How are state regulations complied with and traditional reporting procedures altered to support this new instructional model? Working through these and other relevant issues has created a practical and efficient internal operational design that focuses on accommodating students first and ease of operations second.

Instructional design. The instructional design for the Web Academy provided a set of challenges unlike any other. The school had to respond to both internal staff cries for high-quality teaching and learning as well as external requests for solutions to wide-ranging instructional issues with which traditional educational settings were struggling. These external requests included effectively delivering high-quality content to homebound students, allowing student access to certain courses that traditional school settings were unable to provide them, providing course-retaking options, and giving students access to courses needed in addition to those that could be provided during a traditional instructional day. Traditional education is unable to provide all of the answers to the problems that currently exist within education, making alternative education of critical importance.

The Web Academy has created a successful instructional model for alternative education. Many North Carolina school districts utilize this teaching and learning model because of its flexibility and its success rate. An overview of this model shows that it is focused on creating the most positive learning environment possible under existing circumstances. Key elements are a school-based computer lab and an on-site locally trained facilitator, whose responsibilities are to maintain the lab, assist students, and keep them on task. An additional element is mainstreaming: With few exceptions, all students from alternative learning settings are mainstreamed into Web Academy classes. The school's ability to meet the needs of alternative education has resulted in a very good reputation in the educational world.

Reputation. A good reputation is hard won, but easily lost; it must be consistently maintained. The staff is vigilant, and recognizes any issue that has the potential to do harm to the school's reputation. When such issues arise, the staff is thoughtful and thorough, and very adept at making the best possible decisions.

Commitment to success. The last positive factor within the organization of the Web Academy is the commitment to succeed shared by the staff. Many people think that fear of failure is the secret to success. On the contrary, I think it takes something much more difficult to create: a staff unafraid to succeed. Often, the possibilities of success are more frightening than the possibility of failure. The administrative challenge is to create an operational and personal culture within the school that says, "We are all valued first as human beings. We are then valued for what we can do for the school." Such a culture has been created at the Web Academy.

Stakeholders

Most stakeholders in virtual education are the same as those in traditional education; the difference is that they may have different levels of influence, or different goals within the school models. The universal stakeholders are parents, students, educators (several levels), business, taxpayers, and vendors. Some virtual education stakeholders may not yet realize they are stakeholders, because exposure to virtual teaching and learning is still relatively limited. This limited exposure results in a lack of knowledge about the opportunities and benefits available to potential stakeholders through this instructional medium. It is not surprising that many parents and students are totally unaware of the options available online, but often principals and guidance counselors are also not aware of the problem-solving solutions available through online education.

Goals

A description of desired outcomes for the Web Academy is a description of desired outcomes for a school district model generally. Since the Web Academy offers enrollments to the entire state of North Carolina, its outcomes, goals, purpose, and mission are broader than they would be if it served one district alone. In order to achieve desired outcomes and to maximize resources within the state, the school has helped create a statewide alliance of the major participants in virtual teaching and learning.

The North Carolina Alliance for Online Teaching and Learning (AOTL) was formed in late 2002. Its purpose is to "work together for the improvement and expansion of online teaching and learning for North Carolina's students, faculty, and staff." The members of AOTL are the North Carolina School of Science and Math, the North Carolina Department of Public Instruction, the Web Academy, Learn NC, the North Carolina Center for the Advancement of Teaching (NCCAT), East Carolina University, and the North Carolina Association of School Administrators.

Several important opportunities arise from the creation of AOTL. Not only is each entity better positioned to share access to content and personnel, but perhaps more important, each entity is now positioned to collaborate across educational levels. For example, one project currently underway brings together professional development content created by NCCAT personnel, technology and training expertise from the Web Academy, and certification from East Carolina University. This project is only one example of the synergy that can be created by bringing together individual entities willing to work together for the betterment of education and for the benefit of students, whether K–12 students or teachers as learners.

Whether in a local school district or at a statewide level, three primary factors have critical roles in the new educational paradigm of secondary virtual learning: instructional quality and management, access, and financing of delivery. The ultimate success of the Web Academy and of the school district model will be determined within these critical areas, thus program goals must include continuous focus within these three areas.

Outcomes

Outcomes may be defined in several ways, but in the current educational climate, they are most often defined by student achievement, which in turn is most often defined by achievement outcomes. Public release of achievement outcomes from virtual secondary schools has been rare. There is little information available to make judgments of student success. This lack of information on student outcomes has been and remains a concern to me. My instincts tell me that if there was a wealth of good news on the subject, there would be much published information; because there is not, I have to wonder what the results have been.

Although broad-based outcomes for K–12 virtual teaching and learning are of considerable interest, I can only determine outcomes for the Web Academy. In my doctoral dissertation, *An Investigation Into the Effects of Online Teaching and Learning on Achievement Outcomes at the Secondary Level* (2002), I examined student achievement outcomes on North Carolina–mandated end-of-course tests for three academic years, 1998–99, 1999–2000, and 2000–01. The results of my research indicate that no significant differences exist between the achievement outcomes of Web Academy students in online courses and those of students taking courses in traditional classrooms within the Cumberland County School System over the 3-year time period. These are early data and accordingly no long-range conclusions should be reached. But the data provide an indication that when student achievement outcomes are used as the criteria for outcomes, if the instructional model is sound, online learning can be successful.

CRITICAL COMPONENTS FOR THE SCHOOL DISTRICT MODEL

This book provides focus and direction in the nine initiative components identified by Clark (2001): technology, funding, curriculum, student services, professional development, access and equity, assessment, policy and administration, and marketing and public relations. The challenges facing virtual schools operated by a local school district are numerous and can be found within these initiative components. While each component provides its own unique challenges for the school district model, some challenge the model more directly than do others. The most challenging components for the school district model are funding, curriculum and instruction, and technology.

Funding

While funding is always an issue in education, it provides unique opportunities for confusion when applied to the school district model of virtual education. Funding traditionally comes from two sources, local monies and state monies. Local funding for virtual schools is contingent upon situational determinants within each school district and will vary from district to district based on many changeable factors, such as the amount of money available and the commitment to virtual learning held by the local superintendent and board of education. State funding for virtual schools is more difficult.

Each state involved in virtual learning seems to have its own approach to funding and some approaches seem to be more effective than others. However, I must point out that it is so early in the evolution of this instructional model that few conclusions about funding formulas can be reached; more time and experience with accompanying results are needed. Several examples of state funding designs for virtual schools exist, including a combination of state funds and tuition, formal agreements with individual districts across a state that may take the form of district memberships, and complete funding by the state.

Another state-level funding idea is currently receiving some attention, the idea of using a full-time equivalent (FTE) as part of an ongoing formula to provide a continuing financing stream to support the development and operation of virtual schools. This idea is currently being studied in North Carolina, but Florida has just passed legislation that removes funding for the Florida Virtual School as a line item within the state budget and moves it to the regular school per-pupil funding system. The interesting thing about the Florida plan, however, is that the FTEs will be paid only for students who successfully complete courses with passing grades.

In North Carolina, the idea began as a proposal from the Web Academy. Above the average daily membership (ADM) amounts, the per-pupil funding amount provided to each district by the state department of education, would be additional funding through FTEs. Since most students enrolled in virtual schools are not full-time virtual school students and therefore the ADM amounts are allocated to the traditional schools of record, consequently, no state-level funding goes directly to the virtual school. For example, the full-time enrollment at the Web Academy is usually 20–25% of the total enrollment, but another 1,000 students may be enrolled in an average of 1.5 courses. ADM amounts are received on the full-time students, but no monies are received for students not enrolled full-time. The only ways to make up for the financial shortfall created by this situation are to get supplements from local school district monies or charge tuition, thereby limiting access to badly needed online courses. FTEs would solve this funding inequity.

The FTE funding concept would provide additional ADM monies thereby ensuring a continuing source of funding for the virtual school. An additional benefit to this funding design would be to create a basis upon which to project income allowing for well-designed development and long-range planning (FVS will now be able to do this). The complication that develops from this funding formula is that the FTEs represent new monies above the ADM monies currently being allocated to districts. Practicality then requires that these FTE funds be distributed by the state department of education prior to the individual distributions being made to the local school districts; otherwise, each district would see the funding formula as an attack on their funding.

Curriculum

Curriculum presents another challenge for the school district model of virtual schools. Among the most critical questions that must be answered before a school district seriously considers creating a virtual school are, Which courses will we offer? and Where will we get them? The answers to these two questions have very important design and cost implications. For example, will an entire secondary curriculum be offered or just basic courses? Will Advanced Placement courses be offered? Will remediation-level courses be offered? Once the process of deciding which courses will be offered is complete, then the decision regarding where to acquire the courses remains. Quite simply, there are three options: Write your own; purchase (or rent) from a vendor; or a combination of both. If you write your own, then you commit to a huge task, both financially and in terms of staffing and professional development and support. If you purchase or rent, then you run the risk of relinquishing significant control of your school to vendors. And if you choose a combination of both, then you have a combination of difficulties.

Curriculum was a huge issue for the Web Academy. The process of determining curriculum to be offered by the Web Academy had several steps. First, we knew that we wanted to begin with secondary-level courses, but we were uncertain beyond that broad preference. The deciding factor for us in determining which courses would be developed and the priority given to development was need. What did our school district and the state of North Carolina need to have developed first? That need took us in several directions, but each direction was carefully planned. For example, we recognized the need for Advanced Placement courses, but we identified and prioritized those needed most urgently and began there.

We created curriculum across all core areas and in all areas where North Carolina mandates end-of-course testing. We also included a limited number of electives as part of a marketing strategy to appeal to homeschoolers and students from other school districts. After these decisions were made and priorities had been correctly placed, we decided to write our own courses. We began the process of content creation and, over a period of time, built and expanded offerings as needed.

The Instructional Model

In addition to curriculum, another critical decision is the choice of an instructional model. A successful instructional model must be built around high-quality content, strong instruction and support, and high-quality teacher training supported by efficient and dependable technology. There are three forms that the delivery of online content may take: synchronous, asynchronous, or a combination of the two. Synchronous instruction brings students and teachers simultaneously into virtual classrooms. This usually requires a meeting in a chat room among the teacher and students. The chat room is password and ID protected and convened at scheduled times. Two master schedules are developed each semester, one offering daytime classes, the other offering evening classes. Asynchronous instruction may be delivered without any real-time meetings, for example, via instructor postings online to which students respond at another time. The third choice is a combination of the two.

The refinement of the Web Academy instructional model has been a long-term process, but we remain true to the foundation of the original model, which consisted of both synchronous and asynchronous instruction; it still does. It never made sense to me to expect a 15-year-old student to demonstrate success online with asynchronous instruction alone when the postsecondary data routinely reflects poor outcomes with dropout rates regularly as high as 50% or even higher. How can we expect mid-teens to be successful in online courses with an asynchronous instructional model, which by design requires very limited monitoring and supervision, when adults have such an abysmal performance history with the same model?

The answer seems obvious, yet many instructional models used by secondary-level virtual learning programs still maintain asynchronous instruction alone. If some of the goals of a secondary-level virtual school are low dropout rates and higher performance outcomes, then synchronous instruction must be the critical part of the instructional model.

Some changes may be in the offing. Recently, I have seen a national trend toward a combination of delivery options in virtual school instruction. Some virtual schools that have offered asynchronous instruction alone are adding elements of synchronous instruction; for example, the Florida Virtual School now offers optional synchronous tutoring. I believe that neither the synchronous model nor the asynchronous model alone is sufficient to achieve the student outcome goals that are needed. The current challenge is to continue to refine instructional models that blend synchronous and asynchronous instruction that results in maximum student performance.

Figure 10.1 shows the Web Academy model for traditional online instruction (bottom left) and alternative online instruction (bottom right); hopefully, the visuals will bring the model to life. The same basic model works for both traditional and alternative instruction; the only differences between the two are in the student setting for online instruction and in the

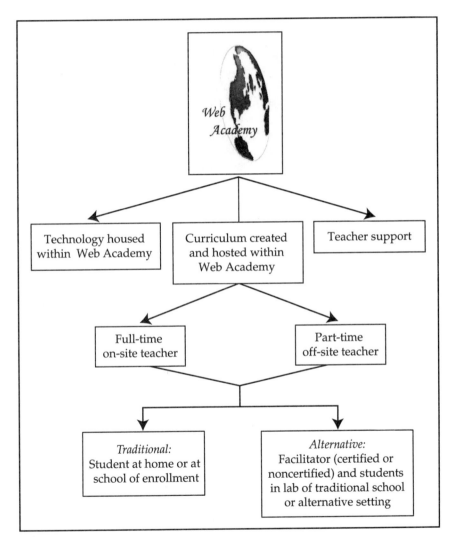

Figure 10.1. Flow chart for traditional and alternative online instruction.

need for an on-site facilitator for alternative programs taught in labs. All students are mainstreamed, but on-site monitoring is essential within the alternative program. The model is simple and allows for local control; simplicity and control are two of the reasons it is successful. It remains easy to understand, and hopefully to duplicate, while simultaneously maintaining local program control.

Instructional delivery is only one part of the instructional model; another is the selection of teachers. Online teachers may be full-time or part-time employees. They may be teachers within the system that operates the virtual school or from outside the system. An instructional model may include either or both types of employees. Regardless of which teachers are hired, they all must be trained to teach online. Some of the teaching competencies that are successful in a traditional classroom will be useful in an online environment; many will not. A rubric of teacher competencies for online instruction at the secondary level must be used. Most such rubrics reflect the required competencies for postsecondary online teaching; these are not appropriate. The teaching and learning environments are very different and therefore require different skills.

Teacher Development

Nothing in education works if teachers can not teach well. The goals of the teacher development program in the Web Academy are to identify, train, and support a base of professional educators sufficient in number and in areas of content expertise to allow for short- and long-term high-quality programmatic development. This encompasses both content creation and online instruction. The Web Academy has three levels of professional development in this area. The first level is a carefully designed 10-hour curriculum at the end of which a traditional teacher may successfully teach online, with ongoing in-house support. Eight of the ten hours are in content design system and operation and two hours are in utilizing the tools of the instructional model. The second level is an additional 10-hour curriculum that builds on and expands the lessons from the first session and results in a traditional teacher being exposed, through the use of specially designed templates, to the writing of content for delivery online and to expanded teaching techniques. The third level is a 10-hour curriculum at the end of which a teacher, with ongoing support, can write content for online delivery and successfully teach an online class.

Teacher development is always challenging, but this is particularly true when teaching teachers the techniques of successful online instruction when their professional backgrounds are in traditional instruction. First, the teachers must know that we recognize this is new to them and we do not expect them to begin as proficient in either technology or teaching online. In other words, they must be made comfortable with the learning environment into which they have been thrust. Second, they must be exposed to the techniques of high-quality online instruction. This consists of elements such as navigating within the chat room, handling large numbers of e-mails, keeping online records (attendance and grades), and utilizing the available instructional tools provided within the model.

An advantage of online instruction is that virtual schools have continued access to teachers who no longer live within the school district. With this access comes the challenge of continuing the necessary training of teachers from extended areas. This needed training is delivered online through training modules and within chat rooms, as well as through monthly online teachers meetings. Each monthly training session focuses on a particular topic and prior information about topics and dates of sessions is made available in time for teachers to plan ahead so that attendance is good.

Once teachers are trained to teach online, decisions are jointly reached about their appropriate levels of participation within the program. They may wish to just teach; they may want to write curriculum; or they may even wish to take on both tasks. The decisions made are based on teacher desires, available funding, and existing program needs. All of these elements combine to bring focus to the teacher development program.

Technology

Effective, efficient, and reliable technology is also critical to the success of local school district model for virtual schools. I use the term *technology* very broadly to encompass not only hardware, but also technical support personnel and a well-designed system for the operational technological elements of a virtual school. Examples of the operational technological elements are how online enrollment is managed and stored, how online student training is delivered in preparation for success in online classes, as well as how passwords and IDs are issued for access to virtual classrooms.

It is not unusual for a virtual school to outsource all of these technology elements, utilizing the hardware, support personnel, and management design of vendors, and thereby simplifying the issue. This approach, however, is a trade-off. By contracting with a vendor for these services, two important elements are lost to the school, namely, a level of school-based control that allows for needed changes to be made quickly, and perhaps more important, the opportunity for the school staff to build a culture of shared success that can come only from traveling the bumpy road of trial and error.

The Web Academy outsources very little. We have a contract with a local company that provides access to a computer expert who has developed a complete understanding of our school and its technology needs. We use this expert on an hourly basis to assist with difficult problems. Additionally, we meet with him, his company owners, and a representative of our local school system technology department on a monthly basis to discuss development ideas, operational problems, or sometimes just to communicate information such as schedules. Communication in the area of technology is as important as it is in the other areas of school operation. By maintaining an open line of communication with all these players, we are able to make needed technology changes and anticipate technology changes that may be needed as growth occurs. Additionally, this regular communication helps maintain a level of trust within the local school district that reduces the friction that might otherwise exist between our school and the school system technology department.

LESSONS LEARNED

Unique Characteristics of the Successful School District Model

How is the successful school district model different from successful state or national models? The elements that create the differences are flexibility, broad-based human capital, and an entrepreneurial spirit.

With the successful local model, there is often a need for speedy adjustments. Purchasing decisions are often made with short lead time, as are course creation decisions. For example, recently we were asked by our school district to facilitate the instruction of an internal program called Math Counts. The request was made one morning about 10:30; by 2:00 that afternoon, needed equipment had been ordered and staff hired to complete the project. We would have been unable to act that quickly without flexibility and without the required human capital immediately available.

Over the years, we have trained hundreds of teachers who provide a broad-based pool of well-trained faculty from which to draw. These teachers provide an invaluable resource. When we need to create content for online delivery or have access to trained online teachers, we have immediate access to professionals who can accomplish whatever task they undertake. Most of these professionals are part-time; some are full-time. The full-time professionals are especially valuable to us because of their wealth of experience and expertise. This knowledge and experience base is at the heart of our entrepreneurial spirit.

The Web Academy is a school, but one of the requirements that makes our school unique is the need to develop in a businesslike fashion. Few public schools have this need or this opportunity. Our human capital base provides the confidence we need to make decisions that are not only grounded in proven educational practice, but in solid business practice.

The Chances of Success Are High

The story of the Web Academy (and years of experience in the delivery of online instruction) demonstrate that this instructional medium can work; have confidence in virtual education because both qualitative experience and quantitative results (admittedly limited) make it clear that virtual learning is likely to play an important role in the educational paradigm of the future. Move with care, but without fear. Intelligent risk taking is essential if a local school district is to successfully create, support, and develop a virtual secondary school.

Structural Obstacles

Two of the major issues revolving around online teaching and learning have been essentially unaddressed. Until the problems of funding and unfriendly state laws and policies are resolved, virtual education will never be as valuable to education as it should be. Some of the most critical needs relate to the relationship among the school system, the proposed virtual school, and the design and operation of the program.

Importance of Preliminary Planning and Networking

Clear focus must be brought to the design of the virtual school. For this to occur, the school system must have realistic expectations of the program and the courage to hire personnel to create the program and then to give them the opportunity to do the job, including sufficient monies, freedom to make school-based decisions, and sustained distance from the program by school board members and central office personnel.

Research the topic, focusing on K–12, not postsecondary information. There is some overlap in the methods used in K–12 and postsecondary, but not much. Arrange site visits with successful schools utilizing the models that you find of interest. Ask questions and create collaborations. Inquire about their willingness to provide ongoing expertise as you build your program. Few things are more valuable than access to experience. Contact and participate in the national organizations active in virtual education.

Finally, as Tip O'Neill used to say, "All politics is local." In this case, "All politics is local" means that a continuing effort must be made to create, develop, and maintain support for the program with the local school district. As local leadership changes, so do priorities. It is critical to have a sufficiently wide base of support for the program so that the absence of individuals is not fatal to the program.

The University of Missouri–Columbia High School: From Independent Study to Accredited Diplomas Online

Kristi D. Smalley

MISSOURI'S ONLINE high school has a long and rich history that shares similarities with other distance education and online course providers. The University of Missouri–Columbia High School (MUHS) is one of many university-based high school programs that have developed online courses as an outgrowth of their traditional correspondence study programs for secondary-level students. More than 30 regionally accredited college and university independent study programs offered traditional correspondence courses at the high school level during the 2000–01 academic year. Most provided a full sequence of courses, and at least seven awarded diplomas. With their distance high school frameworks well established, at least five schools were able to offer diplomas earned entirely through online courses by 2001 (Clark, 2003). In addition to MUHS, other university-based independent study programs with online high school course offerings include those of Indiana University, Texas Tech, the University of Texas–Austin, Brigham Young University, the University of Oklahoma, and the University of Nebraska. Nebraska was the first to offer an independent study high school.

The University of Nebraska's Extension Division truly paved the way for university-based independent study programs. Begun in 1929 in an effort to save small rural schools by supplementing and enriching their curricular offerings, Nebraska's high school correspondence program grew rapidly. According to Van Arsdall (1977), Nebraska registered 14 students from a single school in its first school year, 1929–30. By the 1938–39 academic year, registrations had increased to 1,372 from 117 schools. Nebraska was not only serving isolated schools within its own state boundaries, but its correspondence program was also gaining a very favorable reputation both nationally and internationally. Nebraska's program was recognized as a diploma-granting high school by both the Nebraska State Department of Education and the North Central Association of Colleges and Schools (NCA) in 1967 (Van Arsdall, 1977). More recent statistics indicate that in the 1999–2000 academic year, Nebraska's Independent Study High School had generated approximately 15,000 course enrollments from 6,500 students (Clark, 2001).

THE UNIVERSITY OF MISSOURI'S
INDEPENDENT STUDY PROGRAM

The University of Missouri–Columbia High School is part of the university's Center for Distance and Independent Study (CDIS), an entity that has been in existence in one form or another since 1911. CDIS ("the Center") began by offering university correspondence courses, and it belongs to the university's Outreach and Extension Division—a logical fit in this land-grant university's organizational hierarchy. Historical records show that the Center offered high school courses as early as 1913. The April 1913 issue of the *University of Missouri Bulletin, Extension Series* illustrates Missouri's early efforts at outreach through correspondence education: "The University of Missouri through the United States mail gives you a chance to work for high school credit if you are unable to attend a high school. . . . The University of Missouri belongs to all of the people of the State, and is desirous of serving you. Now is your opportunity to make use of it. It is prepared through the extension division to go to you."

The University of Missouri (MU) first offered high school courses so that teachers could work on meeting increasing teacher certification standards while still teaching. Another goal of the program was to help prospective University of Missouri students meet college entrance requirements. Thus the Extension was fulfilling the university's land-grant mission by providing courses and assisting teachers and students in small rural schools. According to the *Bulletin*, there were 20 different offerings in 1913, including Grammar, Composition, Complete Elements of Algebra, Plane Geometry, Trigonometry, Medieval and Modern History, Beginner's Latin, Second Year German, Agriculture, Economics, and Pedagogy. Although its roots can be traced back to at least 1913, the high school program at MU's CDIS did not really take off until the late 1940s and early 1950s.

At one time, MU had a bricks-and-mortar school that combined high school and elementary school divisions in a single K–12 private school known as the Laboratory School. The elementary school division operated from 1857 until 1978, and until 1904 constituted the entire Laboratory School. The high school division, known as the Teachers College High School, was added in 1904 and operated until 1973. The Laboratory School allowed student teachers to gain practical teaching experience and afforded faculty and students opportunities for educational research (Archives of the University of Missouri–Columbia, 2003). Although there is no longer a functioning high school located there, Townsend Hall has recently been completely refurbished and is in use today by the university's College of Education for classrooms and faculty offices. CDIS records indicate that during the early 1970s there was a proposed partnership between CDIS and the lab school that would allow students to earn credit through independent study and the lab school would issue the resulting high school diploma. The only evidence of such an arrangement is an unsigned memo in the CDIS archives, so one must conclude that no such partnership ever actually occurred.

Another period of growth occurred during the 1970s when CDIS pioneered the use of telephone modems to submit lessons via the Computer Assisted Lesson Service (CALS). CALS, a precursor of today's online independent study courses, was a method of grading objectively scored lessons by having students submit answers via a phone line. A printer would print out the student's results with feedback on what the student got wrong, why it was wrong, and where the student could get additional information to correct any mistakes. The printouts were then mailed to students. The Center received the National University Continuing Education Association's (NUCEA) Significant Achievement Award in 1985 for its use of technology in independent study. At that time, it was the only such award that had been given by NUCEA (Center for Independent Study, 1985). The Center experienced tremendous growth in enrollment during the 1970s and 1980s, and was number one in the nation in terms of university-affiliated independent study program enrollments in 1983–84, with 16,113 course enrollments overall, 11,850 of which were at the high school level (Center for Independent Study, 1984).

Even with the growth that CDIS experienced in its high school courses during the 1980s, it could not maintain its lead in enrollments for long. As is shown in Table 11.1, the 1990s saw the Center's market share shrink with the ever-increasing competition in the field. Precise enrollment numbers were not the main issue, as those numbers naturally fluctuate from year to

Table 11.1. Enrollment in Six University-Based High School Programs of Independent Study

	Univ. of Missouri	Univ. of Nebraska	BYU	Texas Tech Univ. [a]	North Dakota	Indiana Univ.
1989–90	12,218	9,831	9,534	13,803	4,345	6,310
1990–91	11,416	9,751	10,233	17,346	4,331	6,201
1991–92	11,374	10,048	12,207	18,550	4,786	6,186
1992–93	11,064	10,426	13,693	22,412	5,169	6,345
1993–94	10,509	11,892	15,608	25,197	5,906	6,615
1994–95	10,649	12,731	18,517	29,267	8,395	7,506
1995–96	10,178	13,667	23,375	33,166	10,589	8,012
1996–97	10,273	14,120	26,941	39,670	8,907	8,283
1997–98	9,586	15,233	27,675	40,950	9,638	—
1998–99	10,217	14,777	28,946	55,580	8,560	—

Source: National University Continuing Education Association, 1989–90—1998–99.
[a] Enrollments include credits awarded by examination.

year. Missouri's numbers, however, were continuing on a downward slide while similar peer institution enrollment numbers were experiencing an upward trend during the same time period. The Center needed to regain lost enrollments, as well as find and reach out to new potential audiences. Therefore, the Center countered with two important and intertwined developments: the creation of the University of Missouri–Columbia High School (MUHS or MU High School) as an accredited, diploma-granting institution and the offering of online courses.

THE ESTABLISHMENT OF MU HIGH SCHOOL

When an internal review indicated that enrollments in MU's high school–level independent study program were declining, just as they were at other similar programs without a diploma program, the Center hired a new director in 1997 with the expectation that he would begin an independent study high school that would be accredited and grant diplomas. Although the University of Missouri had offered high school–level independent study courses since at least 1913, those courses were only used as transfer credit to another institution. Establishing MU High School in 1999 as an accredited diploma-granting high school enabled CDIS to provide students in Missouri and elsewhere with a complete program, as well as to fulfill the university's land-grant mission in new ways.

Accreditation

Before MU High School could be up and running as a functional high school, several issues needed to be addressed during initial planning stages. Foremost among those issues was applying for and obtaining accreditation as a high school from the regional accrediting agency for Missouri, the North Central Association of Schools and Colleges (NCA). MU High School applied for membership to NCA in early 1999 and was approved for accreditation at NCA's annual meeting held in Chicago in April 1999. MUHS was fortunate to have the guidance of Missouri's NCA state director, Robert C. Shaw, and associate state director, Wayne Walker, whose offices were located on the University of Missouri campus, to assist with the application procedure.

MU High School is classified by NCA (now called the North Central Association Commission on Accreditation and School Improvement, or NCA-CASI) as a "special purpose" school. In addition to distance education institutions like MUHS, other nontraditional schools that fall into the special purpose category include schools in children's hospitals, schools for the deaf, and schools for the blind. Under NCA-CASI guidelines, MUHS has an ongoing school improvement plan and submits an annual report to renew accreditation. It has also formally adopted the following mission statement:

> The mission of the University of Missouri-Columbia High School is to provide courses, through a variety of delivery methods that will complement traditional high school curricula, and provide an accredited diploma program for independent learners of all ages seeking an alternative to traditional high school attendance. (Center for Distance and Independent Study, 2002)

Although not an accrediting agency, the National Collegiate Athletic Association has approved most of MUHS's core courses for establishing initial-eligibility certification of student-athletes.

Diploma Program

MUHS also needed to address ways to maintain its long-standing reputation and the mutual goodwill that existed between it and the traditional public and private schools it served. Although it was adding a diploma program to the services it provided, MUHS knew that the vast majority of those students enrolling in independent study courses would still be those students taking a course or two to use as transfer credit on their transcripts back at their local high school, not to obtain a diploma. Those students may need to take distance education courses to resolve scheduling problems at their local school, restore credits, graduate early, or take a specialized topic not offered at their local school, such as our courses targeted for gifted and talented students. Many small rural schools have group enrollments because they lack certified teachers for subjects such as foreign languages, chemistry, and physics. (In recent years an increasing number of enrollments are coming from virtual charter schools that act as portals to courses from other providers.) Therefore, MUHS took great care to balance its acceptance by public school officials and counselors with its autonomy as a nonpublic school.

In addition, MUHS wanted to satisfy Missouri's Department of Elementary and Secondary Education (DESE) graduation requirements and involve key DESE personnel in its distance education high school plans. Meetings were held with then commissioner of education, Dr. Robert Bartman, and assistant commissioner, Dr. Orlo Shroyer. Although not under DESE's jurisdiction because it is self-supporting through the payment of student fees and hence could not be considered a public school, MUHS purposefully chose to follow DESE guidelines and to keep them informed. MUHS chose to offer a general high school diploma as well as a college preparatory diploma, both following the graduation requirements set forth by DESE. DESE personnel did not have objections to MUHS's offering a diploma, and indicated that such a program would offer a welcome alternative to students who might drop out of traditional high school.

Diploma-seeking students include people of all ages from many different circumstances: adults, students who had dropped out, or students wishing to earn a high school diploma rather than a GED; children from missionary, military, and other families who have relocated overseas due to job assignments; foreign students desiring a diploma from a U.S. high school; homebound students; homeschool students, especially those wanting an accredited high school diploma to help facilitate the college admissions process; students with a traveling lifestyle; professional athletes and Olympic athletes in training; and musicians, child-actors, or other entertainers with rigorous training and practice schedules.

A unique feature of this distance education high school is the employment of field representatives, four retired school administrators who work part-time contacting schools and visiting with school counselors and principals. Not only do they help spread the word about distance education, they give MUHS a more personal touch by providing the schools with a face to associate with the program. These field representatives also soothed some public school administrators' early fears that MUHS would be competing with them for their students. Understandably, many school administrators had feared that online schools would lure their students, and hence their average daily attendance money as well, away from their schools (Lorenzo, 2002). This has never been the intention of MUHS at all, as the school only seeks to complement what the public schools do by providing their students with options they may not have available to them otherwise.

MUHS's course development process also illustrates its commitment to ensuring a high-quality program. All MUHS courses are written by or reviewed and approved by Missouri-certified teachers. These may be retired educators or some of the state's best teachers currently teaching in a traditional classroom. Additionally, the learning objectives for many of the core courses have been voluntarily coded to Missouri's academic standards.

MISSOURI'S ONLINE HIGH SCHOOL PROGRAM

The Development of Online Courses

CDIS began offering online courses in 1997 before MU High School was established. Not only was CDIS hoping to increase the number of enrollments by offering courses in a different format, but there also was a push to include more interactive and multimedia elements in our courses. We began by converting some of our most popular print-based courses into an online format. These online courses contained links to online resources for student exploration. Students were able to submit their lessons online, as well as access their course information and grades over the Internet.

Our greatest obstacles to developing online courses included the expense and drain on personnel resources to do so. We did not hire additional staff specifically for the purpose of developing and expanding an online program. Rather, our course designers and editors were producing online courses in addition to the traditional print-based courses they had already been producing at the high school, elementary, and college levels. This meant that the development of online courses was time consuming with such a limited staff. However, with an increased focus, some priority shifting here and there, and a dedicated staff, it was possible. Additionally, the development of online courses was facilitated by the fact that we already had the infrastructure in place through our long-standing correspondence program to enroll students; to receive, grade, and return their lessons in a timely manner, and to keep accurate and up-to-date student records. Throughout our long history, our technology personnel have developed a tailor-made and fully integrated records management system. Unlike newly established online high school programs that may not already have such infrastructure in place, we found the biggest change was mode of course delivery.

The start was rather slow going, as we only had 9 online courses open for enrollment at the end of the 1997–98 fiscal year, with only 14 student enrollments. We gradually added more online high school courses, and at the end of the 2002–03 fiscal year, we had 56 online courses with a total of 4,927 enrollments. There are more than enough courses for students to complete a sequence of courses leading to a high school diploma entirely online now, if they so choose.

Table 11.2 shows enrollment numbers for the past five years. As can be seen, enrollments in our online courses have increased dramatically, and our total number of high school enrollments has increased as well.

Technology

Because MUHS serves such a wide variety of students under many different circumstances, we chose to make the courses user-friendly and easily accessible. Therefore, most of the online courses do not have overly demanding hardware and software requirements. Students obviously need a computer with Internet access and a recent browser, which they or their

Table 11.2. Enrollment in Online Courses at University of Missouri High School, 1997–2003

Fiscal Year	Online Courses (n)	Enrollments in Online Courses	Enrollments in All High School Courses	Online Enrollments as Share of All Enrollment (%)
1997–1998	9	14	9,850	0.001
1998–1999	15	437	10,268	4.26
1999–2000	18	1,219	12,133	10.05
2000–2001	28	1,811	13,026	13.90
2001–2002	50	3,707	14,753	25.13
2002–2003	56	4,927	15,233	32.34

schools are responsible for providing. Some courses require certain downloads and plug-ins, which for the most part can be obtained from the Internet free of charge, and some courses make use of a CD-ROM.

MUHS chose not to use commercially available course delivery and management platforms such as Blackboard or WebCT. Rather, we developed a course delivery template that is fully integrated into our existing records management database and online submission process. We also already had technology support staff in place who have developed a records management database that is fully integrated with how students can access course information and submit lessons online. This tailor-made system allows students to submit lessons in their online courses and receive immediate grading reports. This information is then automatically incorporated into our database enabling students to access their coursework from any place at any time, proceed at their own pace, and check their records and progress in "real time."

Funding

Although associated with a public university, MUHS does not receive any financial support from governmental tax dollars. The Center for Distance and Independent Study is self-supporting through the payment of student fees for its college, high school, middle school, and elementary school course offerings. In most instances students and their families pay course fees directly to the Center. If the local school district cannot provide a particular course for a student, oftentimes the local school will pay the student's fees.

Curriculum

In order to provide students with as many options and as much flexibility as possible, MUHS offers a wide variety of courses from which to choose. Students can take courses in the four core subject areas (language arts, math, science, and social studies), as well as in specialized topics such as aerospace and women's literature. Most courses are written for typical high school–aged students, but MUHS also offers courses developed specifically for gifted students and a limited number of Advanced Placement courses. As mentioned earlier, although MUHS is not a public high school because students pay fees, we purposefully chose to adopt the state of Missouri's high school graduation requirements for both general and college preparatory diplomas. Not only does this help with consistency and public relations within the state, it also helps ensure that our diploma students receive a balanced education that is equivalent to that offered in the public schools.

To assist students as they work on their courses, MUHS added access to online library resources in the 2002–03 academic year. We have purchased subscription services to *Britannica Online's School Edition* and the *I-Net Library* for all of our high school students, and assembled our own list of links that students can use for research. As far as we know, we are the only university-based independent study program that has purchased subscriptions to online library resources for our high school students.

Student Services

MUHS has a certified counselor who analyzes diploma students' transcripts and provides guidance on which courses are appropriate and needed to meet a student's goals. For students using our courses as transfer credit, we work closely with local school counselors who must approve their students' enrollments in independent study courses. MU High School sends those counselors monthly updates on their students' progress in addition to making a password-protected Web site available to them to check on their students in "real time." MUHS also has a certified high school principal on staff, and student services personnel who can assist students with problems and advise them on how to proceed with their independent study coursework. Students can fax, e-mail, or call the Center at any time on any day of the year.

Professional Development

Since many of our courses are objectively graded and "stand-alone" courses that need very little involvement from the teachers once they are written, for the most part there is very little online professional development for our staff. For instructor-evaluated courses, we orient online instructors on how to retrieve and access student lessons online or by e-mail, how to correct student work, and how to send grading information back to MUHS for entry into our records management database.

Access and Equity

MUHS makes it possible for students to take courses that might not be available to them otherwise and also allows schools to expand and enrich their curriculum with courses that they are unable to provide because of their size, location, or limited teaching staff. Moreover, MUHS offered these courses during the 2002–03 academic year for $125 per semester course (not including any required textbooks), a cost that is much less than the average online high school course fees of $264 per semester course reported in

Clark's 2001 study. Furthermore, at MUHS the cost of online courses is the same as the cost of a print course.

Assessment

Students work through their independent study coursework at their own pace and can take up to 9 months to complete a course. Most courses contain a variety of self-check exercises so that students can practice and monitor their progress before submitting work for a grade. Throughout their coursework, students submit objective assessments (multiple-choice, true or false, or matching questions), which can be submitted and graded online instantaneously, or more open-ended assignments that require a faculty member to grade. Although these faculty-evaluated lessons can be submitted online or by e-mail, the lessons are forwarded on to an instructor for grading. Students must also take exams under the supervision of a CDIS-approved proctor, who is usually a student's local high school guidance counselor or principal. If the student lives in Missouri, exams may be taken at a county extension office. Because the exams are the only proctored portion of our courses, students must earn a passing average on all exams in order to pass MUHS courses.

In our efforts to improve MU High School's quality and effectiveness, we ask students to fill out an optional evaluation form when they complete a course. We use these course evaluations, as well as phone calls, letters, and e-mails to the Center to improve our course offerings and student services. Additionally, we perform annual internal evaluations as part of our NCA school improvement plan and accreditation process.

Policy and Administration

Because MUHS is a self-supporting nonpublic institution, we are not required to adhere to state guidelines. Since we partner with many other public and private schools, however, we have voluntarily accepted some state guidelines such as Missouri's graduation requirements. Moreover, we are accredited by NCA-CASI and participate in their annual accreditation process and their school improvement program. As mentioned earlier, we work closely with public school counselors and require a school's permission when enrolling their students in our courses for transfer credit. These factors, coupled with commissioning Missouri-certified teachers for course development and requiring students to take and pass proctored exams, are important considerations when public and private schools choose to partner with us by using our courses.

Marketing and Public Relations

MUHS uses many different marketing strategies. We print an annual bulletin at the end of each summer that is essentially a course catalog listing our policies, course descriptions, textbooks, and prices. This bulletin is sent to schools nationwide each fall using internal mailing lists as well as purchased mailing lists. Our Web site is an increasingly important and popular marketing tool since people can search for us, find us, and have up-to-date information on our program literally at their fingertips. In addition, we advertise in many magazines and journals, do direct mailings, exhibit at state and national educational conferences, and rely on school visits by our field representatives who serve as our ambassadors and personal liaisons to schools in Missouri and surrounding states.

LESSONS LEARNED

Through our many years of experience in operating an independent study high school study program and our recent development of a virtual high school, we have learned some things that we can offer as recommendations to others. Accreditation by one of the regional accrediting agencies and, if possible, a state department of education is highly desirable for a university-based high school program. This helps assure public schools and students that the program is of high quality, reputable, and accountable. It also will facilitate the transfer of academic credit between high schools and the acceptance of high school credit when students apply to college.

For university-based independent study programs wanting to start an online high school, the importance of establishing and maintaining positive public relations, both on and off campus, cannot be emphasized enough. Great care should be taken to keep the proper officials informed at all times during initial planning of the program, its implementation, and then following up after the program has been established. Much emphasis is placed on educational missions and mission statements in the realm of academia today. Research should be done on the educational mission of your particular institution. Be prepared to explain and defend the existence of a high school independent study program, and how it fits in and helps fulfill the university's mission. With a land-grant university, such as Missouri, this is not an overly difficult task since the program is reaching out not only to Missourians, but also providing educational opportunities for students worldwide. Increased exposure and publicity, and the ability to recruit and attract future students to attend the university are also good selling points on a university campus.

Since public school officials may mistakenly believe that an online high school program will draw students away from their local district, taking their state funding with them, the utmost care should be taken to keep the proper officials, including those at the state department of education, informed of your plans. We already had a very positive working relationship with public schools, especially guidance counselors, within the state. It helped soothe many fears within the public schools by having regular communication with counselors through monthly updates of their students' progress, our field representative visits, and being responsive to the schools' needs. Also, we require the signature of a school superintendent or principal for a student under the age of 18 to be admitted to our diploma program.

It is imperative that an independent study program emphasize how it can serve the needs of public and private schools, how partnerships can exist between the two for mutual benefit, and how they can complement each other's services by providing students with more educational opportunities and options than ever before.

(12)

The LUDA-VHS Model: The Role of the University in Virtual Schools

Charalambos Vrasidas & Richard Chamberlain

GOOD PARTNERSHIPS between universities and K–12 schools and districts are essential for the success of educational innovations and e-learning initiatives. This case study of a partnership between a university's research and development center and local school districts to develop a statewide virtual high school will attempt to illuminate the role that universities can play in fostering successful e-learning in K–12 settings.

Telecommunication technologies permit and encourage interaction among persons on a scale never imagined when correspondence courses were the preferred method of distance education (Vrasidas & Glass, 2002). One recent trend in the field of distance education is the development of virtual high schools that rely on these new technologies.

The Center for the Application of Information Technologies (CAIT) at Western Illinois University commissioned a study to examine the status of virtual high schools in the United States (Clark, 2000b). The study looked at leading projects and provided information on key forces driving state interest in virtual schooling. Clark identified some key characteristics of these virtual high school projects, such as technologies used, funding resources, curriculum issues, student services, professional development for teachers, access and equity issues, assessment, policy and administration, marketing, and public relations. In a more recent study, Clark (2001) found that the trend to develop virtual schools continues to grow and identified a variety of virtual school projects: state-sanctioned projects, university-based virtual schools, virtual school consortia, virtual schools operated by schools and districts, virtual charter schools, and private virtual schools.

K–12 schools are interested in e-learning but do not always have the expertise and resources to develop e-learning projects. Therefore, schools and their districts often seek partners to help them succeed in e-learning. Some of the major reasons behind the need to partner with universities are the following:

- There is a strong push to participate in e-learning due to state mandates and general public interest.
- An outside partner that is expert in the area may be able to help stakeholders get a better understanding of the potential of e-learning (presentations to faculty, school boards, and so forth).
- K–12 schools usually do not have the expert personnel to guide the development, implementation, evaluation, and support of e-learning projects.
- K–12 schools usually do not have experience with learning management systems that enable the development of online courses (e.g., Blackboard and WebCT) and do not have the technology infrastructure to support and host the development of online classes.
- K–12 schools often do not have the funds to support the development of e-learning projects.

Institutions of higher education have been key partners in many school improvement efforts. Partnerships work best when both parties benefit from the relationship. Oftentimes policymakers and planners have a vision of what they would like to develop but are unclear on the process and uncertain what path they need to follow to achieve their vision. Projects often become more concrete for policymakers when they sit down and begin to work out the details regarding development and deployment of an e-learning project with experts from universities. CAIT and Western Illinois University have a long history of successful involvement in distance education and e-learning and have been in partnerships with a variety of institutions, including boards of education, professional groups, government agencies, and corporate settings.

One of our recent partnerships was with the Illinois Community College Board (ICCB). We engaged in a partnership with ICCB to develop GED Illinois Online. The General Education Development Test, or GED test, provides a basis for conferring a high school equivalency diploma on adults who have not graduated from high school. GED Illinois Online was designed to provide educators with resources to work with students in the classroom and give students, who could not normally attend the traditional classes, the resources to study GED materials anytime from anywhere. Members of the ICCB had the vision and will to develop a GED program that could be deployed online. However, they were not clear about what path to follow for developing the project. Their vision became more concrete and the road map for achieving that vision took shape as the steps to complete such a project were defined during meetings with the advisory committee and the CAIT design team. During those meetings policymakers sat with instructional designers, developers, and evaluators to define the scope of the project and establish a production plan. In this early phase of the partnership, the different strengths each partner brought to the table helped define the project. The ICCB gained access to expert knowledge that helped them achieve their goals, and CAIT gained access to content experts and more funding to help improve the quality service it offers to the education community and try out new ideas. A strong theme that emerged from this and other partnerships is that a constant negotiation takes place that shapes the form and nature of the project as well as the benefits for each partner.

THE CONTRIBUTION OF K–12 SCHOOLS AND UNIVERSITIES TO K–12 E-LEARNING

K–12 schools and universities have been collaborating for decades in preparing preservice and in-service teachers for the K–12 classroom. Each brings different strengths to the partnership. K–12 schools bring the content experts, the teachers who will teach the classes and provide access to the students who will serve as the audience of e-learning projects. These schools also bring the real-world view of e-learning projects and a more pragmatic approach to their development. Projects that are developed need to work and serve the needs of their students. Any partnership with K–12 schools places a major emphasis on "user needs." Schools have yearly budgets within which they have to work, and they are responsible to their school boards, administrators, and communities. Therefore, they are constantly scrutinized and innovations like e-learning always come with risk.

The university offers expertise and experience, as well as a technology infrastructure and training for teachers. More specifically, universities offer the following:

- *Educational technologists.* Universities have educational technologists who have the knowledge and expertise needed to successfully plan and implement e-learning projects.

- *Instructional design.* Instructional designers who understand the unique characteristics of the online environment can help design e-learning projects that will capitalize on the potential of technology offering the best learning experience possible to students, teachers, and their communities.
- *Research and evaluation.* The university can provide the rigorous research and evaluation component needed for every program to ensure that it meets its goals and to provide feedback for improving future operations.
- *Technology infrastructure.* Most universities have the necessary technology infrastructure that enables them to plan, develop, and implement e-learning projects. K–12 schools can benefit from this partnership by taking advantage of the technology available at partner university institutions.
- *Training and support for teachers.* Teachers need to be trained to effectively teach and facilitate online learning. Universities can offer ongoing professional development and support for teachers to strengthen their skills and improve the quality of learning experiences students will be receiving.
- *Prior experience.* Because they work with multiple partners, universities can provide concrete examples of other projects that they have worked on that may be similar. Examples from lessons learned from other cases can often be the best teacher in helping all partners gain a better understanding of the project and the process behind its development.
- *A bridge for collaboration.* Because of their regional or statewide mandates, universities are often able to bring together partners that may not have otherwise collaborated.
- *Best practices.* Universities can bring examples of successes and failures from past projects as examples of what does or does not work. This real-world experience goes beyond theory, as it is the result of actual projects that had real outcomes, which in most cases can be quantified.

THE LUDA VIRTUAL HIGH SCHOOL PROJECT

Goal and Partners

The LUDA Virtual High School, or LUDA-VHS, is a project supported by LUDA (Large Unit District Association) Education Foundation in partnership with the Center for the Application of Information Technologies

(CAIT) at Western Illinois University. The goal of the project is to provide opportunities for virtual learning to high school students in the state of Illinois. The LUDA Education Foundation (http://lrs.ed.uiuc.edu/luda) is a nonprofit corporation formed to operate "exclusively for charitable, educational, religious, or scientific purposes." Members of the foundation are school districts in the state of Illinois, members of LUDA, and other education specialists. One of the goals of the organization, as stated in its bylaws, is to develop educational programs, which will permit students to learn in a virtual classroom setting. Students can access the educational programs offered by LUDA-VHS to obtain high school credit toward a diploma.

The major goal of LUDA-VHS is to use technology for developing alternative ways for serving the needs of school districts and providing quality education to high school students in the state of Illinois. The project entered its planning phase in fall 2000 with meetings attended by LUDA representatives and CAIT personnel. The LUDA Education Foundation appointed the LUDA-VHS planning committee, which consisted of members of the LUDA Education Foundation, CAIT personnel, and representatives from LUDA school districts. The planning committee's major role was to work closely with LUDA teachers and CAIT personnel for the design, development, and implementation of a pilot online class.

The pilot online class on consumer education was developed and implemented during the summer of 2001. The pilot class had three goals:

- To resolve the technical, administrative, development, and implementation issues relating to online class development
- To identify a process for online class development
- To identify the lessons learned from this pilot, so that they could be used to develop more courses

Development Process

For the development of the pilot class on consumer education, three LUDA teachers worked closely with the project manager and two instructional designers from CAIT. After class content was developed, teachers were trained in teaching online, using the class tools, and navigating the class Web site. Three sections of Consumer Education were offered online during summer school 2001 at the three schools where the teachers worked. Students met face-to-face with their classmates and teacher during the first day orientation to the course. Class continued online and met again face-to-face at the end of the summer session for the final exam.

Levels of Collaboration

Collaboration for this project took place at multiple levels. Administrators from LUDA and CAIT met several times to discuss the project, its challenges, and offerings. Schools and school districts in the state of Illinois collaborated with each other in developing and coordinating the project and worked collectively on a common goal. All stakeholders in the project wanted this effort to succeed and collaborated effectively. Once the project entered its development stages, schoolteachers and school administrators collaborated with the CAIT design team to develop the classes. Teachers were trained on how to teach online classes and facilitate online discussion groups. CAIT experts worked with teachers and schools to establish the policies to govern LUDA-VHS, as well as the individual course offerings. Once classes were developed, CAIT support stuff collaborated with teachers and students during the offering of the course and supported the technical infrastructure necessary to deliver the classes.

LESSONS LEARNED

The first-year evaluation of the project indicated that a general feeling among all stakeholders was that the project met its goals and all stakeholders were satisfied with the results of the pilot class (Vrasidas, 2003). A good indicator of success in this project is the fact that all stakeholders interviewed, including teachers, principals, superintendents, members of the LUDA Education Foundation and LUDA-VHS planning committee, the CAIT design team, and CAIT administration indicated a high level of satisfaction with the project. The class content and materials were of high quality and rigor. Teachers were satisfied with their students' ability to engage in the class activities and lessons, meet deadlines, work independently, troubleshoot, and ask for help when needed. Students gave high ratings to the class and were pleased with the level of interaction with their teacher. Students felt that their teachers communicated with them regularly and in a timely fashion during the summer session class.

An important lesson is that successful innovations cannot be implemented following a top-down model. Participation of all involved is essential. One of the most important lessons that CAIT learned had to do with the realities of implementation in the K–12 classroom, which helped improve the overall operations of CAIT and its involvement in other K–12 e-learning projects.

THE LUDA-VHS LOCAL MODEL FOR COURSE DEVELOPMENT

The success of the model used by the LUDA-VHS is based on local development and control of classes. From the very beginning of this project, teachers and schools who are most directly affected by the project provided their feedback and input to the production of the project. Their input helped shape the plan for what should be offered and how it would be used. This helped develop a strong sense of ownership and commitment to the project by the participating schools. School districts involved in the development of the class were the districts that participated in the pilot. Teachers who developed the content were the teachers who taught the class in the summer, and they put their best effort forward in making the project a success. Classes for LUDA-VHS are developed by LUDA teachers working within their local school districts and taught by Illinois-certified teachers. LUDA-VHS places emphasis on locally developing and teaching its classes.

Having as foundation the valuable insight from all stakeholders, further buy-in was obtained by schools, administrators, and teachers. Rather than use a centralized model that had students working with a teacher from a central location out of district (or out of state), the LUDA-VHS model allows for local control of the class. This model calls for a teacher from the local district to be trained both in teaching online and in the specifics of the class content. This teacher then offers a class from her or his own school district as part of a regular teaching load. The teacher reports to her or his administrators as usual and remains accountable to the local district. The technology that houses the class is still supported and maintained by the LUDA-VHS, and there is tech support offered by the LUDA-VHS Help Desk, but the class administration and accountability is at the local level. This level of local control is at the heart of the LUDA-VHS model. The university's role is that of a facilitator.

Teacher Training

Teachers need to receive training in how to develop and teach online classes. Here the role of the university is instrumental in helping teachers prepare for the online environment. The training should provide teachers with the opportunities for practicing the principles of online teaching and learning. However, for teachers to be able to participate in training sessions, it requires the support of their school districts. Such support can include release time, reduced workload, and financial incentives.

Teacher Compensation and Support

Participating schools are still working to establish clear policies on how to handle teacher time, pay, and other compensation for those involved in LUDA-VHS. These issues are very important, and the LUDA Education Foundation along with participating school districts need to establish clear policies on how to compensate and support teachers who want to participate in LUDA-VHS. In addition, union issues, such as contractual obligations to teachers, need to be reviewed so that there is no conflict of interest. Unless policies and expectations are clear, teachers will not support the project. Training teachers to develop online content and teach online is not enough. Teachers should be provided with ongoing support to ensure they have everything they need to teach online classes. Part of the teacher support is provided by CAIT at Western Illinois University.

Quality Assurance and Evaluation

As more classes are developed, more schools will join LUDA-VHS, and the project will grow and expand to include large numbers of students. One of the major concerns that emerges is quality assurance. In order to maintain high quality of courses developed and instruction delivered to LUDA high school students, LUDA Education Foundation should establish a mechanism of yearly review of its courses, content alignment with Illinois Learning Standards, and professional development opportunities offered to teachers. The results of every review should be shared with the districts to help them improve their contribution to the project. CAIT can provide the expertise for the establishment of this quality assurance mechanism through its research and evaluation unit. Only through the systematic evaluation of the project will stakeholders be able to make informed decisions on how to improve the project, identify the most appropriate activities and structural characteristics of online courses, better serve the needs of LUDA districts and their students, and maintain a fruitful partnership.

Site Coordinators

Several of the issues associated with LUDA-VHS can be resolved when site coordinators are trained and assigned to each participating school. Several of the suggested tasks recommended for the site coordinator are also tasks that teachers will be performing. Establishing clear structures and procedures to be followed will be beneficial for the success of the project. A site coordinator could be a counselor who will receive training in online classes and would also be able to provide guidance to students in choosing the right class. Each school should have a site coordinator. One of the site coordinators could be the district coordinator or representative who would be the link between the district and LUDA-VHS. Site coordinators need to receive training from CAIT similar to the training that teachers would receive in online teaching and learning. In addition to the educational responsibilities of the site coordinator, another important task would be to serve as the liaison and point of contact between the schools, LUDA, and CAIT. Constant communication among all partners is essential for the success of e-learning partnerships.

CHARACTERISTICS OF SUCCESSFUL
PARTNERSHIPS AND CHALLENGES

In any successful partnership there needs to be a strong commitment to the process, which will be demonstrated by a mutual contribution. Partners need to buy into the project. But unlike other projects and initiatives with partners at state agencies or other institutions, a project like LUDA-VHS will probably not command districts' undivided attention. In our experiences working with multiple districts, they were unlikely to have the staff resources to commit a significant block of several people's time to work on a project. Districts are concerned with issues of curriculum, student behavior, buildings, and faculty. Because such issues command most of schools' attention, some flexibility is necessary in evaluating K–12 and university partnerships. In the case of LUDA-VHS, people working on the project (particularly the teachers) are participating in addition to their regular responsibilities. All stakeholders were committed to developing a quality product that would meet their students' needs. The LUDA Education Foundation was committed to building capacity over a period of time and was interested in the development of a model for designing and delivering online classes. CAIT was interested in the project since the success of LUDA-VHS would mean the development of more classes and more e-learning projects in collaboration with K–12 schools. All participants understood that the development of such a model required the commitment of all stakeholders.

A critical element in any good relationship is the development of trust among partners. Sincere conversations and open dialog on all aspects of the LUDA-VHS helped develop the sense of trust among all stakeholders. However, conversations alone will not develop trust; trust also needs to be based on performance. If districts say they are going to provide release time for faculty and they do it, then that engenders a sense of trust. If a promise is made to develop and deploy a class by a particular date and that deadline is met, this adds to the sense of trust and commitment to the relationship. This sense of trust also creates a sense of shared responsibility. The project's success or failure has an impact on all partners, not just one. The buy-in and commitment to the project needs to come from all partners. Coupled with a shared responsibility is a shared success. When the project succeeds, then all parties involved need to be given credit for the work and be acknowledged for their efforts and contributions.

One of the challenges behind successful partnerships is the possibility that members of the partner institutions might change over time. School districts work locally and are accountable to both the school board and their local community. Their commitment to a partnership may change or be driven by factors that do not directly relate to higher education. The makeup of the local school board may change every 2 years, and with that change there may occur a change in focus related to priorities and commitment to e-learning projects. Most successful projects are also based on good interpersonal relationships among key players. Successful partnerships rely heavily on personal contacts. Good interpersonal communication skills are essential for maintaining good interpersonal relationships. In the case of LUDA-VHS, good relationships among stakeholders were based on prior experiences from collaboration and on the sense of trust and commitment that developed throughout the project.

Classes for LUDA-VHS are developed and taught by Illinois-certified teachers. School districts involved in the development of classes are also the school districts that offer these classes to their students. Teachers who teach the classes come from schools whose students participate in those classes. The LUDA Education Foundation was aware that beginning such an effort would be time-consuming and would require significant commitments. The board was interested in developing courses with the involvement of Illinois-certified teachers. By having LUDA teachers develop the classes, teachers, administrators, and students saw the classes as their own, thus making them more committed to making the project successful. The combination of ownership and commitment to the project was a major factor that led to the project's success. The teachers who developed and taught the class made this project a success. Even though there were several problems with the class implementation, teachers managed to put their best effort forward and did a very good job, regardless of the amount of time it required of them. However, it is important to note that school districts may be more vulnerable to funding issues that may constrain their ability to provide teacher support, release time, travel, or release from a class period to prepare and teach an online class.

A challenge that is crucial in the success of partnerships has to do with a shared vision and alignment of the project's goals with the participating institutions' goals and strategic plans. Much of the support for this project was a result of the alignment among the goals of the project with LUDA's strategic plan, with the participant schools' technology plans, and with CAIT's vision for e-learning. All partners had strong beliefs in the use of technology and in its capabilities in improving student learning. All felt that the project was helping their schools meet their mission for the future. LUDA-VHS was the result of a team effort and all stakeholders believed in the benefits of technology and virtual schooling.

CONCLUSION

Healthy interdependence, a shift from individualism to collaboration and team building, group consensus, and shared decision making and responsibility are fundamental characteristics of any good partnership. Almost 3 years since the launching of LUDA-VHS, the LUDA Education Foundation is still supporting, developing, and deploying classes because it meets these characteristics. The number of classes and sections has grown and so has the number of school districts using LUDA-VHS classes. All of the original members of the LUDA Education Foundation and advisory committee are still active participants. The LUDA-VHS has grown slowly, but continuously. A slow, planned expansion has allowed for systematic revision of the development process, training procedures, and administration of the classes. The partners in LUDA-VHS learned important lessons regarding the cultivation of a common vision, commitment, trust, mutual contribution to the project, the need for teacher training and support, and establishing quality-assurance mechanisms.

South Dakota's Statewide Distance Education Project: Diffusion of an Innovation

Michael Simonson

S OUTH DAKOTA is one of the most rural states in the Union. It boasts a population of just 754,000 residents distributed across a territory measuring approximately 400 miles by 250 miles. Many of the connecting roads are single-lane rural highways, and travel time between the major communities is lengthy.

There is also a growing shortage of teachers in South Dakota, which holds the unenviable record of offering the lowest teacher salaries in the United States (*Argus Leader*, February 18, 2002). Teachers are steadily leaving South Dakota and authorities are discovering that the outward flow of human resources is hard to stem and even harder to replace. Lack of specialized teachers is resulting in a reduction in curriculum offerings across all levels of education.

LAYING THE GROUNDWORK

Wiring the Schools; First Technology for Teaching and Learning Academy; A Vision for the Future

Beginning in 1995, South Dakota leaders began innovative initiatives to advance education, the economy, and technology in support of a commitment to opportunities for every person. In 1996, South Dakota's Governor Janklow made a commitment to education in the state that was unprecedented. First, he directed that each school building in South Dakota be wired for interactive telecommunication for distance education. He called this the Wiring the Schools Project. Every classroom and dormitory room in public and private postsecondary institutions was connected by spring 2000.

In 1997, Governor Janklow initiated the Technology for Teaching and Learning Academy (TTL), an ambitious professional development experience for teachers in South Dakota to help them master the skills needed to use technology effectively in the classroom. The program involved a 20-day summer immersion institute and a series of follow up activities that spanned the next 12-month period. The TTL Academy's purpose was to establish a cadre of highly trained educators across the state, with three critical functions:

- To actively change teaching and learning in classrooms through the integration of technology into curriculum
- To model effective teaching practices using technology
- To assist fellow educators in learning how to use technology

During the summer of 2000, a special event was held in Pierre, the capital of South Dakota. This event was called Governor Janklow's Capital City Conclave on Distance Education. The Governor's Conclave brought 12 national and international experts in distance education to South Dakota to interact with local education leaders. These experts, referred to as the Dakota Dozen, worked with over 50 education "ambassadors" representing all aspects of education in the state. Their efforts were summarized in the *Conclave Proceedings Video* that contained a vision for the future of education in South Dakota. The vision was to infuse technology throughout the state and to provide free, open, and equal access to technologies for learning, first to children, then to the community, and finally to improve the standard of living for all South Dakotans.

The theme of the Governor's Conclave, *Start with the children . . . empower the workforce . . . promote economic development*, was the rallying point during the Conclave for ideas to improve education in South Dakota using distance education. This 10-word theme continues today to be a clarion call for education in the state.

The Connecting the Schools Project

Activated in August 2000, the Digital Dakota Network (DDN) is an interactive video-voice-data network designed to provide interactive instruction between South Dakota's school districts. Schools began to be connected to the Digital Dakota Network in 1999 through the Connecting the Schools Project. The purpose of the project was to continue the effort to put educational technologies to work in the newly wired schools. The project consisted of three phases. In Phase I, the network infrastructure was completed, connecting every school in the state to the Digital Dakota Network, South Dakota's statewide data and video Intranet. In Phase II, data networking was established in schools, and interactive video equipment was placed in middle and high schools throughout the state. Phase III was the creation of a distance learning infrastructure, which included the following:

- Resources and opportunities for educators, students, and the workforce.
- Workshops providing participants with an overview of distance education, teaching techniques, and an understanding of the South Dakota plan for distance education.
- Technology for Teaching and Learning Academies (TTLs), providing intensive training for teachers and administrators to increase technology skills and explore issues related to technology planning, acquisition, and integration in curriculum and instruction.
- Distance Teaching and Learning Academies (DTLs), providing teachers with intensive 3-week sessions on the use of video conferencing equipment and instructional design for distance learning. Specifically, the training of teachers provides competence in core technology skills and the ability to use available technologies to enhance the curriculum, instruction, and assessment. In addition, it was determined that distance education should be used to provide staff development for teachers, including competence in classroom management, school district continuous improvement, and techniques of collaborative learning.

As part of Connecting the Schools activities, schools were equipped with state-of-the-art interactive telecommunication equipment for distance education obtained as a gift from the US WEST Foundation. Approximately 200 schools were equipped with equipment and connected to the Digital Dakota Network. The network was used to provide thousands of hours of instruction and hundreds of educational meetings and staff development programs during its first 2 years of operation. More recently, the state of South Dakota has begun to more fully utilize the network. Educators were trained to be effective at teaching distant learners at the DTLs, special staff development sessions that complemented the TTLs. The Wiring the Schools and Connecting the Schools Projects, and the Digital Dakota Network were funded by the state, or from grants from the private sector, notably the US WEST Foundation.

South Dakota's Approach to Distance Education

Distance education has been variously defined and a number of theories about it have been offered (Simonson, Smaldino, Albright, & Zvacek, 2000). South Dakotans studied this literature and redefined the innovation of distance education. South Dakota's definition is based on a belief about the practice of distance education that may become a model for the future application of this technology in the United States. Distance education is defined in South Dakota as

> formal, institutionally-based educational activities where the teacher and learner are normally separated from each other, and where two-way, inter-active telecommunication systems are used to connect them for the syn-chronous and asynchronous sharing of video, data, and voice instruction (Simonson, 2003).

This definition requires several conditions:

- Local control of the distance education curriculum by school boards, school administrators, and teachers
- Partnerships of educators who plan together, share resources, and cooperate to meet needs
- Implementation of distance education using existing educational institutions
- Instruction planned and coordinated by classroom teachers who are supported by other professionals
- Use of a tiered approach to the delivery of educational experiences that involves regional partnerships and statewide alliances so that hundreds of instructional events can occur simultaneously
- Widespread access to a user-friendly and inexpensive network that permits the flexible offering of a variety of distance education experiences
- Availability of a large number of trained teachers, knowledgeable administrators, and prepared students

In South Dakota, this definition and these principles provide the foun-dation for distance education in the state. The state Department of Educa-tion has the responsibility for what may be the linchpins for the success of distance education in the state—the availability of a large number of trained teachers, knowledgeable administrators, and prepared students.

Distance education is possible because of the immense capacity of the Digital Dakota Network and the large number of teachers trained through the Distance Teaching and Learning Academies and Technology for Teaching and Learning Academies. It is based on several principles:

- Effective teaching strategies for local students are also effective teaching strategies for distance learners.
- Careful and appropriate planning of teaching and learning activities improves learning experiences for both local and distant students.
- Instructional strategies should be matched to desired learning outcomes; a variety of strategies should be used for both local and distant learners.
- Technologies should be flexible and compatible with a variety of teaching styles and should be expandable so that new approaches can be easily incorporated.
- Telecommunication technologies should link teachers with learners, and learners with learners, in as unobtrusive and realistic a manner as possible.
- Distance education is a credible and effective strategy for teaching and learning.

Educational Telecommunication in South Dakota

South Dakota has long been recognized for its commitment to excellence in education. The state is also nationally known for innovation in education. Perhaps the best example of both excellence and innovation can be seen in the pioneering role the state has played in the emerging field of educational telecommunication. In South Dakota, the use of various telecommunication technologies dates back several decades, long before the benefits of this form of educational delivery were widely recognized. The expertise in educational telecommunication gained by South Dakota educators has also resulted in model teacher training programs.

In summary, the technology initiatives in South Dakota are part of a comprehensive plan to infuse technology throughout the state, and to provide technology skills to students, teachers, administrators, government employees, and the workforce. These efforts provided the foundation for the South Dakota Alliance for Distance Education, South Dakota's Star Schools project. According to E. M. Rogers (1995), innovations must be made available before they can be adopted.

THE SOUTH DAKOTA ALLIANCE FOR DISTANCE EDUCATION: SOUTH DAKOTA'S STAR SCHOOLS PROJECT

The South Dakota Alliance for Distance Education: South Dakota's Star Schools Project (SDADE) originated as a consequence of a funded proposal written during the spring of 2001 to the United States Department of Education's Star School Program. The proposal was submitted and funded for $3 million. The funded SDADE proposal has 6 goals, 23 objectives, and 56 activities. The approach taken by the SDADE was to identify partners who would receive contracts to complete SDADE activities. Generally, the purpose of the project was to expedite the adoption of distance education and the DDN by teachers and schools. Star Schools funding made it possible for South Dakota Department of Education leaders to add more diffusion activities to their plan and to expand the scope of existing efforts.

The SDADE Partners

The South Dakota Alliance for Distance Education partners fell into three categories:

- *Management*. The project was administered by the South Dakota Department of Education (formerly the Department of Education and Cultural Affairs).
- *South Dakota partners*. These included the state's public broadcasting system, local education agencies, public universities, professional education organizations, the Technology and Innovation in Education (TIE) project, and the Mitchell Technical Institute.
- *External partners*. Out-of-state partners included the U.S. Distance Learning Association, the Instructional Technology and Distance Education Program at Nova Southeastern University (Florida), and Technology Research and Evaluation Systems (a project evaluation firm).

The intent of having many and varied partners was to expand the impact of diffusion efforts by including more in the efforts. As many education organizations as possible were given the opportunity to become a part of the South Dakota Alliance for Distance Education. Special emphasis was on teachers, especially teacher opinion leaders.

The Evaluation Plan

Evaluation activities relied heavily on both qualitative and quantitative data collection and analysis. Data were collected as diffusion efforts were conducted.

Evaluation personnel systematically monitored all aspects of the progress of the diffusion process and used both formative and summative strategies. Formative evaluation made it possible for education department personnel to adjust aspects of the diffusion process as needed.

The use of qualitative data proved to be an integral part of the evaluation plan. In addition to the use of open-ended survey questions, the evaluation team used methods involving focus groups, interviews, and observational techniques for data collection. Qualitative study provides a way to collect data in close proximity to a specific situation. It provided a richness that enabled the complexity of the situation to be revealed and to go beyond answering the questions of what and how many. Qualitative methods were used to collect data about the factors that influenced use, acceptance, and effectiveness of distance education.

Several additional activities were conducted to support the overall efforts to determine the success of the diffusion process. These activities were more like research than evaluation, but were designed to relate directly to the overall purpose—to determine the status of the adoption of distance education in South Dakota and to identify what events were successful and what activities were needed to continue the adoption of this innovation.

First, a number of site visits were conducted to examine firsthand the schools' use of distance education and the Digital Dakota Network. Thirty-one schools were each visited by two evaluators for about a day. Administrators were interviewed, students and teachers participated in focus groups, and DDN classrooms were visited and photographed (more than a hundred photos were taken). A short, but detailed, report was written about each school and the results of the site visit (Simonson, 2003).

About 6 months after the site visits were completed, 11 school superintendents from the districts visited were contacted and interviewed. The interviews were conducted by telephone over a period of several months. The purpose of these interviews was to determine the role that rural school superintendents played in the process of the adoption of distance education (Calderone, 2003). To that end, the interview included four questions: The first question asked the superintendents how they perceived their role in change related to distance education and the Digital Dakota Network; the second, tapping motivation, asked about reasons for using distance education via the network; the third asked how they envisioned the district using distance education in the future; and the fourth asked how they thought declining population and student census trends would impact the network.

Finally, a survey was sent to a random sample of South Dakota teachers drawn from a list supplied by the state Department of Education. The survey was sent twice, once at the beginning of the project and again near its conclusion. The questionnaire had four sections. The first section asked demographic questions. The second was a modified version of the Hurt, Joseph, and Cook (1977) Innovativeness Survey (IS), a standardized measure of personal innovativeness. The third was a modified version of the Hurt and Tiegen (1977) Perceived Organizational Innovativeness Scale (PORGI), a test used to identify employees' opinions about the innovativeness of their organizations (in this case, the schools where the teachers worked). The IS and PORGI have been used in hundreds of studies and have comprehensive normative data available for comparison purposes (Simonson, 2000). The final section asked specific questions about distance education in the state and the Digital Dakota Network.

Evaluation Results

South Dakota teacher profile. A questionnaire was used to answer the following question:

> What are the characteristics of South Dakota teachers, including their personal innovativeness, their perceptions of their schools' innovativeness, and their attitudes about distance education in South Dakota?

The teachers' responses indicated that the Dakota Digital Network had not yet achieved the level of use of other educational technologies. Teachers were unsure of where and how the use of an interactive technology like this fit into their curriculum. Elementary-level students, they said, had less access to the system than secondary students.

Hopefully, the positive attitudes of educators toward the DDN will evolve toward this teacher's response to the survey:

> The DDN is really going to be something we will be using daily. We just need to adjust our thinking. We have so much technology here, I get excited about what we can do with it; it's taking us a while to get integrated. But it's valuable.

Site visits. In order to truly understand the status of distance education in the schools of South Dakota, one would need to visit many, if not most, of them; the evaluation team attempted to provide this understanding by visiting more than 30 schools. Its comprehensive report on those visits (Simonson, 2003) leaves one with the feeling that teachers are generally optimistic about distance education, but have not yet seen the positive impact of this innovation on themselves, their schools, or their students.

Superintendent interviews. *Themes and patterns of response.* Certain themes and patterns emerged from the responses to the questions. All the respondents thought it was their responsibility to ensure financial support for the Digital Dakota Network, and most of them were directly concerned with using the network to meet student needs for courses not offered in the district; indeed, the perception that student needs were to be met by receiving courses over the network rather than by adding them to the regular curriculum appeared to be the norm in the rural school districts. Also running through the interviews was an expansionary vision for the future, including using the network for professional development for teachers, increasing the use of the network for meetings, getting the community to use the network, new uses of the network for younger children in K–3, and enabling teachers to "meet" with teachers on other networks throughout the district and state. Less encouraging was a frequently mentioned lack of interest in having staff teachers teach over the network, on the part of both the superintendent and the teachers themselves.

Findings. The first interview question related to perception of role. All the superintendents interviewed perceived their role as ensuring financial support to keep the network going. More than half (64%), however, said they were not directly involved in ensuring that the network was operational. Almost half (45%) viewed their role as promoting the network and directly overseeing educational opportunities for students. While most superintendents (73%) perceived their role as encouraging teachers to use the network as a resource and urged the teachers to use it for educational opportunities, almost all of the superintendents said they did not perceive it as their role to encourage teachers to teach over the network.

The second interview question asked about motivation to use distance education. To this question, 82% of the superintendents responded that their motivation to use distance education was based on student needs as assessed within the school district. About 73% were very interested in using it for advanced classes or "specialty" electives, and 45% wanted to use it for courses not offered by the school district. About 27% of the superintendents told the interviewers that meetings were a low-priority use of the Digital Dakota Network, although they also said, in response to the third question, that in the future they would like to use the network for more meetings. Teacher incentives were identified as a motivation for using the network by 55% of the superintendents. But, they went on to say, there were no substantial incentives or rewards for teaching over the network in their districts, so teachers had little motivation to put in the additional time needed to prepare and teach a distance education course.

The third question concerned the superintendents' vision for the future of distance education in their districts. Their responses revealed that almost half (45%) viewed the network as a way to provide professional staff development for teachers. An additional 36% saw community use of the network as becoming increasingly important; 18% thought the network could be used to teach preschool and kindergarten; and another 18% said that because teacher-to-teacher support was successful in their school districts, they felt that more teacher-to-teacher meetings would be an important use for the network.

The fourth question concerned the impact of external factors on the Digital Dakota Network, specifically, the declining population and student census trends. All the superintendents said they either shared information on current and projected trends or made it available to teachers. Some respondents (18%) thought the network was a possible solution to the problem of keeping the school district viable.

Recommendations

As discussed above, the study found that superintendents had a vested interest in the Digital Dakota Network; that they perceived their primary role in the network as ensuring adequate financial support and ensuring that the network was available as an educational resource; and that they had little interest in encouraging teachers within their school districts to teach over the network, and the teachers' motivation to do so was low because the incentives were inadequate. These findings suggest the following recommendations:

1. Encourage school superintendents to take a more active role in motivating teachers to teach distance education courses.
2. Advise school superintendents to set measurable goals for utilizing the Digital Dakota Network and review the goals on an annual basis.
3. Encourage school superintendents to identify "teaching at a distance" opportunities at a high level and mandate that teachers teach at a distance.
4. Support superintendents to be instrumental in setting yearly goals within teacher development plans for teaching at a distance through strategic planning goals and objectives.
5. Provide workshops targeted at superintendents regarding uses of the Digital Dakota Network.
6. Provide school superintendents with organization adoption information and implementation strategies.

7. Involve teachers at some level in the decision-making process for teaching at a distance, at both the local and state level.
8. Provide teacher incentives at the state level to teach at a distance.
9. At a state level, utilize the Digital Dakota Network for on-going professional development programs for teachers, perhaps refresher courses and short in-services that demonstrate the use of the network.

Conclusions

The state of South Dakota continues to evaluate the adoption or rejection of distance education as an innovation over time. The adoption of distance education and utilization of the Digital Dakota Network is considered by South Dakota as an alternative and a new means of solving an educational resource problem in South Dakota (Rogers, 1995). In this study, school superintendents were interviewed by telephone concerning their perception of their role in distance education and the Digital Dakota Network. It can be concluded from the results of this study that distance education in South Dakota has not reached the point of critical mass. Rogers describes *critical mass* as the point at which an innovation such as distance education diffuses without the need for direct intervention by change agents. Schools and teachers are adopting distance education in South Dakota, but it is apparent from the results of the study that continued intervention by change agents from the South Dakota Department of Education is necessary.

The final and summary evaluation statements offered by the team of evaluators that examined the South Dakota Alliance for Distance Education are organized around the five-part AEIOU approach, which focuses on Accountability, Effectiveness, Impact, Organizational context, and Unanticipated consequences. These observations are derived from the many and varied activities of the evaluation team over a multiyear time frame.

ACCOUNTABILITY

Did those involved in the diffusion of distance education activities do what they said they were going to do?

Undoubtedly, the majority of the planned activities of the Department of Education were accomplished. Data collected by evaluators clearly indicated that most of what were identified as activities were accomplished.

EFFECTIVENESS

How well were diffusion activities implemented?

Undoubtedly, the tasks accomplished by those involved with encouraging the adoption of distance education were well done, of high quality, and relevant to the needs of South Dakota educators. It was apparent to evaluators that Department of Education leaders expected and received outstanding and high-quality work.

IMPACT

Did diffusion efforts make a difference?

Impact is by far the most difficult category of evaluation to positively identify. It was recommended by evaluators that relevant activities be continued, and that continuing efforts be made by the South Dakota Department of Education to assist schools and teachers who wish to adopt distance education. Teachers report a high degree of receptivity to this innovation, but indicated that they need continued support through training and incentives. Distance education generally, and the DDN specifically, have had impact, but not to the extent hoped. More distance education activities by the Department of Education technology team are needed.

ORGANIZATIONAL CONTEXT

What structures, policies, or events in South Dakota helped or hindered?

The organizational context that supported diffusion activities was found by evaluators to be quite effective in scope, if not in scale. More of the same kinds of efforts are needed to continue the growth of distance education and use of the DDN.

UNANTICIPATED CONSEQUENCES

What changes or consequences of importance happened as a result of diffusion activities that were not anticipated?

Three interesting consequences are worthy of note. First, a number of new professionals were given the opportunity to become leaders and to exercise considerable latitude in the development of distance education. A number of persons at the South Dakota Department of Education, at public universities, and in schools were given the opportunity to demonstrate their industry and insights about how education in South Dakota in the future might be better practiced. These persons will most likely continue to play leadership roles in the education community in the state.

Second, a nationwide, even international, network of colleagues has been developed because of the activities of the Department of Education. Project staff have presented by invitation at a number of national conferences and in two instances at international events. People make projects successful, and people with a broad range of experiences and professional relationships are more likely to be able to continue the process of educational innovation. South Dakota is blessed with a larger number of such individuals.

Finally, South Dakota has a national reputation. It is recognized as a leader in distance education and in the diffusion of innovations using teachers as the primary change agents in this process. The model of diffusion followed both by design and by chance in South Dakota is a model for other states and regions. They have implemented a successful innovation—distance education—in the state, and the process they followed is a case study for the theory of diffusion of innovations described by Rogers (1995). Other organizations should study the model used in South Dakota.

LESSONS LEARNED: THE DIFFUSION PROCESS IN SOUTH DAKOTA

The Model

In South Dakota, the diffusion of innovation process (Rogers, 1995) was followed. Three characteristics of Rogers's innovation-decision process were stressed in South Dakota: the innovation; knowledge; and persuasion, with particular emphasis on the role of opinion leaders, change agents, and incentives.

The innovation. The Digital Dakota Network was the innovation. It was provided to each school in South Dakota as a fully functional two-way, interactive video network. It was supported by the state at no cost to users.

Knowledge. Teachers, administrators, and eventually even members of the lay community were trained in Distance Teaching and Learning Academies or some modification of this in-depth training activity. During the academies, educators were given the opportunity to try out interactive television and observe firsthand the advantages of this approach to teaching and learning.

Persuasion. *Opinion leaders.* Educators were persuaded to adopt distance education in a number of ways. First, opinion leaders—highly innovative education leaders—were trained in special workshops led by nationally known experts in the field of distance education. Next, the governor hosted a special meeting called Governor Janklow's Capital City Conclave on Distance Education. During this conclave, 12 internationally renowned leaders in distance education were brought to the state where they interacted with 50 education, political, and community leaders who became "ambassadors" for the Digital Dakota Network. These ambassadors were opinion leaders and came from all areas of the state. They were asked to return to their communities and discuss the conclave and support the potential of distance education.

Change agents. A small but highly motivated and trained group of instructional technology and distance education specialists were hired by the Department of Education to promote the use of the DDN. These itinerant technology specialists traveled the state to work with teachers in schools. Their efforts were reminiscent of the county extension workers who historically have diffused agricultural innovations from land-grant colleges to the farmers of a state (Rogers, 1995). Continued intervention by state change agents is needed because distance education has not yet reached the point of critical mass in South Dakota, although efforts to promote adoption have been very successful.

Incentives. A proposal to the U.S. Department of Education's Star Schools Program was written and funded. This grant was used to support teacher efforts related to the adoption of distance education. Thematic units were produced, videos were developed, Web pages were put online, training was offered, and additional classrooms were attached to the DDN to improve the relative advantages offered by the DDN and to show teachers the many opportunities possible because of distance education.

The Results

Evaluation efforts of this project, called the South Dakota Alliance for Distance Education, indicated that it was very successful in speeding the adoption of distance education. Rogers's (1995) suggestions have been used in

South Dakota and have been largely successful. The innovation has been made available, knowledge of its advantages has been disseminated, and adopters have been provided opportunities to observe, try, and make this innovation compatible with existing values about how teaching and learning should occur.

Finally, South Dakota's use of Rogers's theory is a model for other states, regions, and organizations that wish to diffuse distance education effectively. As the old midwestern saying has it, "The farmer does not look down at the ground but at the end of the field to plow straight rows."

PART III

Summing Up

Planning for Success: A Road Map to the Future

Tom Clark & Zane L. Berge

I N THIS CHAPTER we summarize the key issues and lessons learned
that were identified in previous chapters, discuss a basic road map for
success, and look at the implications of key findings for the future. We
seek to answer the following questions:

- How are virtual schools addressing key issues in planning for
  success?
- What are some important lessons learned by different types of virtual schools?
- Is there a basic road map for success for schools considering virtual
  learning?
- What are the implications for the future of virtual learning?

HOW VIRTUAL SCHOOLS ADDRESS KEY ISSUES IN PLANNING FOR SUCCESS

Access and equity are overriding issues for virtual school planners. As
Hernandez points out in Chapter 2, virtual schools offer the promise of
bringing minority and low-income learners equitable access to a challenging curriculum, and a real opportunity for academic success. But research
on the role of virtual schools in closing the access and achievement gaps

has been limited. Virtual schools should recognize the barriers to success-ful participation that minority and low-income students face, and the need to ensure high expectations and effective support mechanisms if they are to succeed. High-need schools still lag in their ability to meet the technol-ogy needs of students studying online. Frequently, virtual schools and local school sites are challenged to provide the range of online and on-site sup-port that is needed to move from access to success. To meet equity goals, more resources must be devoted to dedicated on-site mentors and online teachers, tutors, mentors, and support staff. The question is where these resources will come from.

In Chapter 3, Freedman describes how *technology* acts as the founda-tion of virtual schools. Technologies play a critical role in the creation, delivery, administration, and measurement of the educational services that virtual schools offer. Five technology applications comprise this founda-tion: school portals, student information systems, course management sys-tems, course content, and assessment systems. These systems can "talk" to one another in a cycle of improvement. At the heart of virtual school operation is the course management system (CMS), a complex and ever-changing educational operating system that is the largest nonpersonnel budget item for the virtual school. The higher education experience with the CMS is instructive for virtual school planners. Most CMSs are still course-centric, built around traditional education models. Whether to outsource the CMS operation or run it on local servers is an early key de-cision, and here schools should consider their internal IT capabilities. The CMS decision is a difficult one for virtual school planners, who should devote significant time to this issue. As Freedman notes, in virtual educa-tion, technology is not secondary to education, but underlies it, and helps create a new type of educational culture. In the future, technologies may unite the virtual and the physical school.

At the center of the success formula for most virtual schools lies *fund-ing*. In Chapter 4, Cavalluzzo notes the need to align program goals with a funding model at the beginning of the planning process, paying special attention to the implications of the state's school funding laws. She also points out that the economies of scale available to large programs make them more cost-effective, but warns that planners seeking to form consor-tiums need to consider whether their potential partners have the same goals and can make equivalent investments. Funding is also a key issue in the controversy over virtual charter schools; Cavalluzzo raises questions about the actual cost of operating these schools and about the impact of their funding models on public education.

Determining the best *curriculum* to meet academic and school improve-ment needs through a virtual school is a key issue early on. As noted by

Newman, Stein, and Trask (2003), adopting or developing core and supplemental content and reference resources, curriculum assessment methods, and instructional design and curriculum development processes are among the key tasks in building an effective virtual school curriculum. Our case studies describe various approaches to curricular development. Establishing a curricular model grounded in theory can enhance educational quality; as described by Friend and Johnston in Chapter 7, Florida Virtual School uses a course development model that integrates Gagne's Nine Events of Instruction and Bloom's taxonomy to provide relevant, standards-aligned content and activities. A strong curriculum assessment process was the key to establishing quality across the courses of the LUDA Virtual High School collaborative described by Vrasidas and Chamberlain in Chapter 12, and extensive collaboration between partners made it possible to develop a shared curriculum across many school districts.

Virtual schools must also build their *capacity for instruction*, developing teaching and support staff capabilities to offer core instruction and student tutoring. At Florida Virtual School, all instructors undergo extensive training in using the school's highly facilitated, interactive instructional method and ongoing professional development after that. The Virtual High School developed a strong model for online professional development of its widely distributed teachers, to prepare them as online instructors and mentor them as teachers, as described in Chapter 8 by Pape, Adams, and Ribeiro.

Providing adequate and effective *academic services* is a key issue for virtual schools. Registration, guidance counseling, and transcript and diploma services are core services here, and parents and students may vary widely in their support needs. Virtual schools that work with local schools often partner on academic services; the University of Missouri–Columbia High School described by Smalley in Chapter 11 found such partnerships key in establishing complementary academic services, and the Web Academy described by Jordan in Chapter 10 upped the quality of basic academic services by tapping staff resources that are often overlooked.

Policy and administration issues concern both the policy framework within which a virtual school operates and the operational practices the virtual school uses in program management. Policy and practice are linked. For example, state-level policies on what constitutes school attendance dictate school funding models, which in turn may shape the financial operations of the virtual school. In Chapter 5, Blomeyer and Dawson describe important aspects of policy and practice.

Marketing and public relations can build internal and external stakeholder support for the virtual school and help keep client organizations well informed on key issues. In Chapter 6, Stefanski describes the efforts of Michigan Virtual High School in this area. Beginning with the school's broad program goals and objectives, a cost-effective strategy was developed for promoting a wide array of product offerings to subscribing member schools. A broad range of marketing-mix elements was considered in order to determine the combination that worked best. This included development of a branding strategy that integrated outgoing messages and promotional efforts.

Some virtual schools, especially the larger ones, have developed extensive *program assessment* capabilities. The University of California Preparatory Initiative (see Chapter 2), Florida Virtual School, and the Virtual High School have all commissioned major external evaluations to help improve their programs and meet stakeholder and accountability needs. The South Dakota Alliance for Distance Education project described by Simonson in Chapter 13 successfully used interviews, surveys, and site visits to assess the implementation of its statewide e-learning program.

SOME IMPORTANT LESSONS LEARNED BY VIRTUAL SCHOOLS

The lessons learned by different types of virtual schools reflect their differing purposes. Florida Virtual School is probably the largest and best-known *state-level virtual school*. To grow its enrollments, it has developed national and international markets that help subsidize the cost of offering its courses in Florida. Its extensive enrollments are also a reflection of the high quality of its program and academic services. The FLVS mission focuses on providing a flexible, high-quality education for all learners. Part of the school's purpose is to help the state attain educational equity goals. It conducts extensive outreach to high-growth schools and small, underserved rural schools throughout Florida. Struggling and underserved schools and students receive priority, and the school has managed to maintain an 85% course success rate. State per-student funding is contingent on student success, and Florida Virtual School actively supported the move to this performance-based funding model.

The growth of the *collaborative virtual school* movement can be attributed in part to the success of the Virtual High School, now VHS, Inc. In this model, the local school acts as both virtual school provider and consumer, with each school providing a teacher and course and in turn receiving a classroom of virtual seats for its students. Because such a model cannot work effectively without a strong focus on maintaining quality standards across all courses, instruction, and learning, VHS, Inc., created strong models for teacher development and course quality, including a widely recognized online professional development system for its instructors. The buy-in of school-level partners, which provide consortium and teacher training fees, helped make the Virtual High School a sustainable enterprise after its 5-year federal grant ended in 2002; in working with many partners, effective communication, feedback, and collaboration mechanisms were critical. Other collaboratives must address the same issues to succeed.

Virtual charter schools are part of the educational choice movement promoted by No Child Left Behind. Depending on state charter school law, these quasi-public virtual schools may be funded directly by the state or through deductions in local public school budgets. Much of the American public's focus on virtual schools, positive or negative, is on virtual charter schools. Homeschooling parents have also been divided over the cyber charters, which bring a free public school curriculum and state educational standards into home instruction. In Chapter 9, Baker, Bouras, Hartwig, and McNair examine the partnership between the Colorado Virtual Academy, a statewide virtual school, and K12, Inc., a for-profit company that is one of the major curriculum providers for virtual charter schools. To succeed, virtual charter schools need to offer a high-quality curriculum like K12, Inc.'s. They must support parents with varying levels of homeschooling and teaching experience. K12, Inc., is building curriculum over time through the grade levels, raising interesting questions about how it will support students and working parents as its students grow older. Issues with quality and retention in some virtual charter schools could be addressed through transparent evaluation practices. Since the public as a whole is not supportive of educational choice mechanisms, such as vouchers or virtual charter schools, political savvy and effective public relations skills are important for virtual charter school success.

Many public school districts operate or participate in virtual learning programs, or *virtual public schools*, offering anything from a course or two to a full program online. These local education agencies are usually focused on meeting their own academic and school improvement needs, although in some cases their efforts have given rise to regional or state-level virtual schools. The actual impact of virtual schooling on school improvement is unclear and needs more study. The Cumberland County Schools Web Academy found that intelligent risk taking is essential to successfully create, support, and develop a virtual school program within a public school district. The development of the virtual public school is often hampered by policies and funding rules. Realistic expectations must be created about what constitutes program success. Those starting a virtual public school program should proactively build organizational knowledge through collaboration and peer networking.

University-based virtual schools meet university service and outreach goals. They began as independent study high schools in the 1920s, and have struggled with a slow decline in enrollments in recent years. Some, such as the University of Missouri–Columbia High School, are making a successful transition to online learning programs. Those that have attained both regional accreditation and state approval for their diploma programs may be best positioned for success in terms of enrollments and perceived value. The ability to offer their own diplomas helps university-based virtual schools reach homeschool and out-of-school populations, but the local public school continues to be the key market for many. UMHS administrators have found it critical to reemphasize the win-win relationships they form with budget-conscious local schools, and to clearly distinguish themselves from online charter schools that may drain students and funds. Given university budget shortfalls, university-based virtual schools must focus on positive public relations both on and off campus to ensure continued success.

Virtual private schools are a sixth type of virtual school organization. These schools usually serve a specific type of student not well served by public schools, such as students and parents preferring religious home instruction, but otherwise are similar to virtual public and virtual charter schools. Students and parents have high expectations of these virtual private schools, which often rely wholly on their support. Only a limited number of virtual private schools are regionally accredited or state approved, which helps guarantee transcript acceptance by other schools and by colleges.

University-based and other collaborative virtual schools often exist within *large-scale technology integration programs*. Two chapters describe collaboratives that have dealt with the attendant issues successfully enough to serve as useful templates for others: LUDA Virtual High School and the South Dakota Alliance on Distance Education.

In e-learning initiatives led by universities or state agencies seeking to more broadly support the integration of technology into teaching and learning, universities often act as e-learning providers to schools in their region, providing activities such as professional development in technology integration skills. A recurrent problem has been that some of these universities continue to implement top-down models at a time when schools have expanding virtual options for e-learning services, instead of responding to the new realities of competition in their regional e-learning markets. LUDA Virtual High School enabled Western Illinois University to bring an e-learning model based on local development and control into K–12 schools by creating an online curriculum and learning management system in which local teachers instruct their own students online. Training of on-site personnel, clear policies, and effective coordination were critical to success.

States have made efforts to change local teaching practices toward more integration of technology into teaching and learning, often with limited success. The South Dakota Alliance for Distance Education enabled the state to disseminate and encourage adoption of virtual learning methods by having nationally known experts train education opinion leaders to provide hands-on workshops for local educators. Extensive research showed these statewide efforts were largely successful and worthy of recommendation to other states seeking to improve technology integration in schools.

A ROAD MAP FOR SUCCESS FOR SCHOOLS CONSIDERING VIRTUAL LEARNING

The question, Is there a road map? is more easily answered for the local school considering a virtual learning program than for other types of organizations considering becoming virtual school providers. While our focus here is on the basic steps that the local school should consider, the steps described are applicable to a wide variety of organizations exploring development of a virtual school.

Determine Needs, Then Solutions

The vision of offering a virtual school program must be grounded in the reality of needs, resources, and capabilities. Because of the widespread interest in them, virtual schools are sometimes a solution in search of a problem. Watkins and Kaufman (2002) note that a need is a gap in institutional results, which must be identified so that possible solutions can be identified, prioritized, and justified. It is important not to short-circuit the needs assessment process and jump right to a solution.

For some schools, such as those who simply want to add a course or two to the existing curriculum via an external provider, an extensive planning process is probably not needed. For others, which foresee considerable expense and the establishment of a new educational program, it will pay in the long term to conduct a more thorough planning process up front.

Local Virtual Learning Programs: Follow Your Own Path

It is our belief that academic and school improvement needs should drive the consideration of a virtual learning program by a local public or private school. Before committing to a virtual school solution and considering "build or buy" decisions with vendors and other external parties, schools should lay out the framework:

- Create a school planning group.
- Identify school improvement needs.
- Identify desired student outcomes.
- Target student audiences.
- Identify appropriate curricula to meet needs.

Create a planning group. A small planning group with a shared interest in exploring a possible virtual school program is a good place to start. It is helpful if the group represents a cross section of school or district staff from the beginning. Work with this group to assess needs and capabilities.

Identify school improvement needs. Academic needs should drive the development of any new educational program. A local, regional, or statewide education agency may have specific school improvement needs that it believes a virtual school program can address. Many schools already have this information from school improvement processes. The range of current and potential programs that might help meet the needs should be considered, and the potential role of a virtual school program established. School improvement plans may suggest specific areas where targeted improvement is needed to meet No Child Left Behind goals or other equity goals over time.

Of course, it would be naive not to acknowledge the role that parent, student, and staff interest in virtual schools can play in bringing about the initial consideration of virtual learning options and in fostering a positive climate for virtual schooling. But these interests should be subordinate to school improvement needs during the planning process.

Identify desired student outcomes. Most school improvement plans center around specific student outcomes that need improvement over time, in areas such as student achievement and dropout and graduation rates. Schools are generally required to set annual yearly progress targets for improvement across student subgroups. The education agency may consider using a virtual school program as an option for making progress toward these goals.

Target student audiences. Which student subgroups need to be targeted to improve these outcomes? No Child Left Behind subgroups should be considered, such as minority students, students with limited English proficiency, students with disabilities, students at risk of dropping out, dropouts, expelled students, and students who have failed courses or need other remedial assistance. The role of the school in supporting all learners may also involve reaching out to homeschoolers and offering educational access for homebound students, pregnant students, and new mothers. College preparatory students are a frequent focus of virtual schools. Federal funding can help support minority and low-income student access to online Advanced Placement courses and exam preparation.

Identify curricula. What new or enhanced curricula might be offered to help improve specific outcomes for the students identified? While these preliminary curricular decisions should not be written in stone, they are important in providing an effective focus to the program early on. It is important not to let student or parental interest drive initial curricular decisions. Vendors usually offer a wide range of courses and supplemental materials. Don't let their menus drive your curriculum planning either. Rather, see them as resources that make multiple options possible.

The Virtual School Option

Once school improvement needs, desired outcomes, audiences, and curricula have been considered, it makes sense to begin to focus on whether a virtual school program is an option for meeting these needs:

- Build organizational knowledge of virtual schools.
- Assess readiness of key stakeholders for a virtual school option.
- Prioritize needs related to a virtual school.
- Consider alternatives to a virtual school for meeting identified needs.
- Determine costs and benefits.
- Create a vision.
- Prepare the case for a virtual school.

Build organizational knowledge. It may help to identify and contact administrators of virtual schools created in similar circumstances to meet similar needs. Available listings of virtual schools can serve as one starting point. The local school may want to contact specific virtual schools or vendors identified by its own research or recommended by peer organizations. There are a few annual conferences devoted to virtual schools and many others where it is a topical track, including state educational technology conferences. Conference links posted to related Web sites and archived conference presentations and documents online may help meet virtual school planning needs. In general, schools should conduct a self-directed search for information on the range of solutions before committing to a particular provider or product.

Readiness assessment. Gauge the readiness of the school board and administration (or other organizational leadership) to consider new programs. Identify issues that might impede success.

Prioritize needs. Based upon a review of short- and long-term school improvement needs, technology and strategic plans, and other evidence, what specific school or district needs emerge that might be addressed through a virtual school program?

Consider alternatives. Is a virtual school program a viable option given existing programs or new program alternatives that might meet the same need? Identify the alternatives. Why is a virtual school program the best alternative, or deserving of being included in a range of options for learners? It may help to create a comparison matrix (see Table 14.1).

Determine costs and benefits. How does the virtual school program stack up against other methods of achieving the same goals? For example, if new curricula are available via this option, what are ballpark figures for providing these courses by other methods? What concrete benefits might result if the program achieved its goals?

Create a vision. Discuss how a virtual school program might relate to your preferred future as a school or district. Develop a simple vision or mission statement that summarizes what you hope the program will accomplish. Involve representatives of key internal stakeholder groups, such as administrators, teachers, and the school board in creating the vision.

Prepare the case for a virtual school. A summary document proposing a virtual learning program should be developed for use with the school board and other decision-making bodies of the school. It should integrate the process that led the planning team to recommend the virtual school option.

First Steps

At this point, the school board is poised to make its virtual school decision. If the decision is made to move ahead, some mainly internal efforts remain:

Table 14.1. Comparison Matrix for Virtual High School and On-Site Programs

School Improvement or Strategic Need of School or District	How a Virtual School Program Might Address That Need/Audiences	Existing Programs That Address This Need	Potential Importance of Virtual School Option in Meeting This Need
Improve graduation rate	Target remedial and elective courses to individual student needs	On-site alternative high school On-site summer school	Low to medium
Offer more rigorous courses to improve college prospects of graduates, including NCLB subgroups	Provide additional AP and dual enrollment courses Target AP courses to NCLB subgroups and/or free or reduced-price lunch students	On-site dual enrollment program Two AP courses offered on-site	Medium
Improve achievement of NCLB subgroups on exit exams and college prep tests	Provide supervised virtual coursework in core subjects	Remedial on-site course option	High
Reach out to home-school students to minimize impact on district finances	Target home-school and out-of-district students to generate sufficient enrollments to justify operation	None	Medium

- Set virtual learning program goals and objectives.
- Establish teams in key areas.
- Develop a communication plan, and begin building a positive image and stakeholder support.

Set goals and objectives. Establish goals and objectives. Goals simply clarify your visions. Target objectives are specific activities required to achieve the goals, using baseline data on current status to set quantifiable objectives for attaining a desired status.

Establish teams. Establish teams or subcommittees in different areas, such as curriculum, technology, and budget, as the planning process expands.

Develop a communication plan. Those starting a virtual school program in a school district should proactively address concerns about virtual charter schools and the acceptability of virtual learning through a communication plan that clearly informs key stakeholders, such as the school board, teachers, parents, and the local community, about the actual purpose and activities of the new program. This communication plan is a key part of a long-term marketing and public relations plan.

Build or Partner?

At the same time, many schools will begin seeking partnerships and outsourcing arrangements for at least some virtual school components. The Eduventures model presented by Newman, Stein, and Trask (2003) is a good guide to this process:

- Consider models for short- and long-term needs.
- Consider whether to "build or partner."
- Consider and select virtual learning providers and external partnerships.

Consider models. The planning group might begin by considering possible models for how the virtual learning program might operate in the short and the long term. Different models require the local school to provide different resources and capabilities. For example, offering a few supplemental courses delivered and taught by an external provider will make far fewer demands on staff time and expertise than developing and teaching a new online curriculum locally. But the former model could lead to the latter over time.

Build or partner? This is the point in the planning process where it may be most helpful to consult potential external partners as you consider whether virtual school program components will be handled internally, outsourced, or dealt with through partnerships. Newman, Stein, and Trask (2003) have presented a nice model for categorizing virtual learning program components, which is shown in Figure 14.1.

Consider what resources and competencies are needed and whether the school wants to "build or partner" on each. Teams or subcommittees may be charged with analyzing the gap between current and desired resources and competencies in specific areas. What skills and resources does

Needs Assessment

- Assessment of technology, administrative, and academic needs
- Program funding and financing
- Internal marketing of program
- Evaluation of program needs

Technology Infrastructure	Curriculum	Instruction
• Hardware • Software—learning management system, content management system, administrative applications • Systems integration • Customer IT support • Network management	• Core content • Supplemental content • Reference resources • Assessment capabilities • Instructional design services • Curriculum development services	• Teachers • Academic support (tutors) • Guidance services • Professional development— online teaching strategies

Program Management

- Curriculum and instruction management
- Business and operations management
- Program oversight and coordination
- Continuous evaluation of program performance

Back-end   Front-end
(e.g., systems)   (e.g., teachers)

Figure 14.1. Virtual learning program components. *Source*: Reproduced from *What Can Virtual Learning Do for Your School?* [Web document](Figure A), by A. Newman, M. Stein, and E. Trask. Copyright © 1993 by Eduventures, Inc. Reprinted with permission.

the school currently possess, and which ones might it plan to develop internally? Does the school have time-sensitive deadlines and milestones it needs to attain? This may affect its "build or partner" decisions (Newman, Stein, & Trask, 2003).

Many virtual learning programs are funded with the expectation that they will begin operations by a specific date. Faced with such time frames, many virtual schools choose to begin their programs by outsourcing most functions. These early commitments may constrain their ability to choose the best path for the virtual school later on. But grounding the virtual school program in school improvement needs and considering multiple partnering options can help the school retain ownership of the process.

Consider and select virtual learning providers and external partnerships. No road map can be provided for this stage in the process. Potential partners may have emerged early in the process as the school itself investigated virtual learning options. An opportunity to join a partnership, such as a multischool collaborative, has spurred many local virtual school efforts. At this stage the school should be ready to make informed choices about partners and providers. Many providers in the virtual learning arena have become "e-learning solutions providers," seeking to serve all outsourcing needs of the local virtual school program through a single contract. Schools should consider functions and prices carefully to determine how many vendors to use and what they can do themselves.

Assessing Progress and Demonstrating Success

The success of virtual school program implementation depends on effective program design. The program should be operated on the basis of clearly specified program objectives, which reflect desired outcomes linked to school improvement needs. Program assessment and monitoring is critical for determining whether implementation has been effective in meeting stated objectives, and should provide information for a regular process of revising the program to meet changing needs.

Schools should also consider early on how they will know whether they are achieving their missions and purposes. This will help them avoid surprises down the road that derail program success.

- Institute performance assessment measures at the beginning.
- Continually evaluate the program for improvement and justification purposes.
- Demonstrate and communicate your success.

IMPLICATIONS FOR THE FUTURE OF VIRTUAL LEARNING

The vast majority of virtual school activity today consists of teacher-led courses, often tied to the regular school calendar, using the same kind of unit and exam structure found in regular education. These courses are delivered via networked, Internet-connected desktop or laptop computers. Most virtual schooling for high school credit either is supplemental to regular K–12 school curricula or seeks to provide an acceptable alternative course of study, and therefore providers must conform to the standard educational model. While innovation in educational structure can be seen around the edges, today's teachers, administrators, and parents continue to be locked into the agrarian school year and age-cohort–based educational system of their youth.

For the small minority of students whose parents can stay home or otherwise supervise their participation in homeschooling, virtual learning has expanded educational opportunities. There is now the freedom to develop an individualized home study curriculum that reflects family beliefs and values while incorporating the strengths of standards-based learning. But these families are faced with the dilemma of having to agree to quasi-public education rules to participate in a state-funded virtual charter school. Virtual private schools may meet their needs, but at a higher cost and often with less acceptability of the credentials earned.

Students in regular high schools can supplement their curriculum with online courses. High school students typically add an optional online course to their schedules and have a period scheduled for participation in the virtual class. Moreover, they often continue their work outside the regular school day. Today's students live in a virtual learning environment not bounded by the classroom walls. These proficient technology users often see the Internet as a "virtual backpack, locker, and notebook" (Levin & Arafeh, 2002, p. 13).

In the future, more parents may be able to support a type of virtual school that represents a blend of on-site and virtual, in-school and out, even public and private. One often sees parents today checking up on their children at all hours of the day via cell phone, chatrooms, and e-mail. When today's students are themselves parents, a new type of learning may arise, where some parents supervise a day of community-based, team-oriented virtual learning activities for their high school children from work, rather than in stay at home mom or dad mode. This approach requires a highly active involvement of the parent as counselor, mentor, and friend, a parental role with which today's students are more familiar and comfortable than previous generations. The concept of the public school as responsible for children in the parents' absence would be replaced with the concept of shared responsibility among student, parent, and school for individualized education. Students might be able to add accredited online courses from religious or other agencies (usually on a fee-per-course basis) through public-private portals, while receiving a quality public education.

For most students, school-based virtual learning will continue to be the main model. The best future for virtual learning in schools depends on a paradigm shift in how students learn and in the school itself. The local public or private school can remain a major player in the process, as a community learning center, center of supervised social activities, and source of online and on-site instruction and resources. Workable funding models will be needed. With varying abilities, backgrounds, and levels of parental support, many students today appear to need external structure and motivation to succeed—or is that assumption about students a self-fulfilling prophecy? One key lesson of today's virtual schools may be that given a balance of authority and responsibility for their own learning, most students can gain the skills and knowledge they need to succeed in the new century.

References

Adsit, J. (2003). *Funding online education: A report to the Colorado Education Programs Study Committee.* Denver, CO: Colorado Cyberschool Association. Retrieved May 30, 2004, from http://www.cde.state.co.us/edtech/download/osc-fundingonline.pdf

Alt, M., & Peter, K. (2002). *Private schools: A brief portrait.* Retrieved May 30, 2004, from Almanac of Policy Issues Web site: http://www.policyalmanac.org/education/archive/private_schools.shtml

Anderson, A. B., Craciun, K., Anthes, K., & Ziebarth, T. (2002). *State notes: Charter school finance.* Retrieved May 30, 2004, from http://www.ecs.org/clearinghouse/24/13/2413.htm

Apex Learning. (2003). Online courses—purchase. Retrieved May 30, 2004, from Apex Learning Web site: http://www.apexlearning.com/offerings/online/online_purchase.asp

Archives of the University of Missouri–Columbia. (1904–2003). Record group 8C, record sub-group 8, records title UMC; College of Education; Laboratory School; Administrative Records and Memorabilia. Retrieved May 30, 2004, from http://muarchives.missouri.edu/c-rg8-s8.html

Augenblick, J., Myers, J., & Anderson, A. (1997). Equity and adequacy in school funding. Financing Schools [Special issue]. *The Future of Children, 7*(3), 63–78.

Barker, K., & Wendel, T. (2001). *E-learning: Studying Canada's virtual secondary schools.* Research Series #6. Kelowna, British Columbia, Canada: Society for the Advancement of Excellence in Education. Retrieved May 30, 2004, from http://www.excellenceineducation.ca/publications/A_006_FFA_MID.php

Barnett Reed, J. (2004, February 13). Home is where the school is: But should the public pay for it? And how much is too much? *Arkansas Times,* pp. 11–13.

Becker, H. J. (2000, January). *Findings from the teaching, learning and computing survey: Is Larry Cuban right?* Paper presented at the School Technology Leadership Conference of the Council of Chief State School Officers, Washington, DC. Retrieved May 30, 2004, from www.crito.uci.edu/tlc/findings/ccsso.pdf

Berge, Z. L. (2001). From project management to strategic planning. In Z. L. Berge (Ed.), *Sustaining distance training: Integrating learning technologies into the fabric of the enterprise* (pp. 1–12). San Francisco: Jossey-Bass.

Bielick, S., Chandler, K., & Broughman, S. (2001, July). *Homeschooling in the United States: 1999–2001* (NCES No. 2001-033) Washington, DC: U.S. Department of

Education, National Center for Education Statistics. Retrieved May 30, 2004, from http://nces.ed.gov/pubs2001/2001033.pdf

Bigbie, C. L., & McCarroll, W. J. (2000). *The Florida high school evaluation. 1999–2000 report*. Tallahassee: Florida State University, College of Education Center for Study of Teaching and Learning. Retrieved May 30, 2004, from http://www.flvs.net/_about_us/pdf_au/fhseval_99–00.pdf

Blomeyer, R. (2002). *Online learning for K–12 students. What do we know now*. Retrieved May 30, 2004, from the North Central Regional Education Laboratory Web site: http://www.ncrel.org/tech/elearn/synthesis.pdf

Boss, S. J. (2002, January 8). Virtual charters: Public schooling, at home. *The Christian Science Monitor*, p. 14. Retrieved May 30, 2004, from http://www.csmonitor.com/2002/0108/p14s1–lepr.html

Calderone, T. (2003). *Superintendent's perceptions of their role in the diffusion of distance education*. Unpublished doctoral dissertation, Nova Southeastern University, Fort Lauderdale, FL.

California Department of Education. (2003). Retrieved May 2003, from California Department of Education Web site: http://www.cde.ca.gov

California State University Institute for Education Reform (1999, August). *The Advanced Placement Program: California's 1997–98 Experience*. Sacramento: Author.

Cavalluzzo, L., & Higgins, M. (2001). *Who should fund virtual schools?* Retrieved May 30, 2004, from Appalachian Technology in Education Consortium Web site: http://www.the-atec.org/docDownload.asp?docID=23

Cavalluzzo, L., Fauntleroy, C., & Eline, M. (2003). *Contemplating a public virtual school in your district*. Retrieved May 30, 2004, from http://www.the-atec.org/Archive/conferences/documents/vste_2003_update.pdf.

Cavanaugh, C. S. (2001). The effectiveness of interactive distance education technologies in K–12 learning: A meta-analysis. *International Journal of Educational Telecommunications, 7*(1), 73–88.

Center for Digital Education and the U.S. Department of Education. (2003). *Virtual Schools Forum Report: A Report on the Virtual Schools—A Policy Forum, October 21–22, 2002, Denver, Colorado*. Retrieved May 30, 2004, from NACOL Web site: http://www.nacol.org/docs/DenverVSF_FINAL.pdf

Center for Distance and Independent Study. (2002). *University of Missouri–Columbia high school diploma program student handbook*. Columbia: University of Missouri. Retrieved May 30, 2004, from http://cdis.missouri.edu/MUHighSchool/studenthandbook.htm

Center for Independent Study. (1984). *Report of progress, 1983–1984*. Columbia: University of Missouri.

Center for Independent Study. (1985). *Report of progress, 1984–1985*. Columbia: University of Missouri.

Clark, T. (2000a). *Online professional development: Trends and issues*. Macomb, IL: Western Illinois University, Center for the Application of Information Technologies. Retrieved May 30, 2004, from http://www.dlrn.org/educ/prof_dev.pdf

Clark, T. (2000b). *Virtual high schools: state of the states*. Macomb, IL: Western Illinois University, Center for the Application of Information Technologies.

Retrieved May 30, 2004, from http://www.cait.org/shared_resource_docs/vhs_files/vhs_study.pdf

Clark, T. (2001). *Virtual schools: trends and issues.* Phoenix, AZ: WestEd/Distance Learning Resource Network. Retrieved May 30, 2004, from http://www.wested.org/cs/we/view/rs/610

Clark, T. (2003). Virtual and distance education in American schools. In M. G. Moore & W. G. Anderson (Eds.), *Handbook of distance education* (pp. 673–699). Mahwah, NJ: Erlbaum.

Clark, T., & Else, D. (2003). Distance education, electronic networking, and school policy. In D. R. Walling & J. F. Jennings (Eds.), *Virtual schooling: Issues in the development of e-learning policy* (pp. 31–45). Bloomington, IN: Phi Delta Kappa Educational Foundation.

Clark, T., Lewis, E., Oyer, E., & Schreiber, J. (2002). *Illinois virtual high school evaluation, 2001–2002. Final report.* Springfield: Illinois Mathematics and Science Academy/Illinois State Board of Education. Retrieved May 30, 2004, from http://www.imsa.edu/team/ivhs/pdfs/IVHS_FinalRpt.pdf

Collett, S. (1999, July 19). SWOT analysis. *Computerworld 33*(29), 58. Retrieved May 30, 2004, from http://www.computerworld.com/news/1999/story/0,11280,42968,00.html

Colorado Center for Teaching, Learning and Technology. (2002). United States Open e-Learning Consortium [Project Web site]. Retrieved May 30, 2004, from http://www.ctlt.org/projects/us_open_e_learning/

Core Knowledge Foundation. (2004). About core knowledge. Frequently asked questions. Retrieved May 30, 2004, from http://www.coreknowledge.org/CKproto2/about/FAQ/information.htm

Creighton, T. (2003). *The principal as technology leader.* Thousand Oaks, CA: Corwin Press.

DeBell, M., & Chapman, C. (2003). *Computer and Internet use by children and adolescents in 2001* (NCES No. 2004-014). Washington, DC: U.S. Department of Education, National Center for Education Statistics. Retrieved May 30, 2004, from http://www.nces.ed.gov/pubs2004/2004014.pdf

Dodge, B. (1996). Distance learning on the World Wide Web. In B. Brandon (Ed.), *The Computer trainer's personal training guide* (pp. 223–242). Indianapolis, IN: QueE+T.

Doherty, K. M. (2002, May 9). Students speak out. *Education Week Online, 21*(35), 19, 20, 22–24. Retrieved May 30, 2004, from http://www.edweek.org/sreports/tc02/article.cfm?slug=35florida.h21

Ericson, J., Silverman, D., Bernam, P., Nelson, B., & Solomon, D. (2001). *Challenge and opportunity: The impact of charter schools on school districts.* Washington, DC: U.S. Department of Education, Office of Educational Research and Improvement. Retrieved May 30, 2004, from http://www.ed.gov/rschstat/eval/choice/district_impact.doc

Evans, W., Murray, S., & Schwab, R. (1999). The impact of court-mandated school finance reform. In National Research Council (Ed.), *Education Finance, Issues and Perspectives* (pp. 72–98). Washington, DC: National Academy Press.

Florida Virtual School. (2004). *FLVS fact sheet.* Retrieved May 30, 2004, from: http://www.flvs.net/_about_us/facts.htm

Gagne, R., Briggs, L., & Wagner, W. (1992). *Principles of instructional design* (4th ed.). Ft. Worth, TX: HBJ College Publishers.

Hannum, W. (2001, September/October). Professional development for teaching online. *Technology Source* [Online journal]. Retrieved May 30, 2004, from http://ts.mivu.org/default.asp?show=article&id=898

Hendrie, C. (2003, June 11). Florida raises cyber school's fiscal status. *Education Week.* Retrieved May 30, 2004, from http://www.flvs.net/_about_us/spotlight-ed-week-6-2003.htm

Hernandez, F., et al. (1998). *VHS feasibility study.* Santa Cruz, CA: University of California–Santa Cruz.

Hurt, H., & Teigen, C. (1977). *The development of a measure of perceived organizational innovativeness.* Communication Yearbook I. New Brunswick, NJ: International Communications Association.

Hurt, H., Joseph, K., & Cook C. (1977). Scales for the measurement of innovativeness. *Human Communication Research, 4*(1), 58–65.

Jordan, A. (2002). *An investigation into the effects of online teaching and learning on achievement outcomes at the secondary level.* Unpublished doctoral dissertation, Fayetteville State University, Fayetteville, NC.

K12, Inc. (2001, November). K12 Internet Academy declared Pennsylvania's "highest quality" virtual education option [Press release]. Retrieved May 30, 2004, from http://www.k12.com/news/press_releases/110001.html

Kafer, K. (2003). *Progress on school choice in the states.* Retrieved May 30, 2004, from The Heritage Foundation: Policy Research & Analysis Web site: http://www.heritage.org/Research/Education/bg1639.cfm#pgfId-1017951

Kearsley, G., & Blomeyer, R. (2004). *Preparing K–12 teachers to teach online.* Retrieved May 30, 2004, from http://home.sprynet.com/~gkearsley/TeachingOnline.htm

Kennedy, L. S. (2002). CyberTeaching: the real thing! Comparison of an online secondary physics class and a traditional physics class. *Action Research Exchange, 1*(2). Retrieved May 30, 2004, from http://chiron.valdosta.edu/are/vol1no2/PDF%20article%20manuscript/kennedy.pdf

Kirby, E., & Roblyer, M. (1999, October). A glimpse at the past, an eye to the future: A review of three video-based distance education programs. *Learning and Leading with Technology, 27*(2), 46–52.

Kleiner, A., & Lewis, L. (2003). *Internet access in U.S. public schools and classrooms: 1994–2002* (NCES No. 2004-011). Washington, DC: U.S. Department of Education, National Center for Education Statistics. Retrieved May 30, 2004, from http://www.nces.ed.gov/pubs2004/2004011.pdf

Lane, C. (2000). *Funding sources and methods for K–12 distance education.* Retrieved May 30, 2004, from http://www.dlrn.org/library/dl/funding.pdf

Levin, D., & Arafeh, S. (2002). *The digital disconnect: The widening gap between Internet-savvy students and their schools.* Washington, DC: Pew Internet & American Life Project/American Institutes for Research. Retrieved May 30,

2004, from http://www.pewinternet.org/reports/pdfs/PIP_Schools_Inter
net_Report.pdf

Lorenzo, G. (Ed.). (2002). *The California virtual school report: A national survey of virtual education practice and policy with recommendations for the state of California.* Retrieved May 30, 2004, from http://www.edpath.com/images/ VHSReport.pdf

Maeroff, G. L. (2003). *A classroom of one.* New York: Palgrave MacMillan.

McKenzie, J. (2001, March). How teachers learn technology best. *From Now On, 10*(6). Retrieved May 30, 2004, from http://www.fno.org/mar01/howlearn .html

Metiri Group. (2003). *enGauge 21st century skills: Literacy in the digital age.* Retrieved May 30, 2004, from http://www.metiri.com/features.html

Michigan State University. (2003, July 28). MSU study: Children who spend more time online do better in school [Press release]. Retrieved May 30, 2004, from http://www.ascribe.org/cgi-bin/spew4th.pl?ascribeid=20030728 .063351&time=07%2018%20PDT&year=2003&public=1

Minorini, P. A., & Sugarman, S. D. (1999). School finance litigation in the name of education equity: Its evolution, impact and future, in equity and adequacy. In National Research Council (Ed.), *Education Finance, Issues and Perspectives* (pp. 34–71). Washington, DC: National Academy Press.

Morris, S. (2002). *Teaching and learning online: A step-by-step guide for designing an online K–12 school program.* Lanham, MD: Scarecrow Press.

National Education Association. (2002). *Guide to online high school courses.* Retrieved May 30, 2004, from http://www.nea.org/technology/images/02onlinecourses .pdf

National Education Association. (2003). *Rankings and estimates: Rankings of the states 2002 and estimates of school statistics 2003.* Retrieved May 30, 2004, from http://www.nea.org/edstats/images/03rankings.pdf

National University Continuing Education Association. (1989–90—1998–99). *Independent study program profiles* [Annual report]. Washington, DC: NUCEA.

Na Ubon, A. (2003, March). *Supporting the creation of social presence in asynchronous text-based online learning communities.* Unpublished second-year thesis proposal, Department of Computer Science, University of York, York, UK.

Newman, A., Stein, M., & Trask, E. (2003, September). *What can virtual learning do for your school?* Boston: Eduventures. Retrieved May 30, 2004, from http: //www.eduventures.com/research/industry_research_resources/ virtlearning.cfm

No Child Left Behind Act (NCLB). (2002). Accessed May 2003, from http://www .ed.gov/policy/elsec/leg/esea02/index.html

North American Council for Online Learning (NACOL). (2003, April 21). New K–12 organization named; board of directors announced [Press release]. Retrieved May 30, 2004, from http://www.nacol.org/docs/nacol_press_ release.pdf

North Central Regional Educational Laboratory (NCREL). (2002, April). Virtual schools and e-learning in K-12 environments: Emerging policy and practice

[Special Issue]. *Policy Issues*, no. 11. Retrieved May 30, 2004, from http://www.ncrel.org/policy/pubs/html/pivol11/apr2002d.htm

Ohio Federation of Teachers (OFT). (2002, May 20). Coalition seeks ruling in charter school suit. *OFT Update: Special Edition*, no. 34. Retrieved May 30, 2004, from http://www.chtu.org/oft/update34%205-20-02.html

Optimal Performance, Inc. (2001). *The Florida Virtual School parent survey, 2000–2001*. Retrieved May 30, 2004, from http://www.flvs.net/_about_us/pdf_au/flvs_parent_survey_results.pdf

Peak Group. (2002, June). *Virtual schools across America: Trends in K–12 online education 2002*. Los Altos, CA: Author.

Rasheda Daniel et al. v. State of California et al. (1999, July), Los Angeles Superior Court. Retrieved May 30, 2004, from http://www.legalcasedocs.com/120/250/190.html

Roblyer, M. D. (1999). Is choice important in distance learning? A study of student motives for taking Internet-based courses at the high school and community college levels. *Journal of Research on Computing in Education, 32*(1), 157–172.

Rogers, E. M. (1995). *Diffusion of innovations* (4th ed.). New York, NY: Free Press.

Rose, L. C., & Gallup, A. M. (2000). 32nd annual Kappan/Gallup Poll on the public's attitudes toward the public schools. *Phi Delta Kappan, 82*(1), pp. 41–57. Retrieved May 30, 2004, from http://www.pdkintl.org/kappan/kimages/kpollv82.pdf

Rose, L. C., & Gallup, A. M. (2002). 34th annual Kappan/Gallup Poll on the public's attitudes toward the public schools. *Phi Delta Kappan, 84*(1), pp. 41–56. Retrieved May 30, 2004, from http://www.pdkintl.org/kappan/kimages/k0209pol.pdf

Sandham, J. L. (2001, May 10). Technology counts 2001: Across the nation. *Education Week*. Retrieved May 30, 2004, from www.edweek.org/sreports/tc01/tc01article.cfm?slub=35intro_states.h20

Schank, R. (1999, June). *The rise of virtual education*. Keynote address at the National Education Computer Conference, Atlantic City, NJ.

Schnitz, J. E., & Azbell, J. W. (2004). Instructional design factors and requirements for online courses and modules. In C. Cavenaugh (Ed.), *Development and management of virtual schools* (p. 261). Hershey, PA: Information Science Publishing.

Shaw, D. (2000). The great equalizer. *Curriculum Administrator, 36*(2), 32–38.

Simonson, M. (2000). Updated scales. *Quarterly Review of Distance Education, 1*(1), 69–76.

Simonson, M. (2003). *Distance education in South Dakota: School site visit reports*. Pierre: South Dakota Department of Education and Cultural Affairs.

Simonson, M., Smaldino, S., Albright, M., & Zvacek, S. (2000). *Teaching and learning at a distance: Foundations of distance education*. Upper Saddle River, NJ: Merrill.

Smith, S., & Pettersen, J. (2002, September). School funding—what's enough? *State Legislatures*. Retrieved May 30, 2004, from http://www.ncsl.org/programs/pubs/902school.htm

Stanford Research International (SRI). (1998). *An evaluation of The Virtual High School after one year of operation.* Retrieved November 12, 2004, from www.govhs.org

Stanford Research International (SRI). (1999). *An evaluation of The Virtual High School after two years of operation.* Retrieved November 12, 2004, from www.govhs.org

Stanford Research International (SRI). (2000). *The online course experience: Evaluation of The Virtual High School's third year of implementation.* Retrieved November 12, 2004, from www.govhs.org

Sugarman, S. D. (2002). Charter school funding issues. *Education Policy Analysis Archives, 10*(34). Retrieved May 30, 2004, from http://epaa.asu.edu/epaa/v10n34.html

Thomas, K. (2002, January 16). California kids lag in tech access: Minn., Conn., most prepared. *USA Today* [Final edition], p. D6.

Tinker, R., & Berman, S. (1996). *The virtual high school: A technology innovation challenge grant proposal.* Hudson, MA: Concord Consortium.

U. S. Census Bureau. (2004, March 18). *Census Bureau projects tripling of Hispanic and Asian populations in 50 years.* Retrieved May 30, 2004, from http://www.census.gov/Press-Release/www/releases/archives/population/001720.html

U.S. Department of Commerce. (2000, October). *Falling through the net: Toward digital inclusion.* Retrieved May 30, 2004, from http://search.ntia.doc.gov/pdf/fttn00.pdf

U.S. Department of Education. (1997). *A study of charter schools: First-year report.* Retrieved May 10, 2003, from http://www.ed.gov/pubs/charter/index.html

University of Missouri Bulletin, Extension Series, 1(1). (1913, April). Columbia: University of Missouri.

Vail, K. (2001, September). Online learning grows up. *Electronic School* [Online journal]. Retrieved May 30, 2004, from http://www.electronic-school.com/2001/09/0901f1.html

Valdez, G., McNabb, M., Foertsch, M., Anderson, M., Hawkes, M., & Raack, L. (2000). *Computer-based technology and learning: Evolving uses and expectations.* Retrieved May 30, 2004 from http://www.ncrel.org/tplan/cbtl/toc.htm

Valentin, E. K. (2001, Spring). SWOT analysis from a resource-based view. *Journal of Marketing Theory and Practice, 9*(2), 46–54.

Van Arsdall, J. E. (1977). *The stated and operative objectives of the University of Nebraska extension high school program, 1929–1975.* Unpublished doctoral dissertation, University of Nebraska, Lincoln.

Varvel, V., Lindeman, M., & Stovall, I. (2003). The Illinois Online Network is making the virtual classroom a reality: Study of an exemplary faculty development program. *Journal of Asynchronous Learning Networks, 7*(2). Retrieved May 30, 2004, from http://www.aln.org/publications/jaln/v7n2/pdf/v7n2_varvel.pdf

Vrasidas, C. (2003). The design, development, and implementation of LUDA Virtual High School. *Computers in the Schools, 20*(3), 15–25.

Vrasidas, C., & Glass, G. V. (2002). A conceptual framework for studying distance education. In C. Vrasidas & G. V. Glass (Eds.), *Current perspectives in applied information technologies: Distance education and distributed learning* (pp. 31–56). Greenwich, CT: Information Age Publishing.

Watkins, R., & Kaufman, R. (2002). Strategic planning for distance education. In M. G. Moore & W. G. Anderson (Eds.), *Handbook of distance education* (pp. 507–517). Mahwah, NJ: Erlbaum.

Waxman, H. C., Lin, M. F., & Michko, G. M. (2003, December). *A meta-analysis of the effectiveness of teaching and learning with technology on student outcomes.* Naperville, IL: NCREL. Retrieved May 30, 2004, from http://www.ncrel.org/tech/effects2/waxman.pdf

Web-based Education Commission. (2000, December). *The power of the Internet for Learning.* Retrieved May 30, 2004, from http://www.ed.gov/offices/AC/WBEC/FinalReport/

Wiggins, G., & McTighe, J. (2001). *Understanding by design.* Upper Saddle River, NJ: Prentice-Hall.

Winners of the Stockholm Challenge Award 2001 Announced. (2001, December). Retrieved May 30, 2004, from http://www.govhs.org/vhsweb/Press.nsf/0/EDD97A6C9575689506256BBB0049E1D5?OpenDocument

World Wide Web Consortium (2003). *W3C World Wide Web consortium . . . in 7 points.* Retrieved May 30, 2004, from http://www.w3.org/Consortium/Points/

Young, J. (2003, May 29). *Florida Virtual School.* Presentation at Exploring Virtual Schools symposium [Innovations in Education Exchange Series], Orlando, FL.

Zucker, A., Kozma, R., Yarnall, L., & Marder, C. (2002). *The Virtual High School: Teaching generation V.* New York: Teachers College Press.

About the Editors and the Contributors

Zane L. Berge, Ph.D., is an associate professor of education at the University of Maryland, Baltimore County.

Tom Clark is the president of TA Consulting, an Illinois-based firm that provides research and evaluation services for business, education, and government. Dr. Clark is cited in *Who's Who in America* for his work in distance and virtual learning.

Ruth Adams is the dean of curriculum and instruction for Virtual High School (VHS, Inc.).

Jason D. Baker is an associate professor of education at Regent University in Virginia Beach, Virginia.

Robert L. Blomeyer is a senior program associate in the Center for Technology at the North Central Regional Education Laboratory/Learning Point Associates in Naperville, Illinois.

Cathy Bouras is a high school science instructor. She holds a master's degree in secondary science education as well as a master's degree in administration and educational leadership.

Linda Cavalluzzo is an economist at the CNA Corporation, in Alexandria, Virginia, a not-for-profit institution that conducts high-level, in-depth research and analysis to inform the work of public sector decision makers.

Richard Chamberlain is the associate director of the Center for the Application of Information Technologies (www.cait.org) at Western Illinois University, and has over 15 years experience working with distance learning technologies.

Matt Dawson, Ph.D., is a program associate in the Center for Technology at the North Central Regional Education Laboratory/Learning Point Associates in Naperville, Illinois.

Gordon Freedman is the founder of Knowledge Base, LLC, a consulting company in education, technology, and policy. Knowledge Base works with state, national, nonprofit, and corporate entities to solve current problems and analyze future needs.

Bruce Friend is the chief administrative officer of Florida Virtual School, an online public school offering middle and high school courses. In 2003 he received the U.S. Distance Learning Association's award for Outstanding Achievement by an Individual.

Susan M. Hartwig is the assistant principal of North Vista Elementary School, a public school in Florence, South Carolina.

Francisco J. Hernandez, Ph.D., is the vice chancellor for student affairs at the University of California–Santa Cruz. He is the founder and executive director of the University of California College Preparatory Initiative, an e-learning project providing online college prep courses to high school students.

Sharon Johnston, Ed.D., the director of curriculum for Florida Virtual School for 7 years, is now the school's director of grants and research. Dr. Johnston is a National Board Certified teacher and a College Board consultant.

Allan Jordan, Ed.D., is the Cumberland County Schools director of online teaching and learning and principal of the Web Academy in Fayetteville, North Carolina. He currently serves as the chairman of the North American Council for Online Learning (NACOL).

Earlene R. McNair, M.PH., is a nutritionist supervisor and nutrition educator at the Norfolk Department of Public Health in Norfolk, Virginia. She is also a doctoral student at Regent University's School of Education in Virginia Beach, Virginia, concentrating in Distance Education.

Liz Pape is the CEO of Virtual High School (VHS, Inc.). She is a founding board member of the North American Council for Online Learning (NACOL).

Carol Ribeiro is the operations manager for Virtual High School (VHS, Inc.).

Michael Simonson, Ph.D., is a program professor at Nova Southeastern University in the Instructional Technology and Distance Education program.

Kristi D. Smalley is the principal of the University of Missouri–Columbia High School. MU High is part of the Center for Distance and Independent Study, a unit of the university's Extension Division.

Ronald Stefanski is currently the director of business and partner development for the Michigan Virtual University, and its K–12 initiative, the Michigan Virtual High School.

Charalambos Vrasidas is an associate professor of learning technologies at Intercollege, Cyprus, and coordinator of Research and Evaluation at the Center for the Application of Information Technologies at Western Illinois University.

Julie Young is the president and CEO of Florida Virtual School, one of the largest providers of Internet-based courseware and instruction for middle and high school students in the world.

Index